I0763093

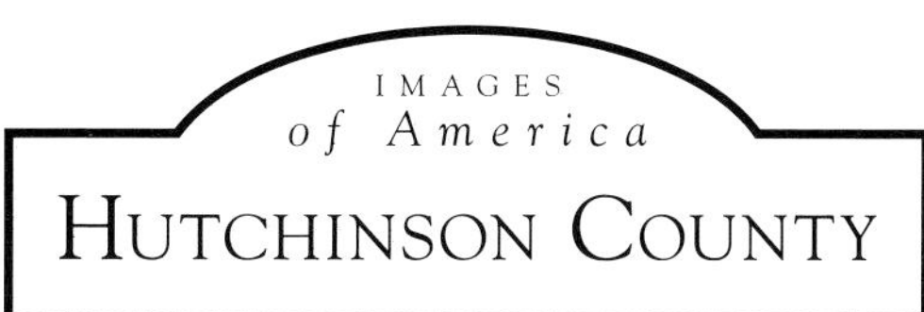
IMAGES
of America
HUTCHINSON COUNTY

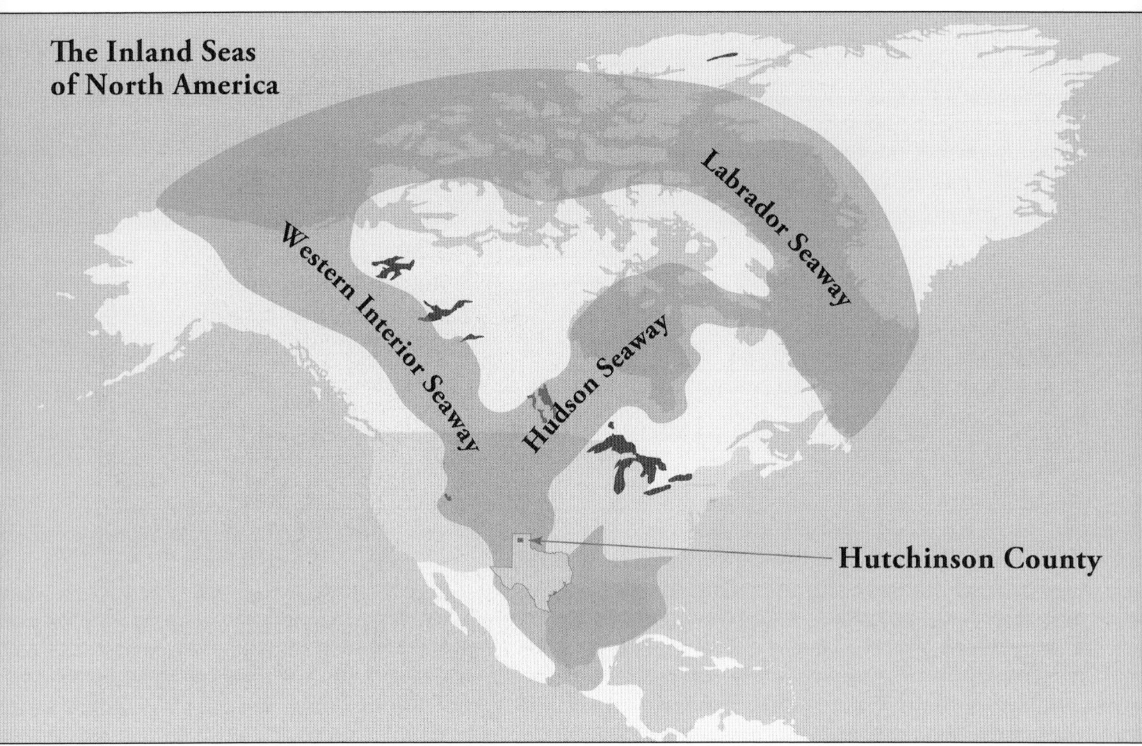

The central part of North America has flooded several times during the last 500 million years. At times, a shallow seaway has been open from the present-day Gulf of Mexico to the Arctic Ocean. The Permian formations in Hutchinson County were deposited in this sea approximately 299 to 251 million years ago. The earliest residents of the county are from the Cambrian era. Invertebrate fossils of trilobites, cephalopods, snails, clams, and corals found here are sometimes as much as 400 million years old. (Illustration by Clay Renick.)

On the Cover: This grainy, slightly out of focus image captures the spirit of Hutchinson County's early days. Ranchers and farmers set up in this area of the Texas Panhandle as early as 1876. The first oil well was completed in Hutchinson County on the C.L. Dial Ranch in 1922, but it was not until 1926 that the oil boom occurred that put Hutchinson County on the map nationally. From 1876 to 1922, this region of Texas was remote and sparsely populated. That all changed when oil was discovered and the tranquil life of ranching and farming collided with the capitalistic fervor of wildcatters, speculators, and roughnecks. These two cultures have existed side by side since that time. (Courtesy of Hutchinson County Historical Museum.)

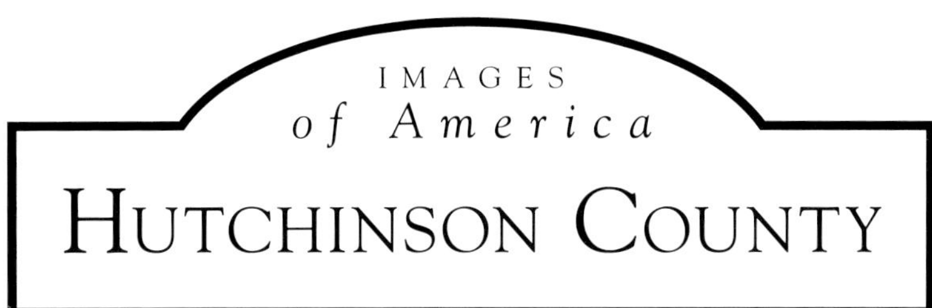

Clay Renick on behalf of
the Hutchinson County Museum

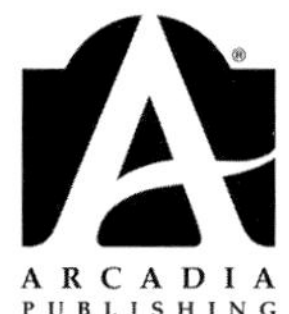

ISBN 978-1-4671-0858-4

Published by Arcadia Publishing
Charleston, South Carolina

Printed in the United States of America

Library of Congress Control Number: 2022935294

For all general information, please contact Arcadia Publishing:
Telephone 843-853-2070
Fax 843-853-0044
E-mail sales@arcadiapublishing.com
For customer service and orders:
Toll-Free 1-888-313-2665

Visit us on the Internet at www.arcadiapublishing.com

Contents

Acknowledgments

Thanks to former Hutchinson County judge Faye Blanks for hiring me in 2012 to be the director of the Hutchinson County Historical Museum in Borger, Texas. I work diligently each day to live up to her expectations. I have always loved history, and her willingness to offer me this position has helped me realize just how much. Thanks, Judge Blanks.

Thanks to the current Hutchinson County Commissioners Court, which allowed me to write this book. Your approval gave me the confidence I needed to embark on this adventure. Thanks for believing that I was the right man for the job, which I have undertaken by utilizing the collective efforts of my predecessors who collected, documented, and recorded a great deal of the history of our county. The research was already done—all I had to do was compile it.

Thanks to Lynne Hopkins, who was the museum's administrator when I assumed the duties of director. Lynne had been the administrator for many years, and she showed me the ropes, told me where the bodies were buried, shared the institution's secrets, and let me take the credit for all of our successes. Without her assistance and guidance, I seriously doubt if I would have succeeded or could have kept the job this long. Thanks, Lynne!

I would also like to thank the founders of the museum and the Friends of the Hutchinson County Historical Museum. These concerned citizens provide their time, effort, and advice to help make the museum the best it can be. The founders had the vision to establish the museum, the tenacity to bring it to life, and the determination to make it sustainable. My tenure as director has been a joy and is the best job I have ever had—I have never had a job that I love as much as this one! Thanks to the founders and friends of the museum.

Most importantly, I would like to thank my wife, Lisa. Her faith in me, our shared interests in history, and her never-ending support have allowed me to be a better man than I would have been without her. Lisa is a public school teacher. She never stops teaching! She took me on as one of her students and has taught me to expect the most that life has to offer—and to be content with what I can achieve. I am a lucky man to have such a wise counselor as my life partner. Thank you, Lisa—my best friend, counselor, guide, and wife!

Unless otherwise noted, all images appear courtesy of the Hutchinson County Historical Museum.

Introduction

The modern history of Hutchinson County extends back to the beginning of the state of Texas. Mexico became independent from Spain in the 1820s and welcomed foreigners to the almost unpopulated region then known as Texas. American pioneers, led by Stephen F. Austin, set up on the Brazos River, and soon, the Americans outnumbered the Mexicans living in the area. By the 1830s, the Mexican government's attempts to control the American settlements led to rebellion. In March 1836, Texas declared its independence from Mexico and fought for the right to govern themselves.

Mexico established Béxar County and named it San Fernando de Béxar in honor of the heir to the Spanish throne, Fernando VI. It was one of the 23 Mexican administrative divisions of Texas at the time of its independence from Spain. Villa de San Fernando de Béxar was the first civil government established by the Spanish in the province of Texas. The municipality was created in 1731, when people settled near several missions that had been established around the source of the San Antonio River. The new settlement was named after the Presidio San Antonio de Béjar, the Spanish military outpost that protected the missions. The presidio was founded in 1718 and named for the second son of the duke of Béjar, a city in Spain. The modern city of San Antonio, Texas, was also named after San Antonio de Béjar.

In 1836, Sam Houston was elected president of the independent Republic of Texas. Texas citizens supported the entrance of Texas into the Union. The US Congress delayed formal action on Texas's admission for more than 10 years due to the likelihood of it joining as a slave state. In 1844, Congress agreed to annex Texas, and on December 29, 1845, Texas entered the United States as the 28th state—and a slave state. This helped to set off the Mexican-American War.

When Texas declared its independence from Mexico, the former administrative divisions became counties. Béxar County was established on December 20, 1836, with San Antonio as the county seat. The newly formed Béxar County stretched from the Rio Grande to the Panhandle and west to El Paso and covered most of the western edge of settlement in Texas. Since 1860, when the partitioning of Béxar County began, 128 counties have been established.

Hutchinson County was established on August 21, 1876, when 53 counties were formed from Béxar County. At that time, it was attached to Roberts, Wheeler, and Carson Counties, respectively, for administrative purposes.

By 1900, the Hutchinson County area's population had increased to 303. Farmers were beginning to move into the area, but the economy continued to be dominated by cattle ranching, with almost 30,000 cattle recorded in the Hutchinson County area in 1900. In the spring of 1901, a movement began for the county's organization. Elections were held on April 25, and on May 13, Hutchinson County was organized with the small town of Plemons as its seat of government. W.H. Ingarton was elected county judge, and William (Billy) Dixon, the Adobe Walls hero who had operated the county's first post office on the Turkey Track ranch, became the first sheriff.

Hutchinson County is located in the north central Texas Panhandle. Bounded on the north by Hansford County, the east by Roberts County, the south by Carson County, and the west by Moore County, its center is at approximately N 35°50' latitude and W 101°20' longitude. It contains 871 square miles of plains and broken terrain. Altitudes in the county range from 2,750 to 3,400 feet above sea level. The county's average annual rainfall is 19.9 inches; the average minimum temperature is 22 degrees Fahrenheit (in January), and the average maximum is 93 degrees Fahrenheit (in July). The growing season averages 187 days. The Canadian River is fed by numerous small creeks and springs and angles across the county from southwest to northeast. In the southwest, the river was dammed to form Lake Meredith. Broken land along the river and its tributaries forms fertile valleys. The northern part of the county is high rolling plain. About $15 million average annual income in the county is derived from wheat, corn, alfalfa, and grain sorghums grown there. Beef cattle, hogs, and poultry are also raised in the county, and irrigated land totals more than 40,000 acres.

Since the 1920s, petroleum has been the county's chief industry. The southern part of Hutchinson County is the center of oil, gas, petrochemical, and synthetic rubber production in the Texas Panhandle. It is also home to one of the world's largest pump stations for natural gas, which supplies metropolitan areas northwest to Denver and east to Indianapolis. State highways 136, 152, and 207 merge at Borger, and several farm and ranch roads provide access to outlying communities.

Hutchinson County was named for Texas pioneer jurist Anderson Hutchinson (1798–1853), who was born in Greenbrier County, Virginia, on April 7, 1798. Hutchinson and his wife, Mariana, arrived in Austin in the independent Republic of Texas on June 23, 1840. He opened a law office and found immediate success, then was appointed judge of the Fourth (Western) District in 1841.

Judge Hutchinson was holding court in San Antonio when the town was captured by the Mexican Army on September 10, 1842. When the army withdrew, they took Hutchinson, the jurors, court attachés, witnesses, and attorneys with them. The group was sent to Perote Prison in Mexico. Hutchinson was released on March 29, 1843, and taken aboard the USS *Vincennes* at Vera Cruz before being returned to Pensacola, Florida. On June 10, 1843, on account of illness and injury resulting from being held at Perote Prison, Hutchinson tendered his resignation to President Houston. Anderson Hutchinson died in 1853.

Today, Hutchinson County is still a remote, rural place. Natural beauty abounds along the Canadian River breaks and in its many tributary canyons carved by creeks and springs over millennia. Wildlife of many varieties can be found throughout the county, which is a big place—871 square miles in area, approximately 29 miles wide by 30 miles deep. By comparison, the state of Rhode Island covers 1,045 square miles.

According to the US Census Bureau, the county's population is 20,617, which equals an average of 23.6 people per square mile, making Hutchinson County the definition of a wide open space. County residents are friendly, and their work ethic is strong. The phrase "a day's work for a day's pay" is the mantra of most who live here. Hutchinson County is a good place to live and work, and guests will receive a warm welcome when they visit.

One

PREHISTORY

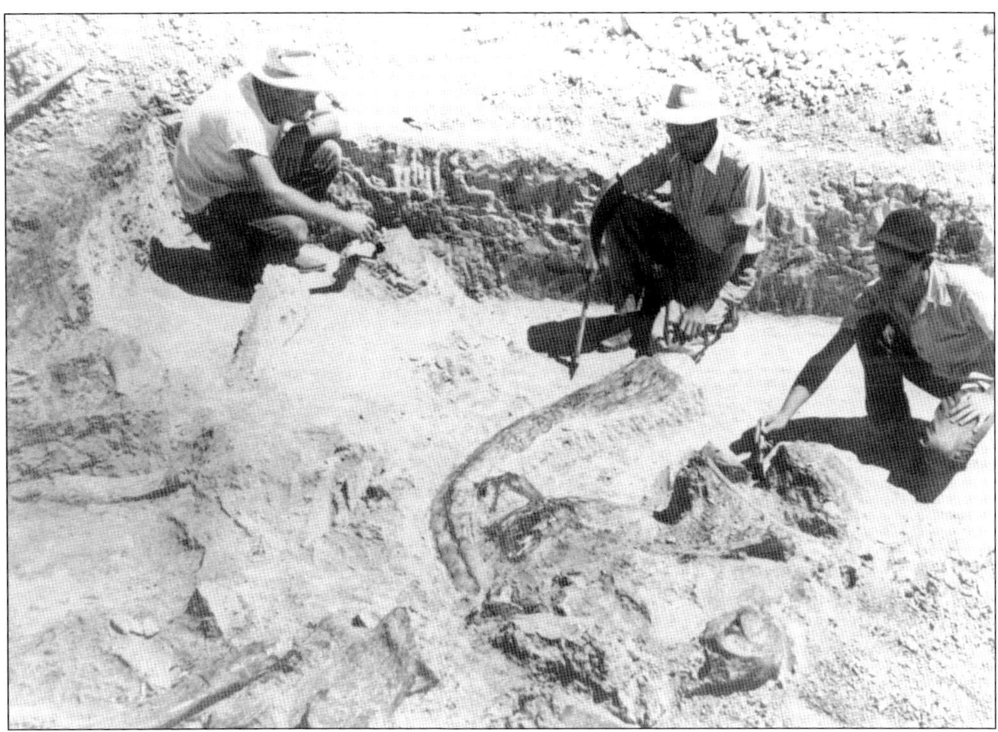

In 1951, Jack Hughes (center) and two other archeologists excavated this specimen just north of where the Sanford Dam is today. Mammoths roamed in great numbers in Hutchinson County as late as 12,000 years ago.

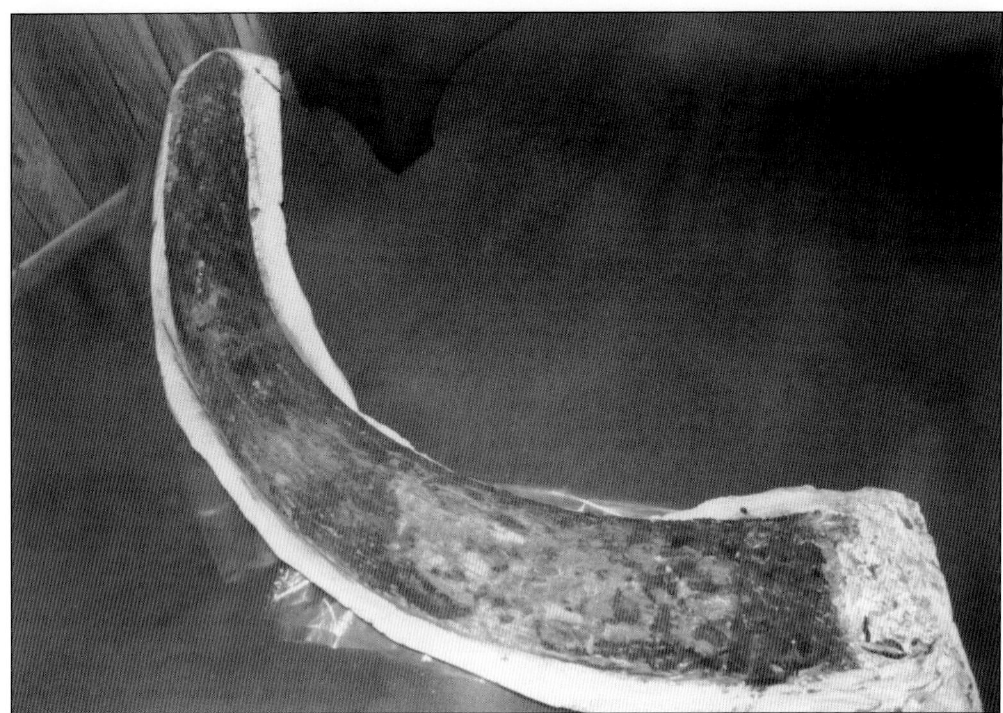

This mammoth tusk was excavated by local amateur archeologist James Bruce. Bruce located this tusk, excavated it, and encased it in plaster to protect it prior to moving it to his home for display.

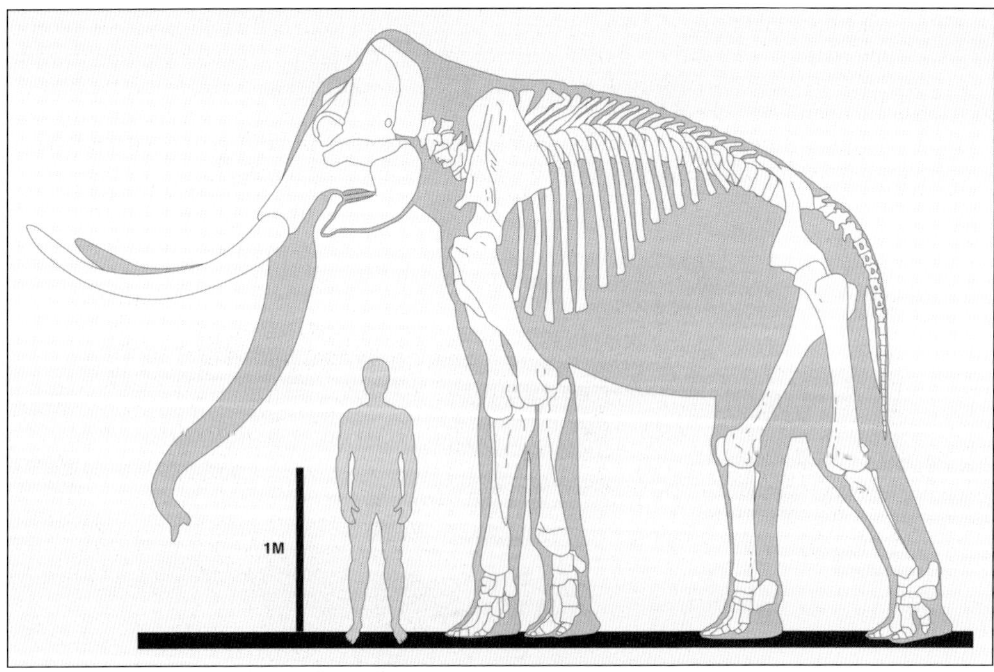

This illustration shows the scale of mammoths compared to humans. Mammoth skeletons found in Roberts County, less than 100 miles from Hutchinson County, had man-made flint spear and arrow points embedded in the bones, proving man and mammoth existed at the same time.

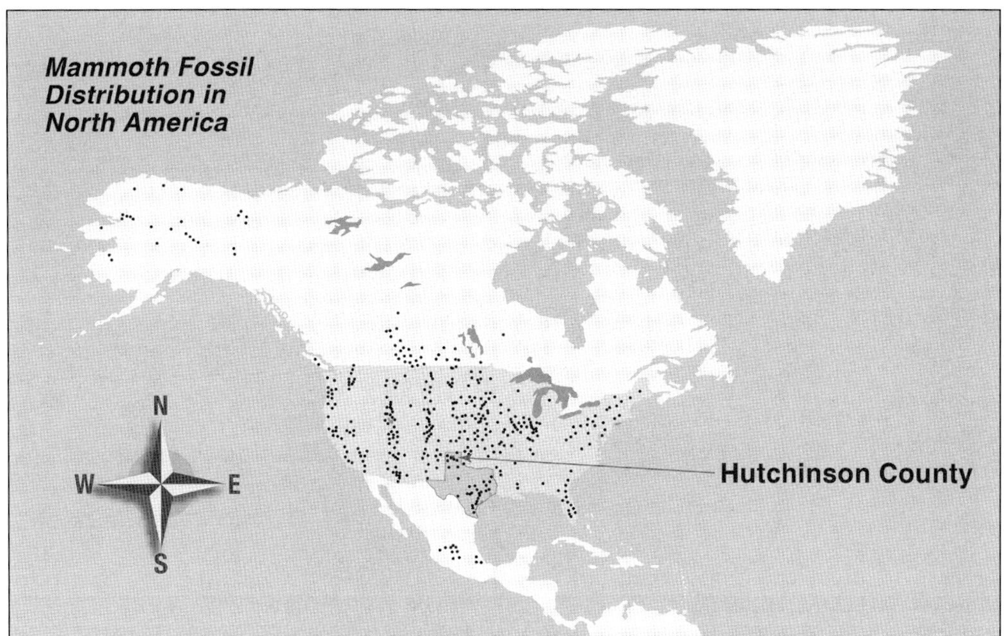

This map shows where mammoth remains have been discovered throughout North America. The section of a mammoth tusk below shows a series of growth rings not unlike the rings of a tree. These rings create a record of growth in yearly, weekly, and even daily increments. Thick rings represent a single year and are made up of a dark band (winter) and a light band (summer). (Above, illustration by Clay Renick.)

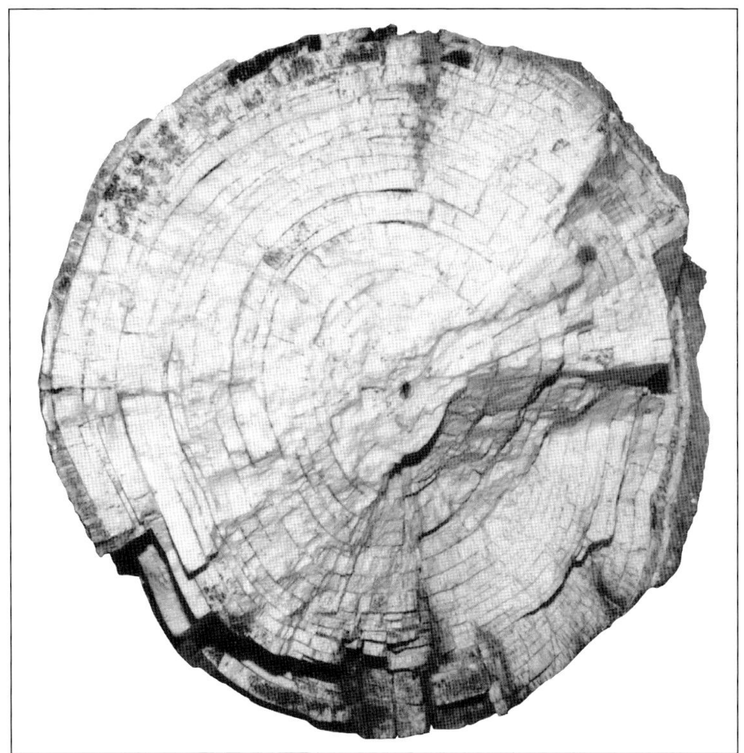

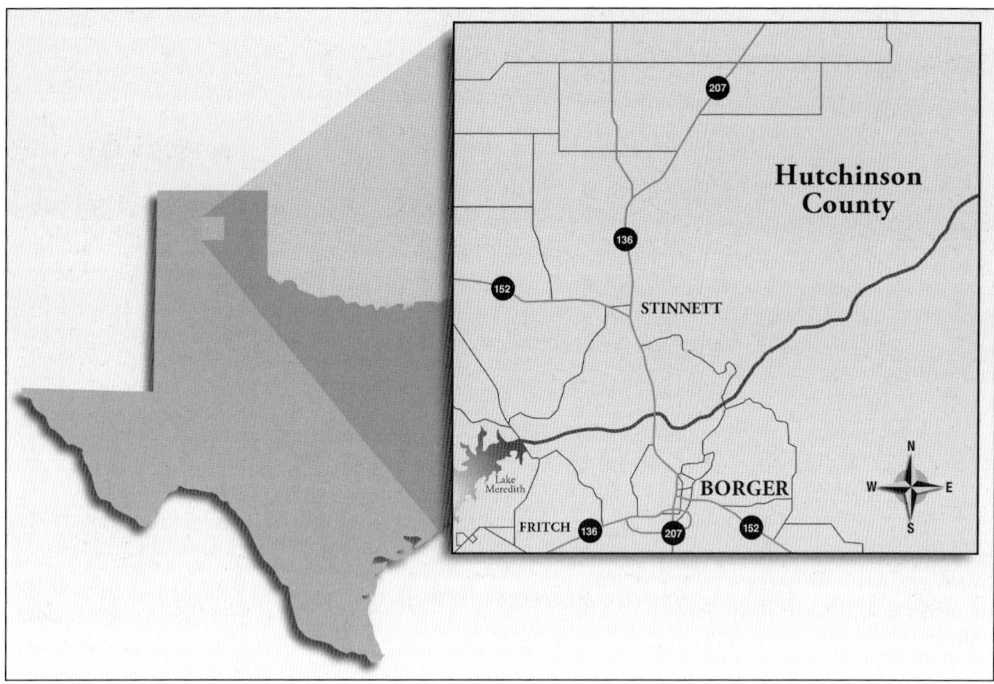

Hutchinson County is in the north central Texas Panhandle. The county contains 871 square miles of plains and broken terrain, and altitude ranges from 2,750 to 3,400 feet above sea level. The Canadian River makes its way across the county from the southwest to the northeast and is fed by springs and small creeks along its way. The watershed of the river is known as the breaks. The many canyons of the breaks form fertile valleys adjacent to the river. The northern part of the county is high, rolling plain. (Both illustrations by Clay Renick.)

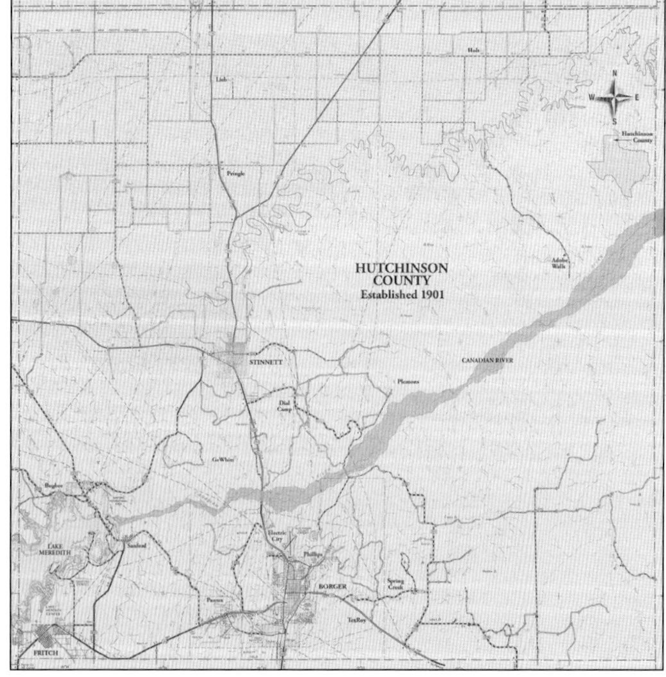

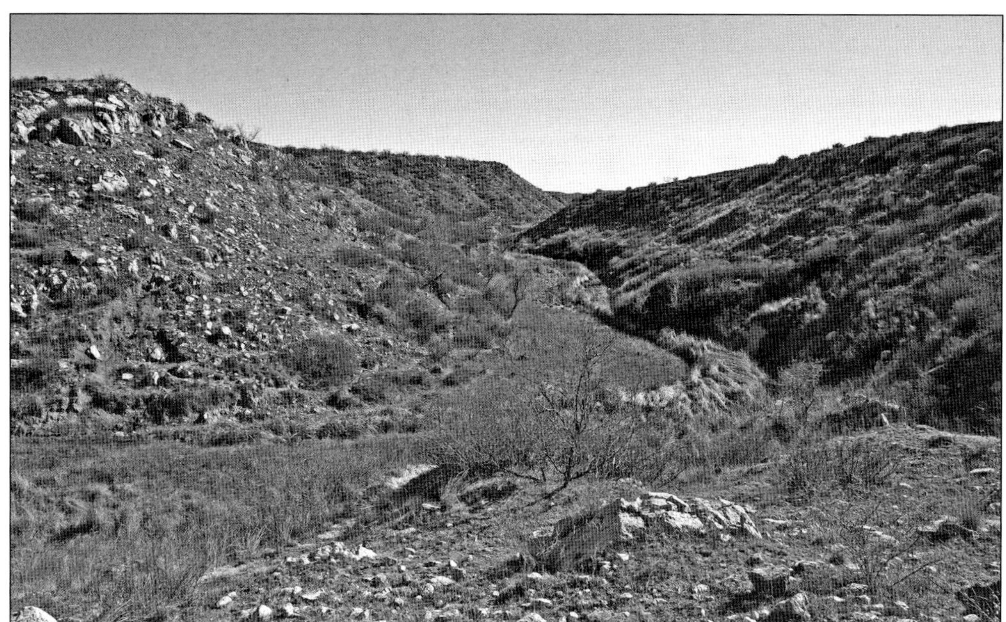

Collectively known as the Permian red beds, most of the colorful red sandstone and white dolomite sedimentary rock layers exposed in the breaks along the Canadian River in Hutchinson County were deposited on the coast and floor of an inland sea approximately 260 million years ago during the Permian Period, when what is now the Texas Panhandle was located near the equator and part of the supercontinent Pangaea. Red beds are colored by the small amounts of iron oxides and clay minerals they contain. (Photograph by Clay Renick.)

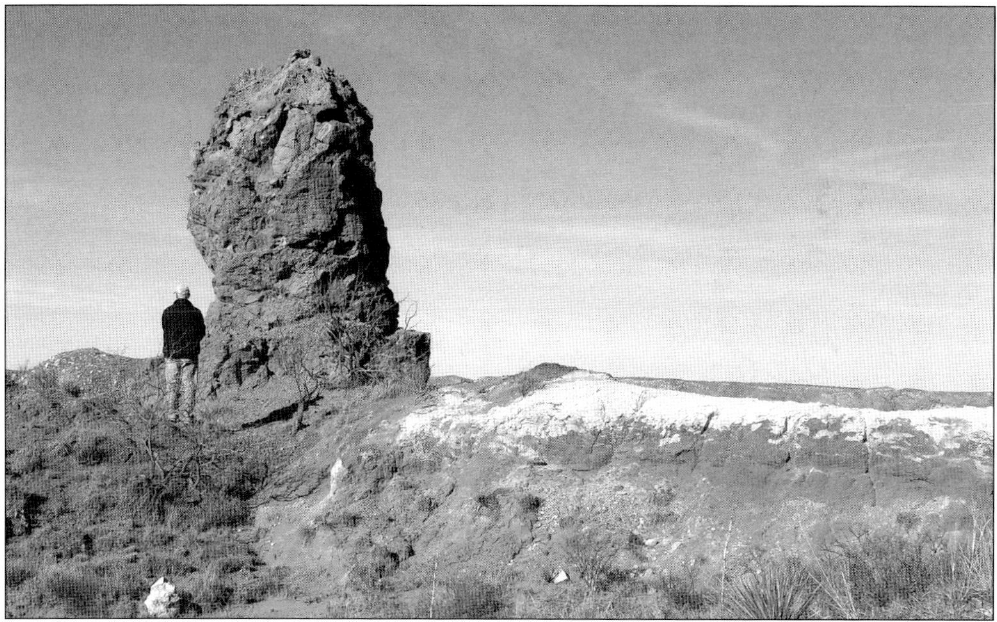

Geological structures known as chimneys, such as this one, formed when water moved between the sedimentary layers and transported minerals that later solidified. Chimneys withstand erosion because the minerals that formed them are harder than the surrounding materials that erode over time. The figure in the foreground provides a sense of scale for the formation.

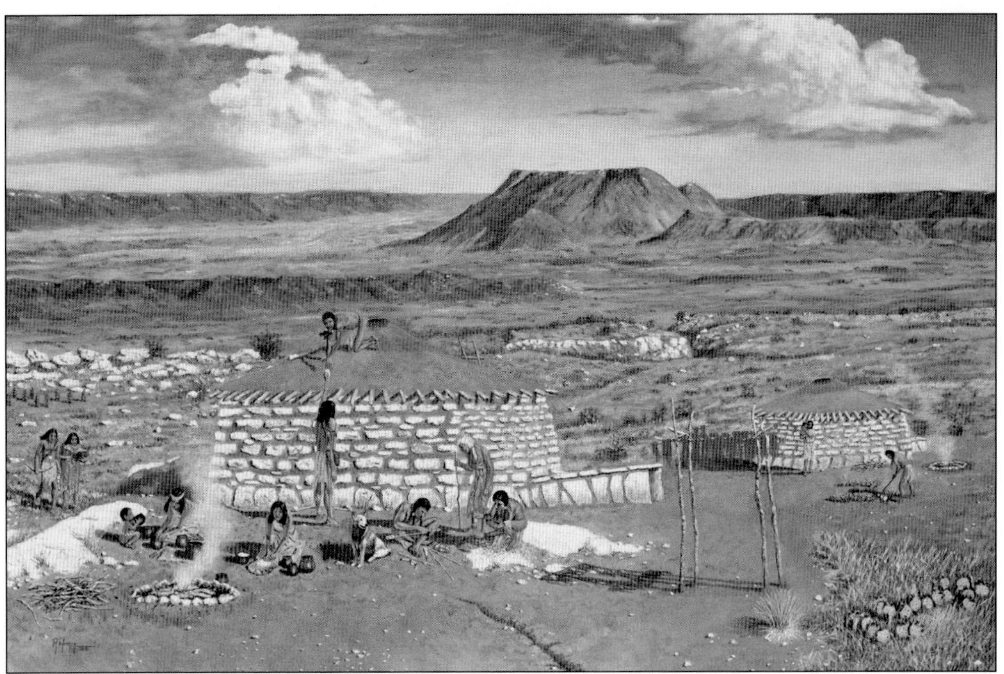

The Antelope Creek culture inhabited the Texas and Oklahoma panhandles between 1150 and 1450. Along the Canadian River in Hutchinson County, the Antelope Creek peoples mined flint found in the white dolomite layer at the top of the canyons to make stone tools. They also traded flint with other tribes. The culture used the local rock to build their homes. Ruins of their settlements, such as the one shown below, can be found throughout Hutchinson County and much of the Texas Panhandle. The above painting was created by local artist Richard Hogue. (Below, photograph by Clay Renick.)

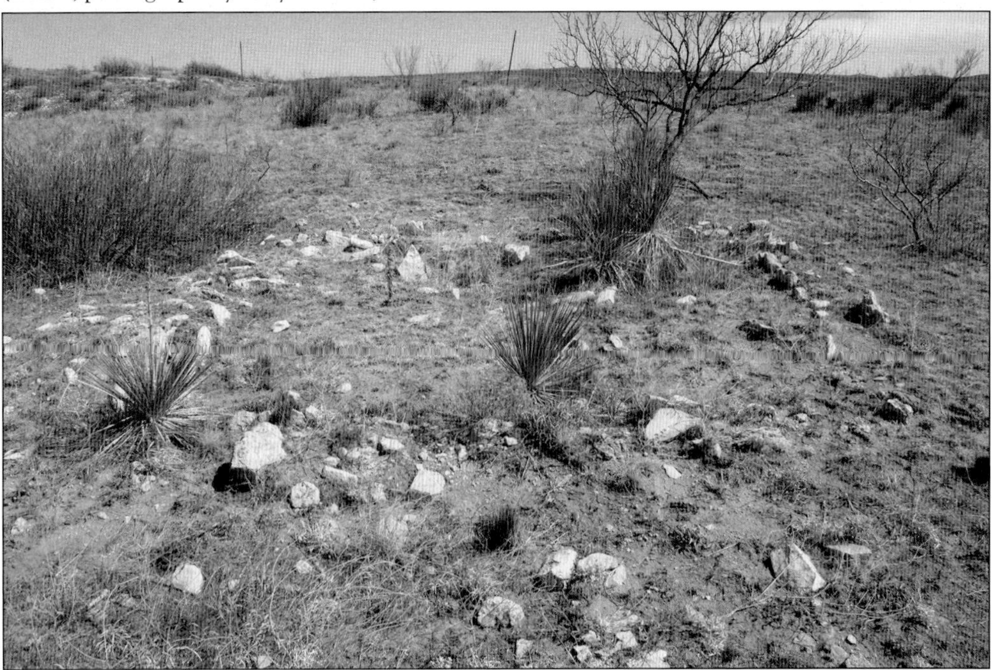

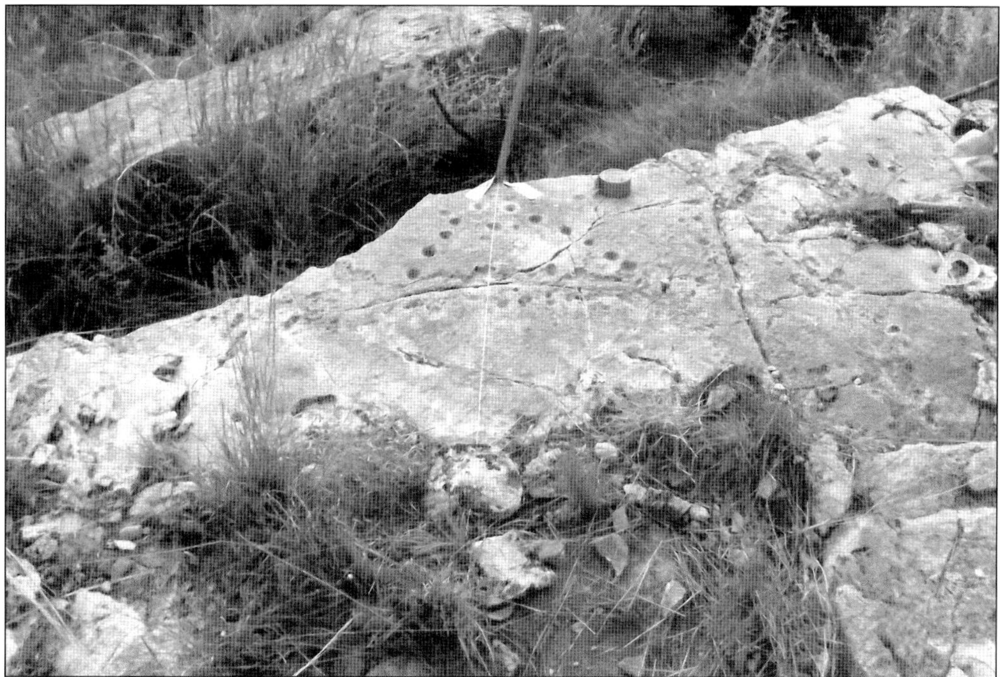

This stone calendar, found on the north side of the Canadian River in western Hutchinson County, is believed to have been made by Antelope Creek culture. The shadow of a stick across the rock at daybreak, when related to the cup-shaped depressions carved into the rock's surface, marked the spring and summer solstices—the periods of the year when people plant and harvest, respectively. Recently discovered, this calendar helped archaeologists to better understand the previously unknown sophistication of the Antelope Creek culture.

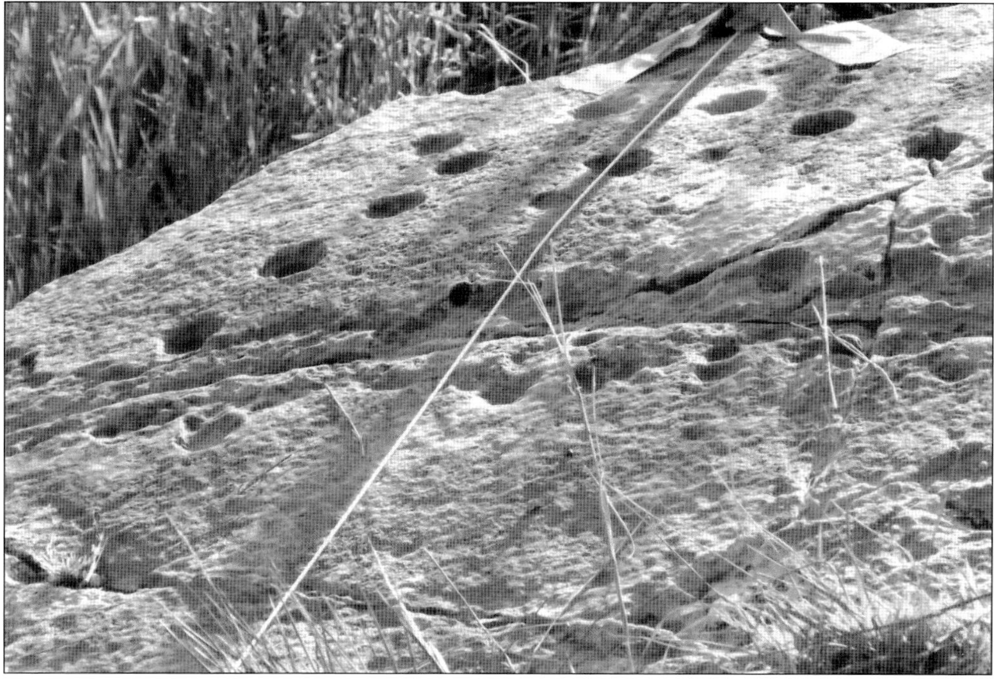

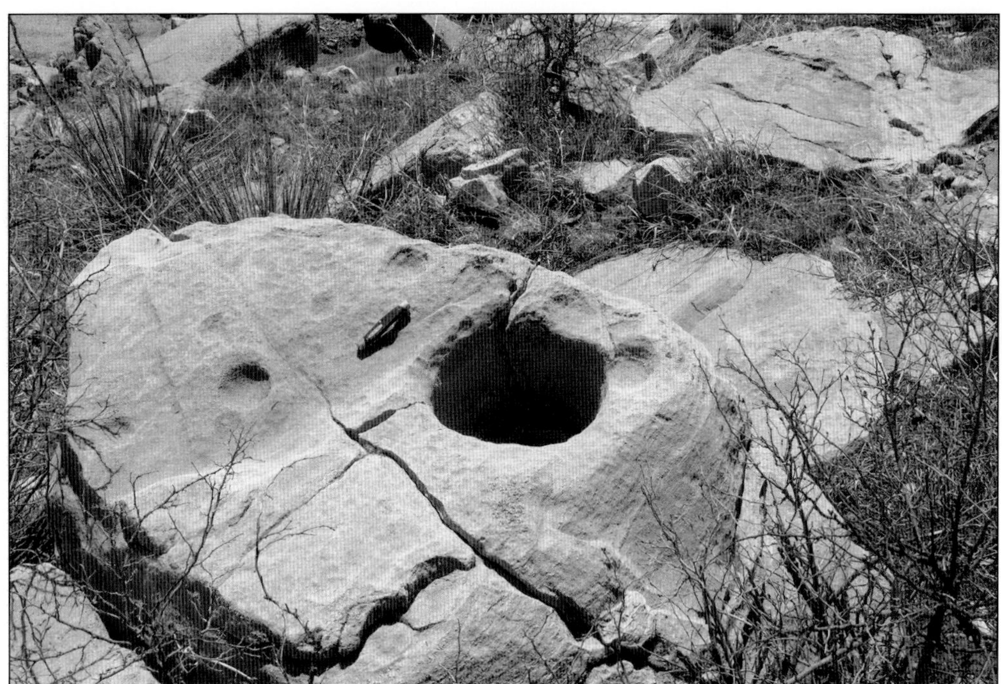

The bedrock mortar shown here was used by Antelope Creek peoples on the Dial Ranch north of the Canadian River in central Hutchinson County. The Antelope Creek people would grind grains, nuts, seeds, and meat to produce pemmican, a food source that would last for days on the plains. The pocketknife in the photograph is included for scale. (Photograph by Clay Renick.)

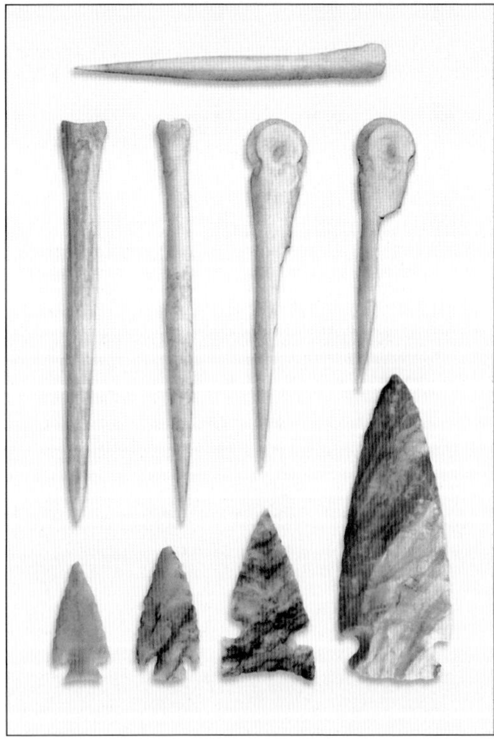

The tools of the Antelope Creek culture may seem crude by today's standards, but they were efficient and effective. Stone and bone resources were widely available and allowed the culture to flourish in this harsh environment for centuries. These are needles made from the bones of the prey they hunted and flint arrow points made from the abundant supplies of flint that formed millions of years ago in the sedimentary dolomite stone along the cliff tops of the Canadian River valley.

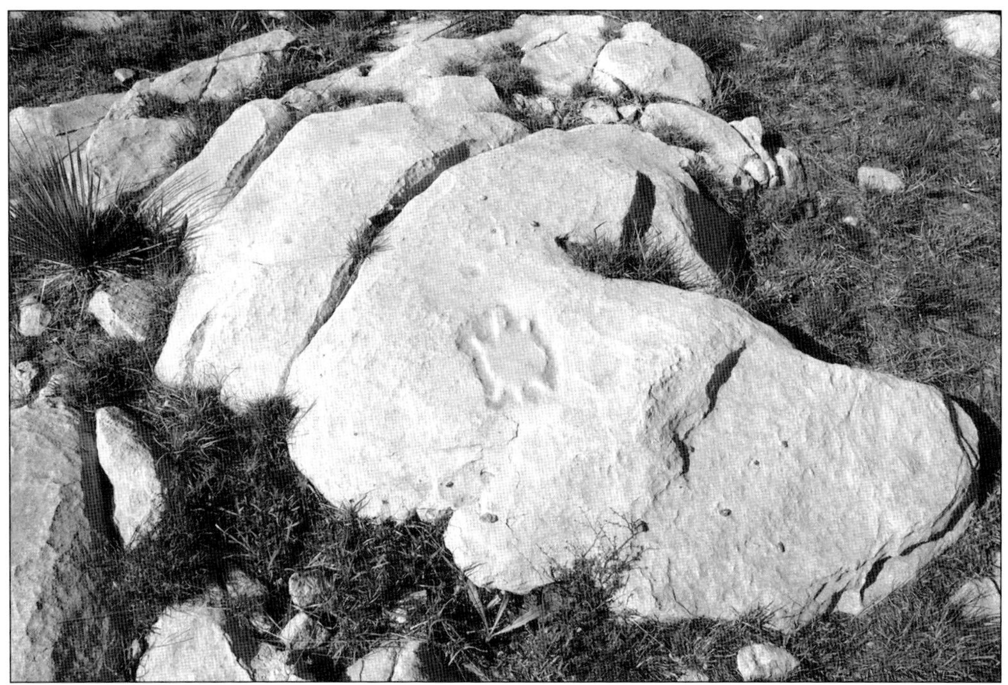

The Antelope Creek people lived in what is now Hutchinson County from 1150 to 1450. They established villages, mined flint for toolmaking, and hunted and farmed along the Canadian River. The Alibates Flint Quarries National Monument was formed to protect and interpret their history. The turtle petroglyph shown above was created by an Antelope Creek culture artist. The Works Progress Administration (WPA) took part in archeological excavations in the 1930s conducted by Floyd Studer, who is pictured below (in the dark suit at left). (Above, photograph by Clay Renick.)

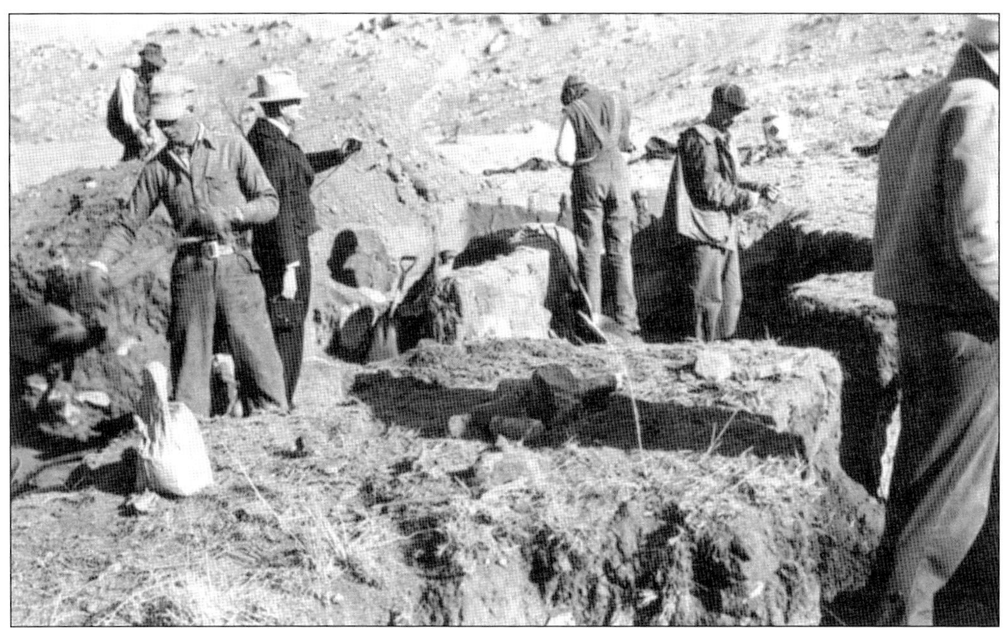

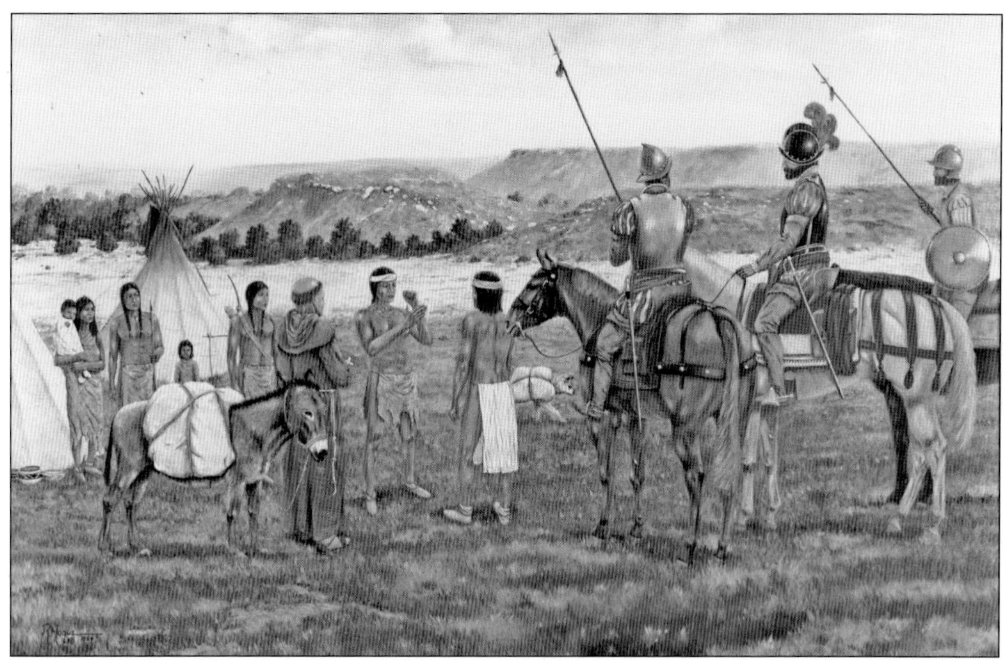

In this painting by local artist Richard Hogue, Francisco Vásquez de Coronado and members of his expedition are shown talking to Native Americans who lived along the Canadian River in what is now Hutchinson County. In 1540, the viceroy of New Spain (present-day Mexico) was Don Antonio de Mendoza, a friend of Coronado. After hearing exaggerated descriptions of the golden cities of the north from Catholic priest Father Marcos de Niza, Mendoza and Coronado outfitted an expedition to find and conquer the rich cities to the north, particularly Cibola and Quivira. Around 300 Spaniards and as many as 800 Native Americans volunteered to join the expedition. Coronado and Mendoza invested their fortunes in the venture.

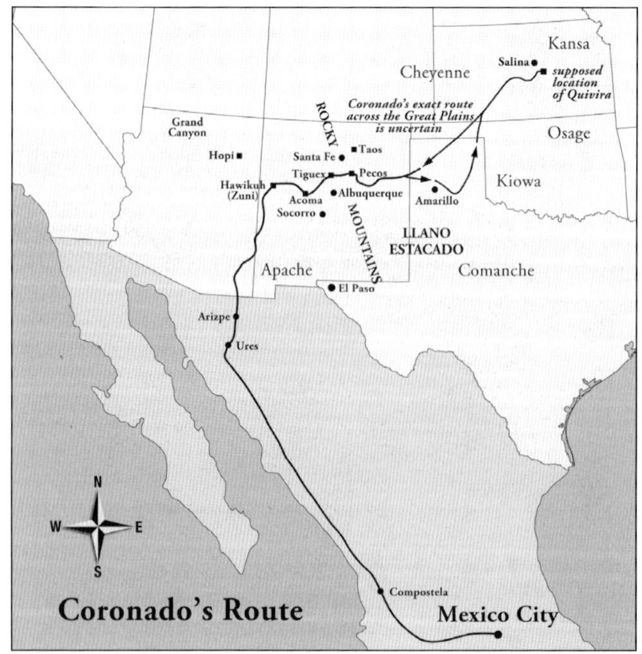

Although the Coronado and Mendoza expedition discovered and described vast expanses of new country and many new cultures, it was a dismal failure. Most of the expedition's members returned to Mexico deeply in debt and angry at Coronado, their weak and flawed leader. This map shows where Coronado's trail crossed the Texas Panhandle. Artifacts from Coronado's expedition have been found in Hutchinson County. (Illustration by Clay Renick.)

Two

THE WILD WEST

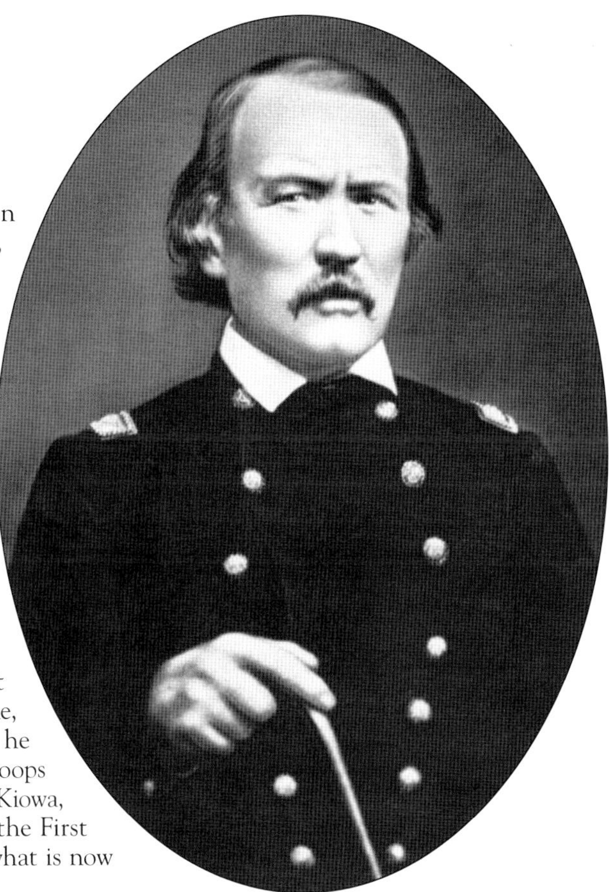

Christopher Houston Carson (December 24, 1809–May 23, 1868), better known as Kit Carson, was a frontiersman, fur trapper, wilderness guide, US Army officer, and an Indian agent. He became a legend in his own lifetime through biographies, news articles, and exaggerated versions of his exploits. Carson's understated nature was surprising because of his often-witnessed fearlessness, combat skills, and tenacity. His presence had a marked effect on the rapid westward expansion of the United States that took place during his life. He was famous for much of his life. It has been noted that Carson did not like, want, or understand the fame that he experienced during his life. He led troops against warriors from the Comanche, Kiowa, Cheyenne, and Arapaho tribes at the First Battle of Adobe Walls in 1864 in what is now Hutchinson County.

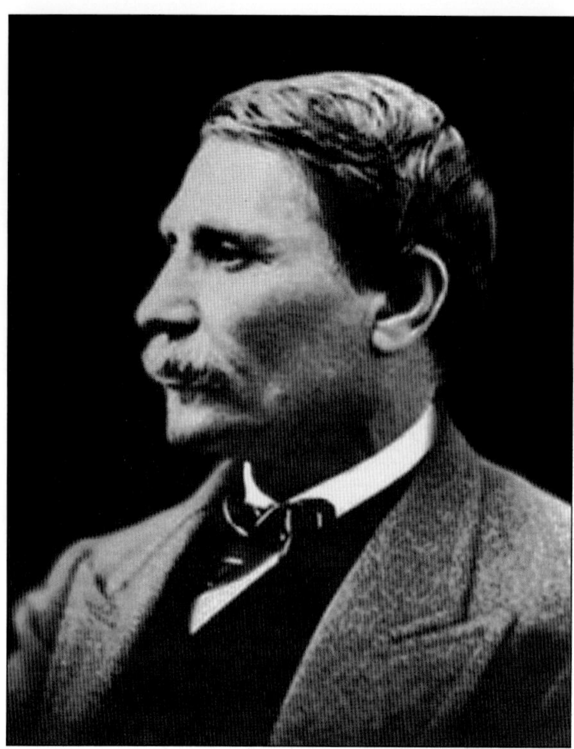

Edward Fitzgerald "Ned" Beale (February 4, 1822–April 22, 1893) was a Naval officer, an Army general, an explorer, a frontiersman, an Indian affairs superintendent, a rancher, a diplomat, and a friend of Kit Carson, Buffalo Bill Cody, and Ulysses S. Grant. Beale was the grandson of Commodore Thomas Truxtun, one of the first six commanders appointed to the new US Navy by Pres. George Washington, and later served as an Army officer and fought in the Mexican-American War, emerging as a hero of the Battle of San Pasqual in 1846. He achieved national fame in 1848 when he carried the first gold samples from California to the east, contributing to the gold rush of 1849. Beale sailed with Capt. Robert F. Stockton's squadron to Texas, where they met with the Texas Congress, which accepted annexation by the United States.

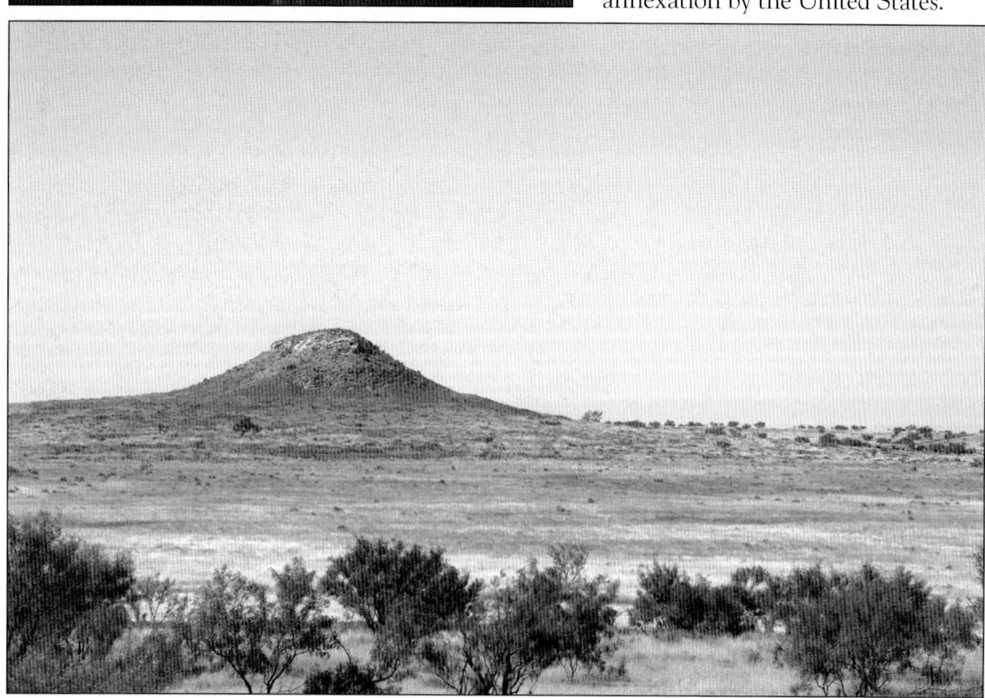

This is the geological and geographical structure known as Ab's Knob, named for Absalom Redding, a man who was once enslaved by Ned Beale and served as his point man on the route of the wagon road across the rugged, unknown territory of the southwestern United States. (Photograph by Clay Renick.)

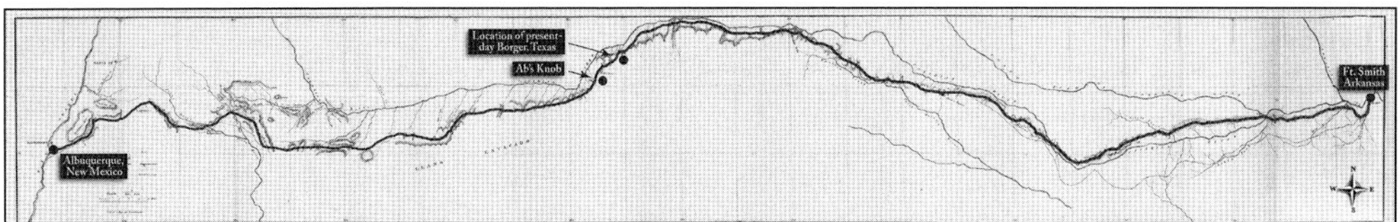

In 1857, Pres. James Buchanan appointed Ned Beale to survey and build a 1,000-mile wagon road from Fort Defiance, New Mexico, to the Colorado River on the border between Arizona and California. Beale used camels imported from Tunis as pack animals during this expedition as well as on another expedition in 1858 and 1859 to extend the road from Fort Smith, Arkansas, to the Colorado River. The camels could travel for days without water, carried much heavier loads than mules, and could thrive on forage that mules would not eat. The camels scared horses and mules, and the Army soon ended the camel experiment. Nevertheless, the wagon road built by Beale became a popular trail during the 1860s and 1870s. This survey marked out for the first time a usable highway along the 35th parallel that is still in use today. The general route of the Beale Wagon Road was followed by US Route 66, the Santa Fe Railway, and Interstate 40. The above map shows a section of the Beale Wagon Road between Fort Smith and Albuquerque, New Mexico. Portions of the original Beale Wagon Road are still visible on the prairie west of Borger, and the trail crosses the Frank Phillips College campus. (Courtesy of the Southwest Collection, Texas Tech University.)

The Hutchinson County Historical Commission and the Texas Historical Commission placed a historical marker on the Frank Phillips College campus in 2015. Due to the notoriety of the use of camels on this route, it became known as the "Beale Camel Trail" and is now listed as the Thirty-Fifth Parallel Route in the National Register of Historic Places. (Photograph by Clay Renick.)

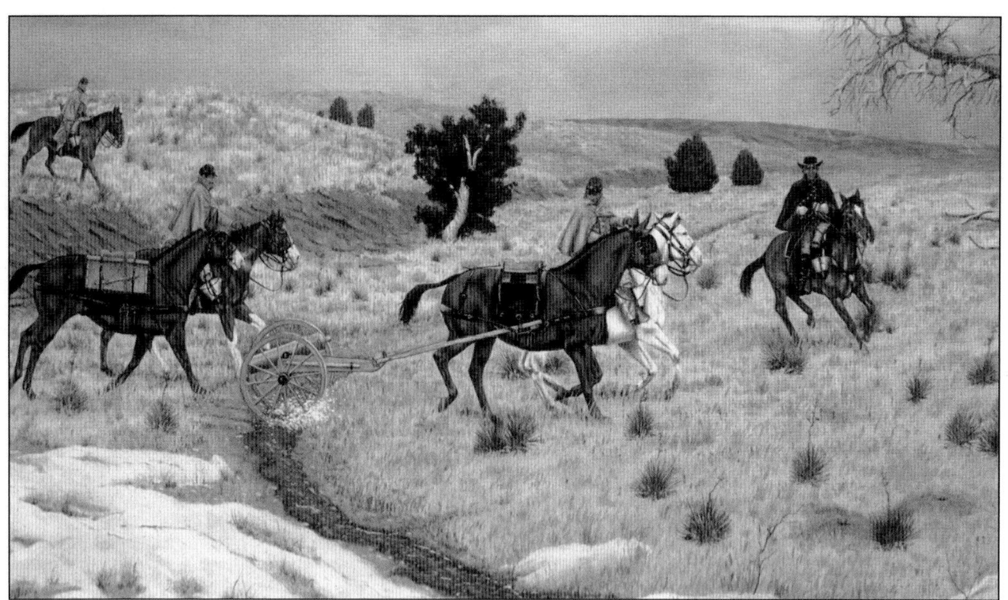

Kit Carson led a military regiment from Fort Bascom, New Mexico, to Adobe Walls to confront Kiowa and Cheyenne raiders on the Santa Fe Trail. He and his troops fought members of the two tribes at the First Battle of Adobe Walls on November 25, 1864. This painting was created by local artist Richard Hogue.

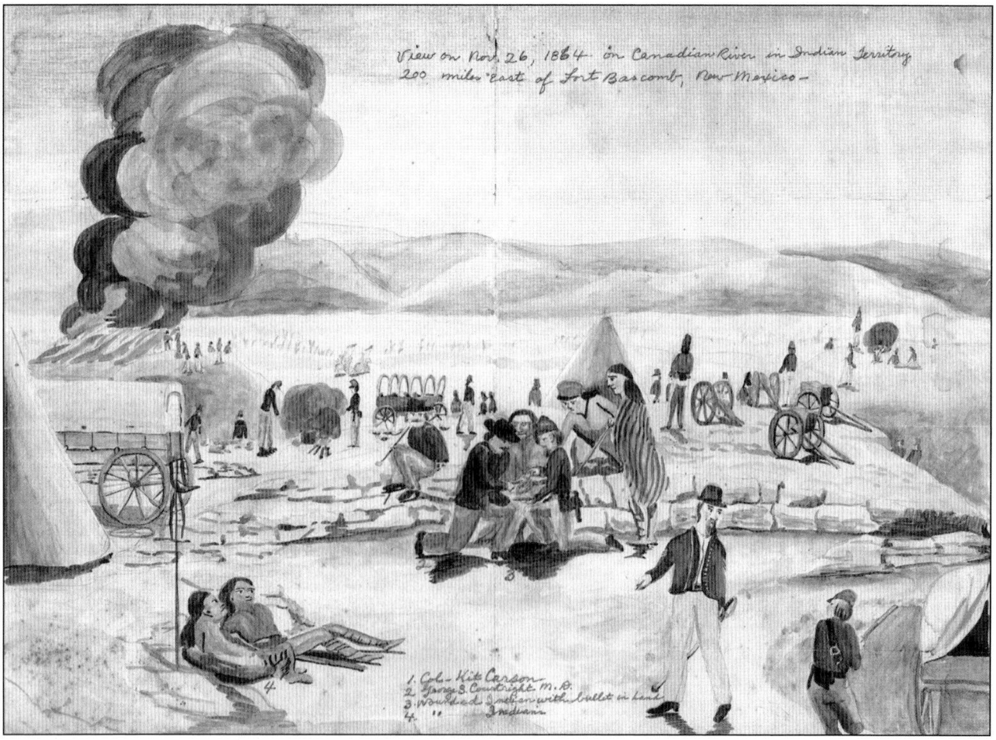

This watercolor painting, "Day After the Battle of Adobe Walls," was made by an unknown soldier in Kit Carson's command. Dated November 26, 1864, it was given to Dr. George S. Courtright, Carson's doctor at the battle. (Courtesy of Alvin Lynne.)

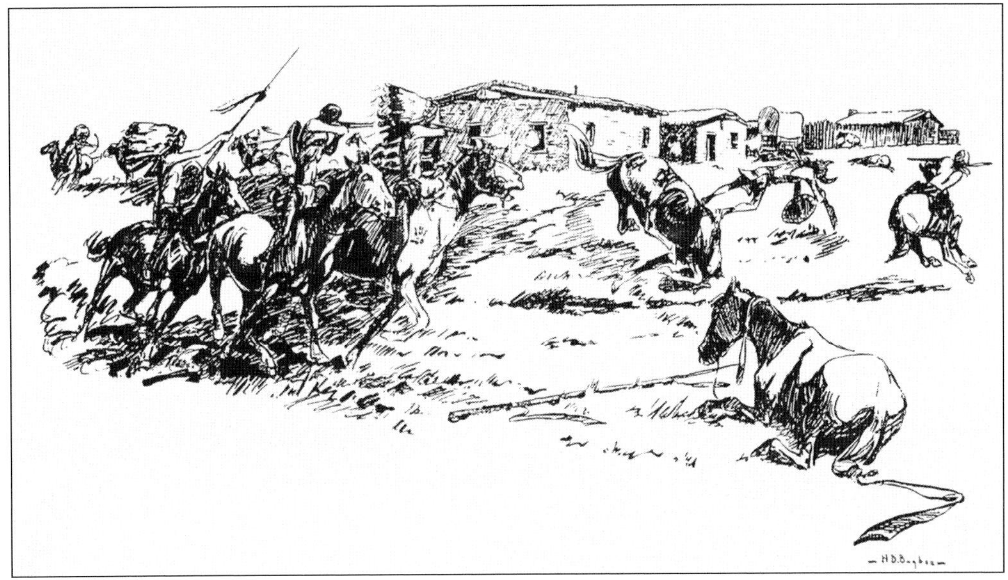

Renowned Western artist Harold Dow "H.D." Bugbee drew this pen-and-ink sketch depicting the Second Battle of Adobe Walls, which occurred in 1874. Bugbee was the cousin of Hutchinson County pioneer Thomas Sherman Bugbee, founder of the Quarter Circle T, the second ranch in the Texas Panhandle. Bugbee was a noted artist who by the mid-1920s had his work displayed in galleries in Denver, Chicago, Kansas City, and New York. In 1951, he became the first curator of art at the Panhandle-Plains Historical Museum—a position he held until his death on March 27, 1963.

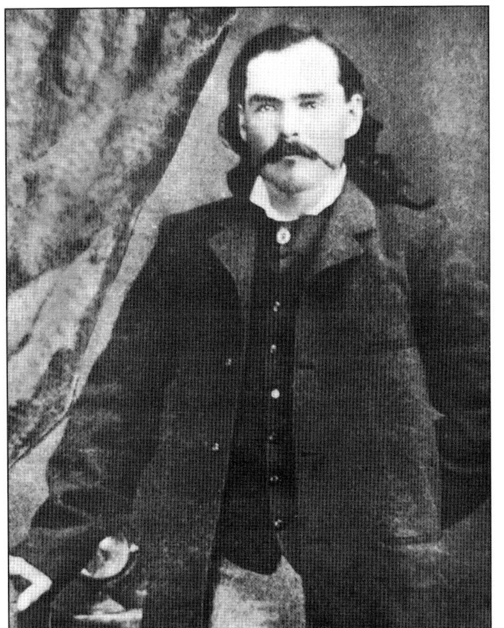

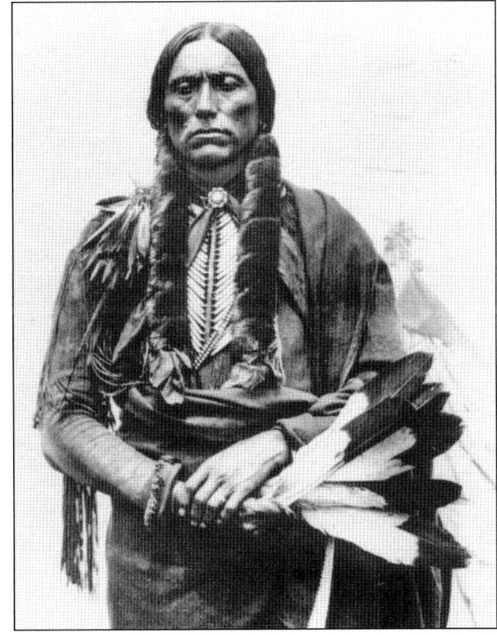

Billy Dixon, pictured at left at age 23, and Comanche chief Quanah Parker, at right, faced off at the Second Battle of Adobe Walls on June 27, 1874. Both men were formidable adversaries and the stuff of legends. The battle lasted for several days and ultimately ended in a draw, but it precipitated the Red River War later that year, which led to the forced removal of the Plains tribes from the land they had roamed for centuries and opened the West to those who had forced the Indigenous peoples out.

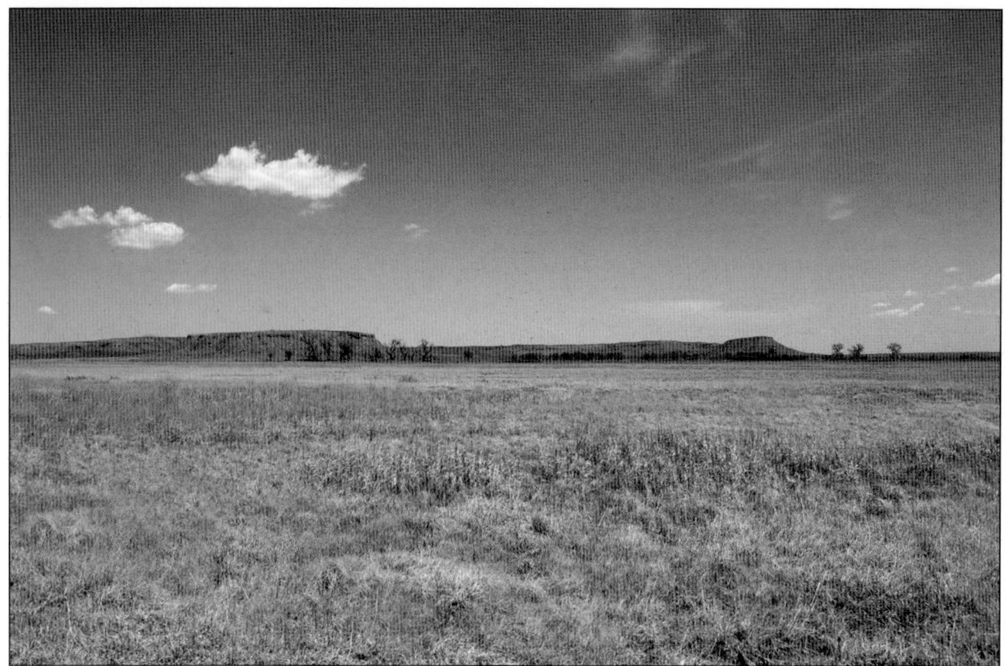

Billy Dixon's "long shot," which ended the Second Battle of Adobe Walls in 1974, was made from near where this photograph was taken. Dixon's remarkable shot dropped a Native American from his horse atop the butte on the left at a range of almost 1,800 yards. (Photograph by Clay Renick.)

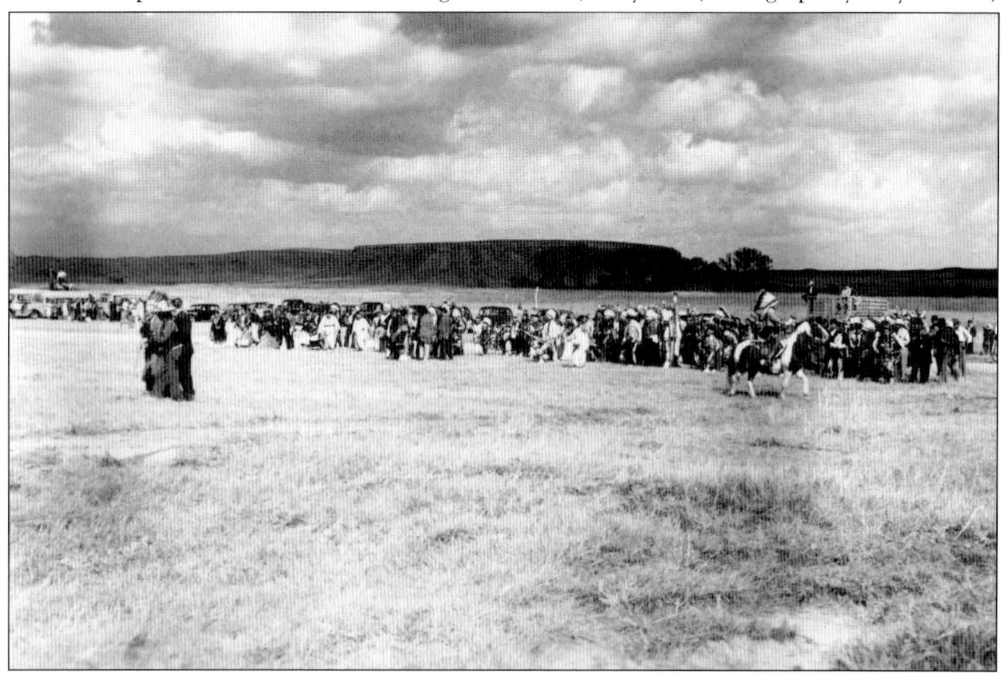

In 1941, a granite monument was set to honor the Native American warriors who fought at the Second Battle of Adobe Walls. As many as 10,000 people attended the three-day observance. Members of the Comanche, Kiowa, Cheyenne, and Arapaho tribes came from Oklahoma to attend the ceremony.

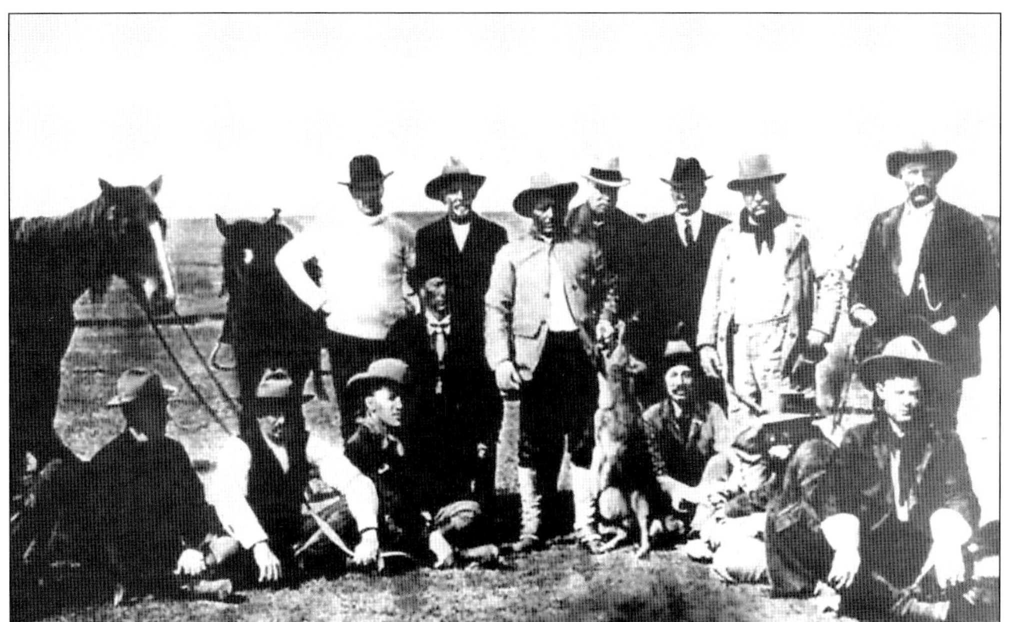

Teddy Roosevelt traveled through Indian Territory on his way to a Rough Riders reunion in San Antonio, Texas, in April 1905, before Oklahoma became a state in 1907. He made speeches at railroad stops in small towns between Vinita and Durant, Oklahoma, near the reservation where Comanche leader Quanah Parker was residing. When he was returning from the reunion, Roosevelt was giving a speech to thousands of people in Fredrick, Oklahoma, when he noticed Parker in the crowd. Roosevelt called Parker to the podium to shake his hand and later invited him to join his hunting party on a 480,000-acre area of open range known as the Big Pasture in present-day Tillman County, Texas, and Comanche and Cotton Counties in Oklahoma. Members of the party included the president's doctor, Dr. Alexander Lambert; several former Rough Riders; cattle ranchers; and Parker. In the above image from the hunt, Roosevelt is second from right in the back row (standing), and Parker is standing in the center. Parker is pictured at right toward the end of his life; he died in 1911.

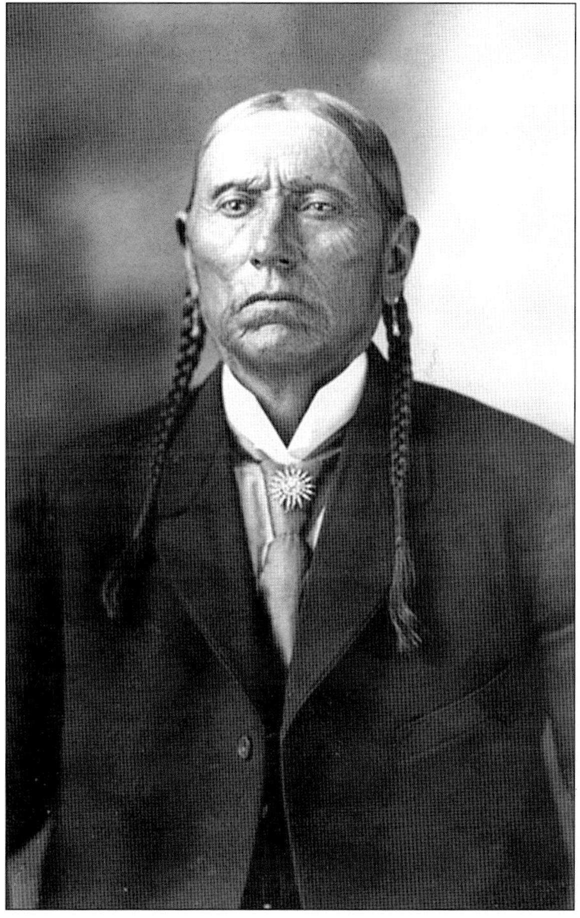

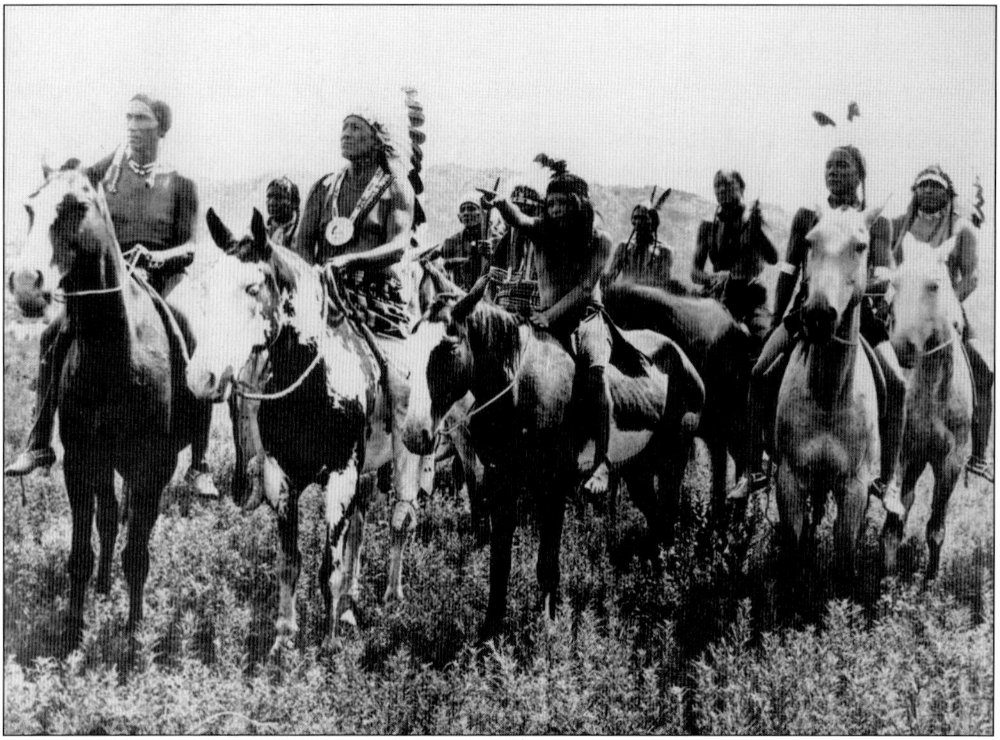

Among those pictured here are one of Quanah's sons, White Parker, Hunting Horse (Kiowa), Cecil Horse, Ochi (Kiowa), Wolf Tail (Kiowa), and Frank Skinny (Kiowa).

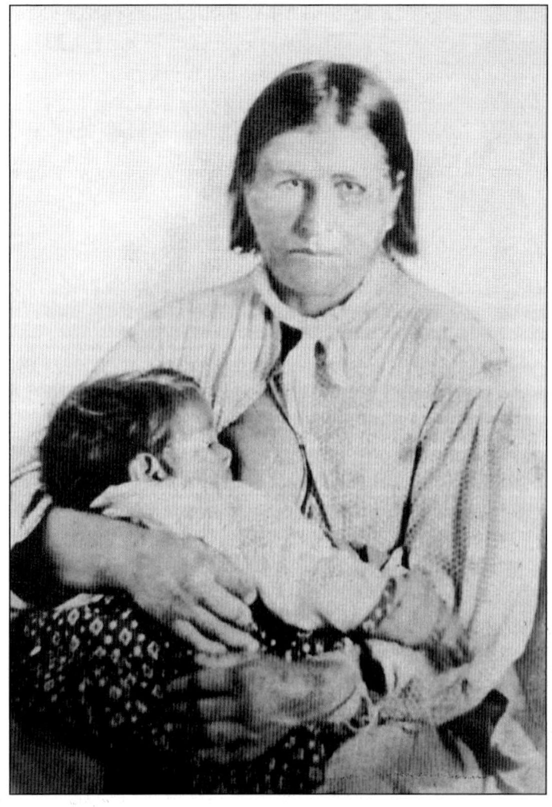

Cynthia Ann Parker is pictured with her daughter Topusana (Prairie Flower). This photograph was taken shortly after Parker was captured at the Pease River south of present-day Quanah, Texas, in 1860.

Billy Dixon was born in 1850 in West Virginia. He headed west at age 14 and served as a mule skinner, scout, buffalo hunter, and soldier. In 1883, he built a home near the Adobe Walls battle site. Dixon served as postmaster, the first sheriff of Hutchinson County, state land commissioner, and justice of the peace. In 1894, he married Olive King of Virginia. The Dixons moved to Cimarron County, New Mexico, where he died and was buried in 1913. In 1929, his body was exhumed and reinterred at Adobe Walls. For his participation in the Battle of Buffalo Wallow on September 12, 1874, Dixon and six other men in the battle were awarded the Congressional Medal of Honor.

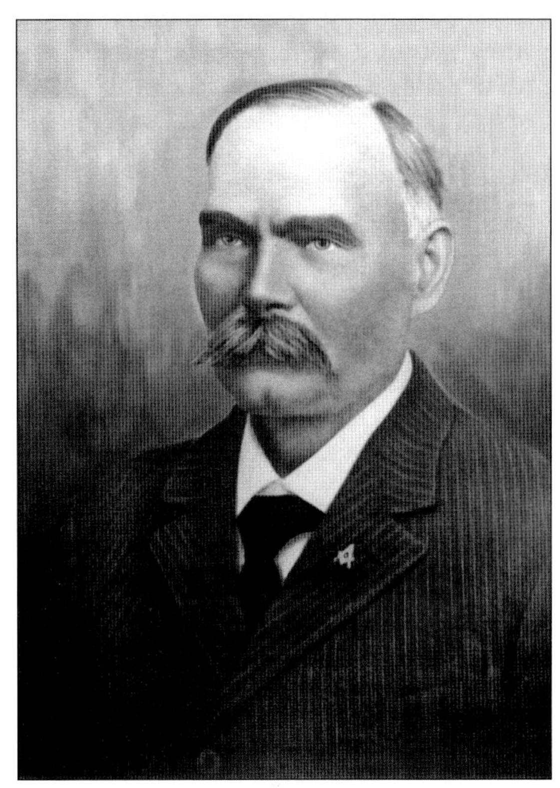

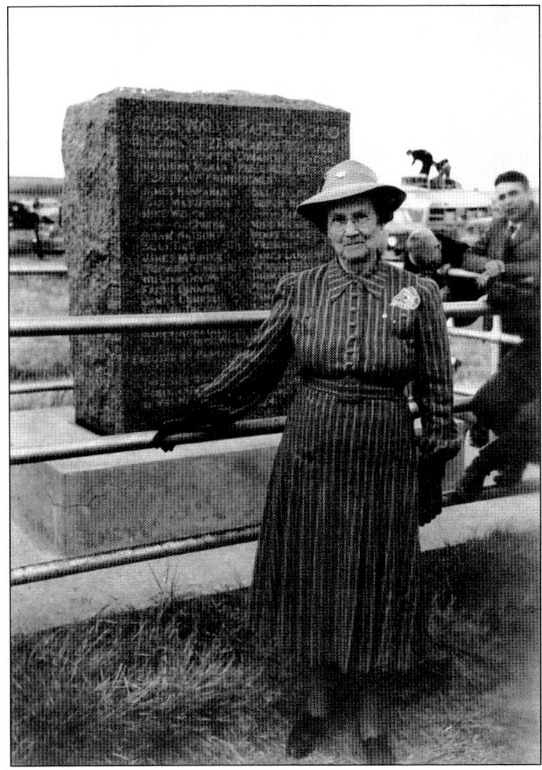

Olive Dixon is seen at Adobe Walls in 1941 for the setting of the Indian monument. She was the teacher at the school pioneer rancher James A. Whittenburg organized for his own children to attend in 1890. She met Billy Dixon while there and they married in 1894. Before Billy's death in 1913, Olive wrote and published *The Life of Billy Dixon*, his recollections as a buffalo hunter and army scout. The book has become an important source of Panhandle history. Olive Dixon led the effort to place historical markers at the Adobe Walls and Buffalo Wallow battle sites in 1924. She later worked as a staff writer and reporter for the *Amarillo Globe-News* until her death in 1956.

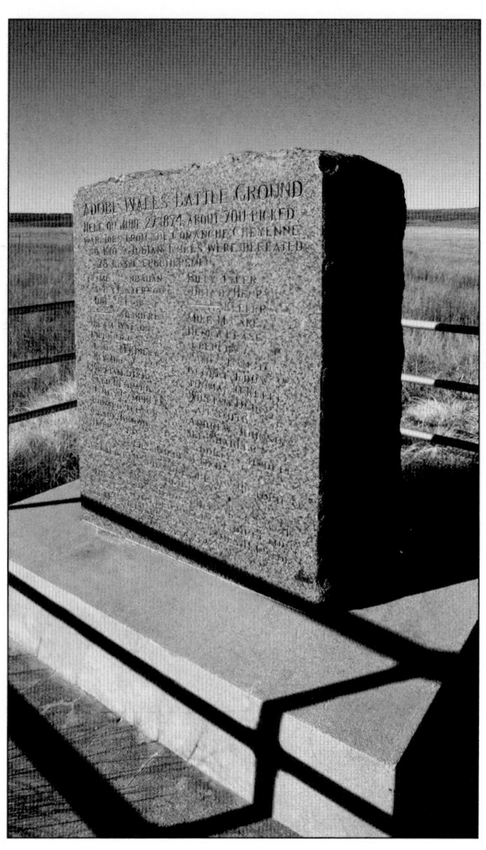

On June 27, 1924, a celebration was held to observe the 50th anniversary of the second Battle of Adobe Walls at the battle site in Hutchinson County. A granite marker—inscribed with the names of those who took part in the battle—was unveiled during the celebration. W.T. Coble and his wife, owners of the Turkey Track Ranch (where the site is located), deeded five acres to the Panhandle-Plains Historical Society in Canyon to permanently preserve the historic location. The society later founded the Panhandle-Plains Historical Museum on the campus of West Texas A&M University in Canyon. (Photograph by Clay Renick.)

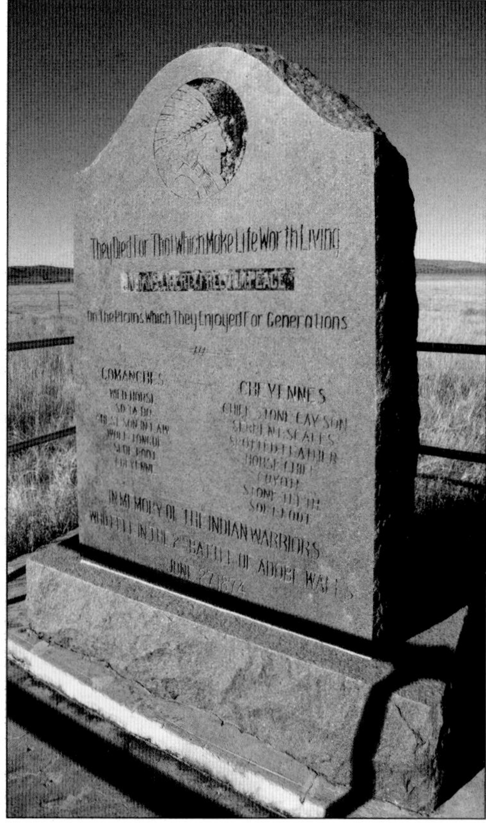

In 1939, after learning that a monument to honor the buffalo hunters who had fought in the Second Battle of Adobe Walls had been erected on the battle site in 1924, members of the Comanche, Kiowa, Cheyenne, and Arapaho tribes inquired if they might place a monument to honor warriors from their tribes who had also fought in the battle. Authorities enthusiastically agreed that they were welcome to do so but told them that funding was not available for the project. The tribes offered to fund the project, providing granite that was harvested from the Wichita Mountains on a tribal reservation in southwestern Oklahoma, and hired a Native American sculptor to carve the monument. They transported and set the marker, which was unveiled in a three-day festival held on the site and in Borger. Members of all four tribes traveled from Oklahoma, joining as many as 10,000 people who came to attend the dedication of the monument at Adobe Walls in 1941. (Photograph by Clay Renick.)

Three

Pioneer Ranchers and Farmers

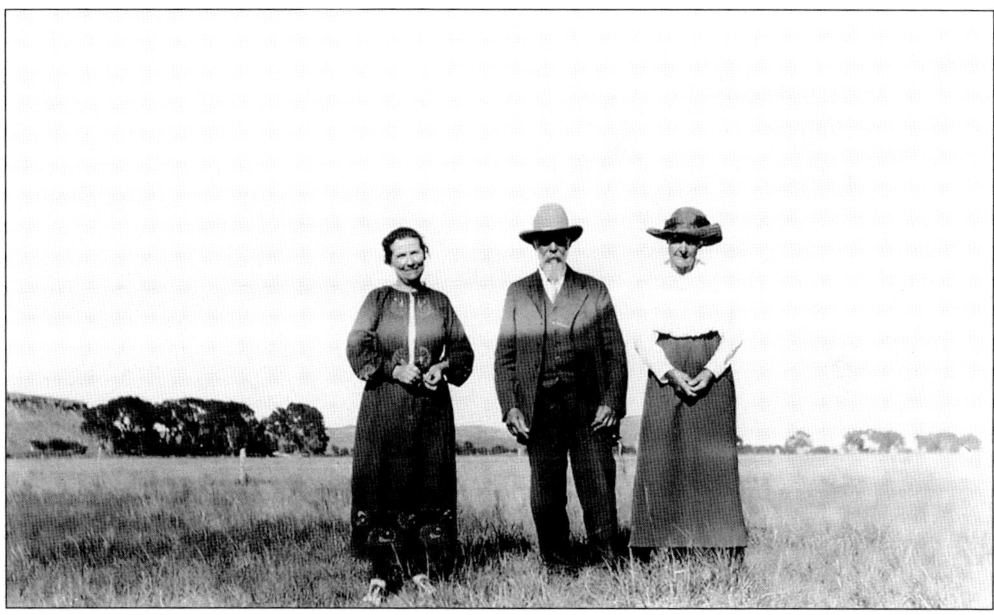

Olive Dixon (left) is pictured with James and Edith Cator near the Adobe Walls battle sites. James and Bob Cator came to America intending to farm in Kansas, but they found farming was much less profitable in America than it was in England. The brothers become buffalo hunters because that business was much more profitable and demand for buffalo hides was great. They built a house and started a store in Hansford County on North Palo Duro Creek. They named their new enterprise Zulu Stockade, because they thought the territory was as wild as the Zulu lands of Africa. Zulu Stockade was near Adobe Walls, the site of the last battle between whites and the Indians. Olive's husband, Billy Dixon, came to the area with the buffalo hunters who built the Adobe Walls trading post and fought in the second Battle of Adobe Walls there in 1874. The battle site is northeast of Borger and 17 miles south of Spearman, in Hansford County.

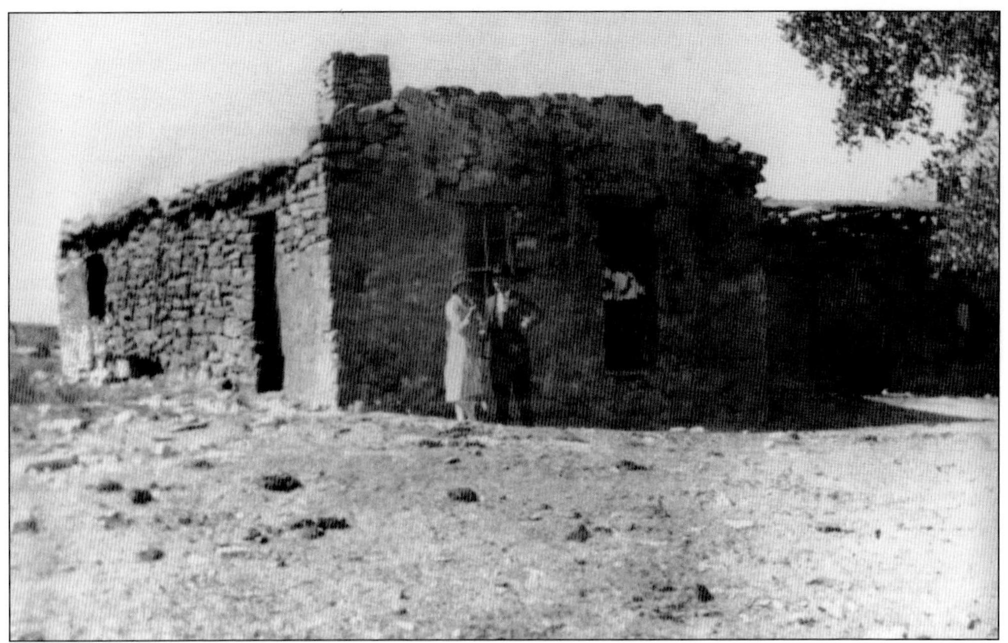

Thomas Sherman Bugbee was one of the first ranchers in what would later become Hutchinson County when he moved to the area with his family in 1876. Bugbee started the Quarter Circle T Ranch, the second ranch in the Texas Panhandle, with 1,800 head of cattle. The Bugbees lived in a dugout while they built a rock house north of the Canadian River and about five miles west of Adobe Walls. Fearing the return of the Native Americans they had displaced, they built the walls 25 inches thick with two gun ports in every room. The house became known as Bugbee Fort. Bugbee's daughter Ruby was the first white child born in Hutchinson County. In 1881, the ranch and its 12,500 head of cattle were sold to Hansford Land and Cattle Company, and it became part of the Turkey Track Ranch.

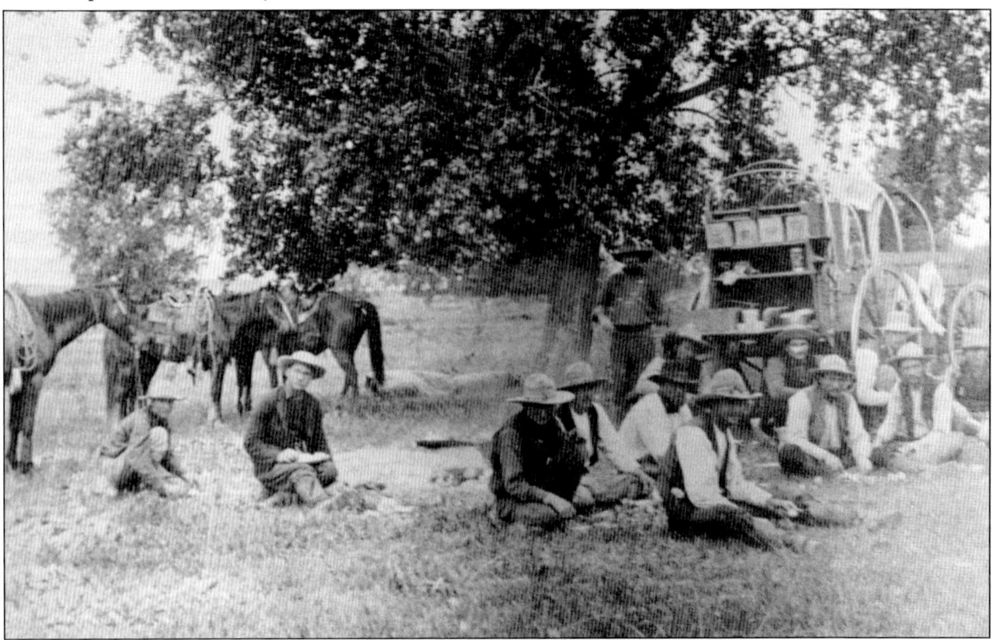

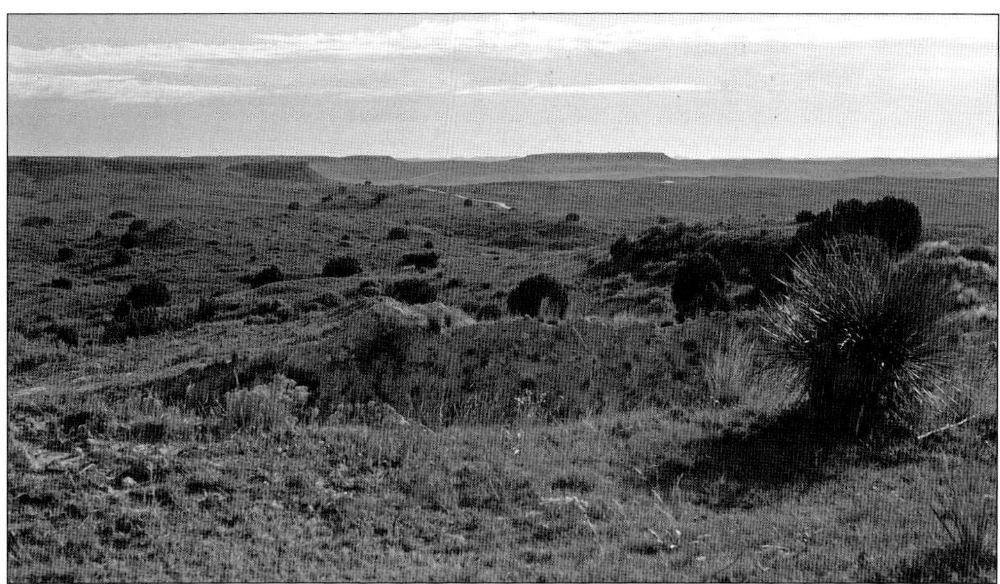

The Turkey Track Ranch was established in 1878 by Richard McNalty from Colorado and was one of the first five ranches in the Texas Panhandle. Hansford Land and Cattle Company, an English syndicate run by J.M. Coburn of Scotland, acquired the ranch in 1883 and also purchased T.S. Bugbee's Quarter Circle T Ranch and William Anderson's Scissors Ranch near Adobe Walls. By 1890, Hansford Land and Cattle owned 85,000 acres, leased 350,000 acres, and had an average head count of 30,000 cattle. In 1903, Kansas banker Charlie Patton and two partners bought the ranch. Patton bought out his partners in 1910. In 1916, William T. Coble purchased the ranch and began using the Turkey Track brand. Coble's daughter Catherine married J.A. Whittenburg II, son of George Whittenburg and grandson of James Andrew Whittenburg, who owned the MM ranch at Plemons, south of Turkey Track. Turkey Track Ranch offers some of the greatest varieties of wildlife in Texas. With miles of water, it has large populations of quail, dove, white-tailed deer, mule deer, pronghorn antelope, ducks, geese, and—of course—wild turkeys. (Both photographs by Clay Renick.)

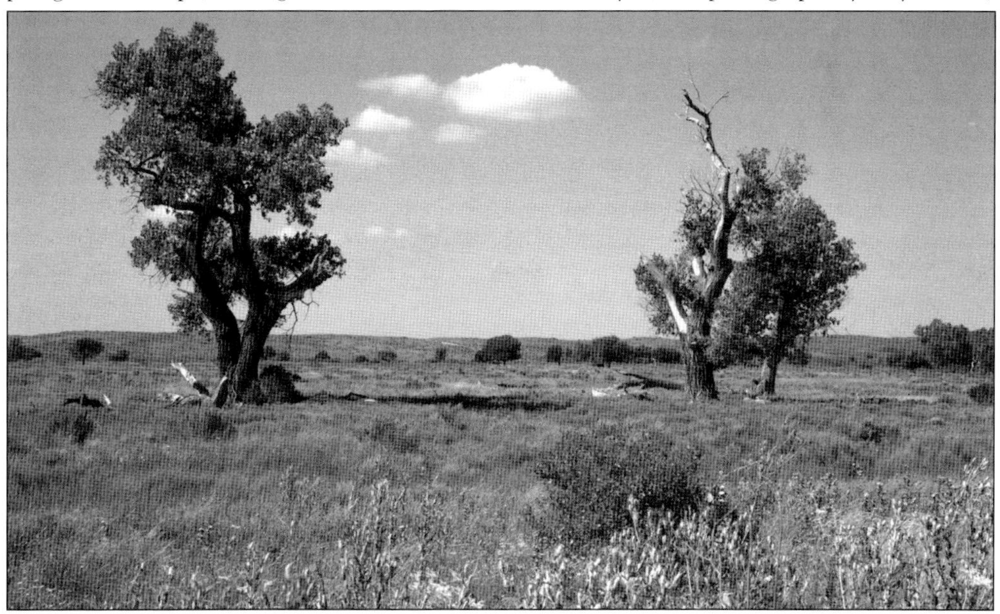

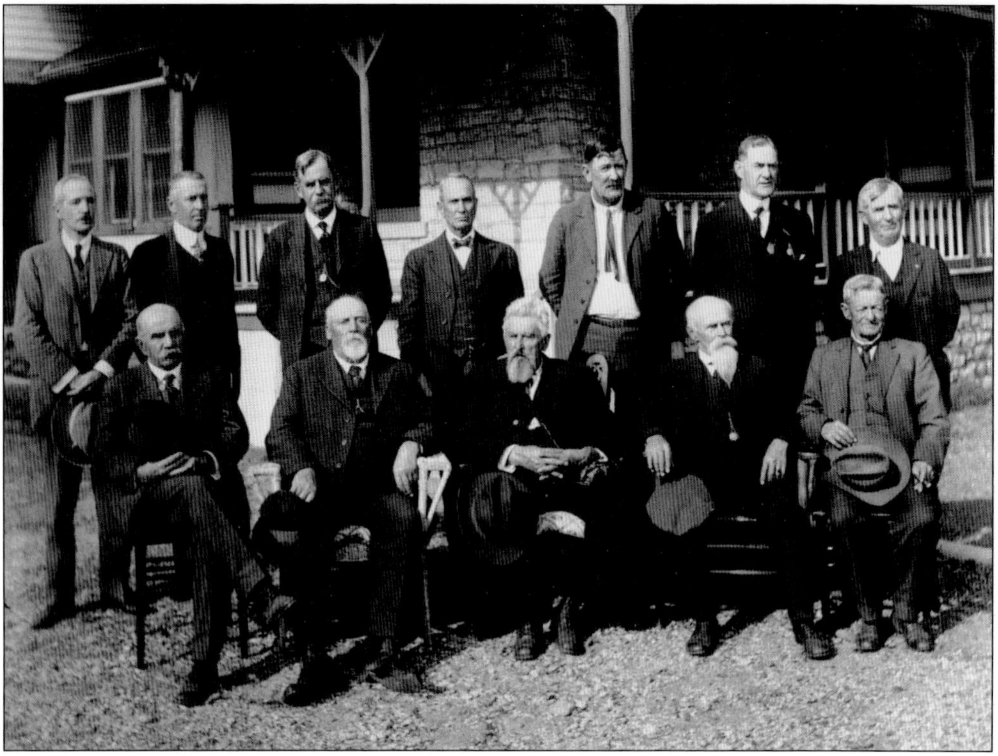

This photograph of "The most notable group of pioneers ever assembled in the Panhandle" was published in the *Amarillo Daily News* on March 4, 1925. It shows members of the Panhandle Stock Association attending a meeting at the JA Ranch in November 1921. From left to right are (seated) Vas Stickley, Thomas Sherman Bugbee, Colonel Charles Goodnight, Captain G. W. Arrington, and Judge O.H. Nelson (standing) M.K. Brown, Whitfield Carhart, T.D. Hobart, Henry Taylor, J.W. Kent, W.H. Patrick, and George Dunn.

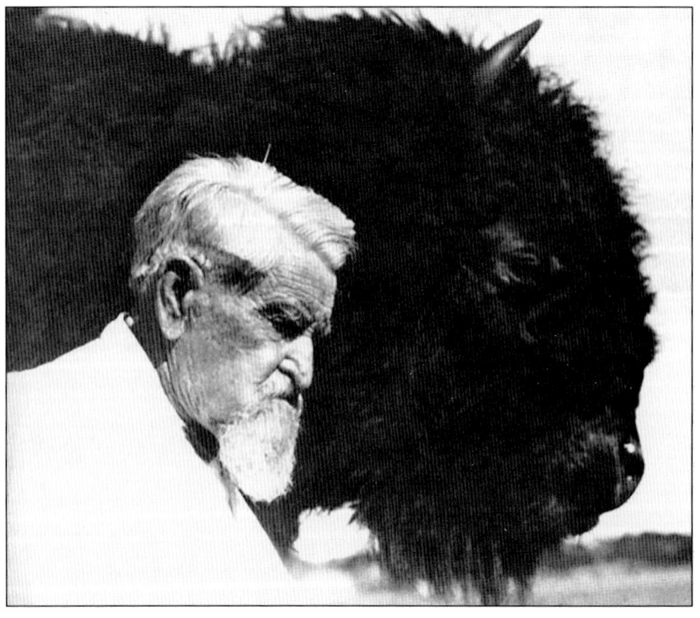

Charles Goodnight established the first ranch in the Texas Panhandle, the JA Ranch, in 1876. Later that year, Thomas Sherman Bugbee founded the Quarter Circle T Ranch, the Panhandle's second ranch and Hutchinson County's first cattle ranch. Goodnight was a visionary pioneer who unsuccessfully tried to crossbreed cattle and buffalo in an attempt to produce hardier animals who would be able to withstand the harsh conditions found on the Great Plains.

At age 19, Samuel Burk Burnett, who is pictured with Comanche chief Quanah Parker, bought 100 head of cattle wearing the 6666 brand and thus became owner of the brand. Burnett and Parker had an agreement that allowed Burnett to graze his cattle on 300,000 acres of Indian lands in Texas and Oklahoma. In 1901, as the free-range grazing era was coming to an end, Burnett bought the 8 Ranch near Guthrie and the Dixon Creek Ranch south of Borger and began his legendary empire. The 6666 Ranch is now in its second century of operation and was sold to new owners in 2021.

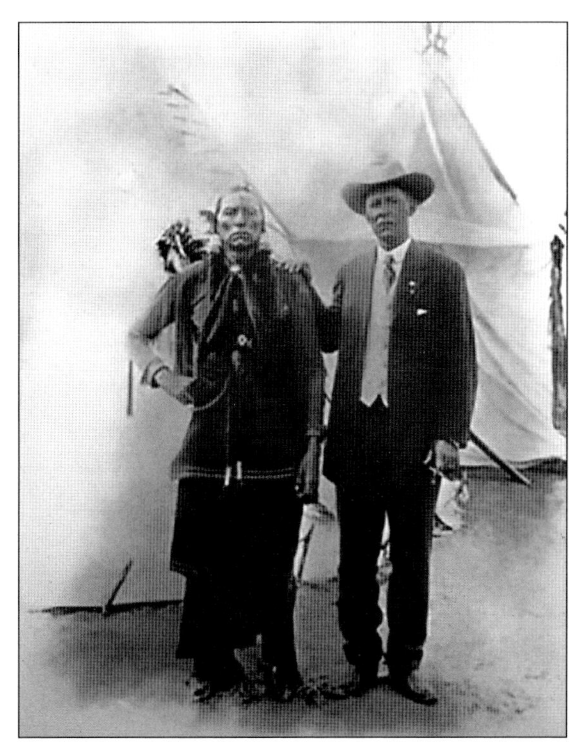

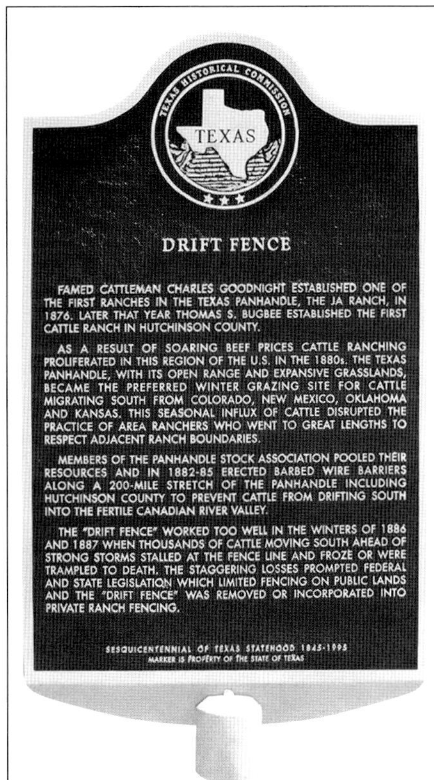

Even though the Texas Panhandle is a very large area, many of the early ranchers realized that there was strength in numbers and formed the Panhandle Stock Association to protect their interests. They erected a drift fence to prevent free-range cattle from migrating into the Canadian River valley from the north. During the winters of 1886 and 1887, the fence stopped the movement of thousands of cattle, causing them to freeze or be trampled to death; it was soon removed. This Texas historical marker, placed north of the Canadian River in Hutchinson County, tells of a significant episode in the long, complex story of ranching in the Texas Panhandle.

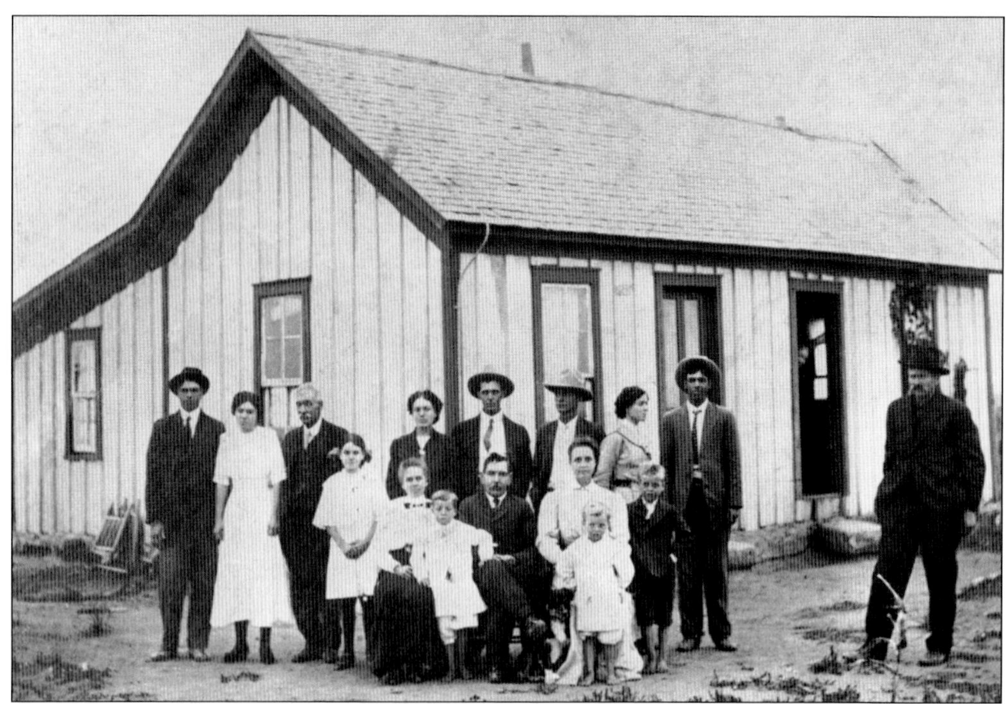

Isaac and Capitola McCormick came by wagon to what is now Hutchinson County in 1899. Isaac purchased four sections of public school land, and the McCormicks and their eight children lived in a covered wagon and a tent while they built a house. Later in 1899, local residents met at the McCormick house to organize Hutchinson County. The house was built with lumber transported by wagon from Panhandle, 35 miles south, and across the Canadian River. The house was built northeast of where it stands today and is one of the oldest buildings in the county. Isaac and Capitola raised 10 children in this humble four-room house; Capitola and one of the couple's daughters are pictured below in front of the house in 1927.

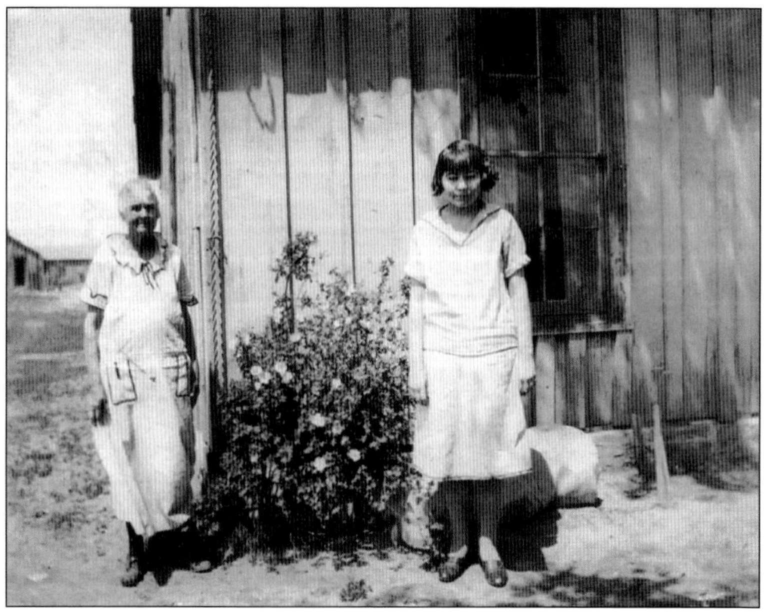

Blanche and Edgar Britain are shown at their ranch east of Stinnett with an antelope they raised as a pet. Edgar graduated from Amarillo High School in 1925 and went to Texas A&M, Texas Tech, and the University of Texas. He later moved to Hutchinson County to ranch and farm. He leased the old Bivins estate, bought a herd of cattle, and established the Lazy E Ranch. In 1932, he married Blanche Groves. They were active in community affairs and cared deeply about Stinnett. They donated the historic McCormick house, which had originally been built on their land, to the City of Stinnett so it could be preserved as a county landmark. Ownership of the house was later transferred to Hutchinson County. The historic structure would probably not exist today without the Britains' generosity and interest in the county's history.

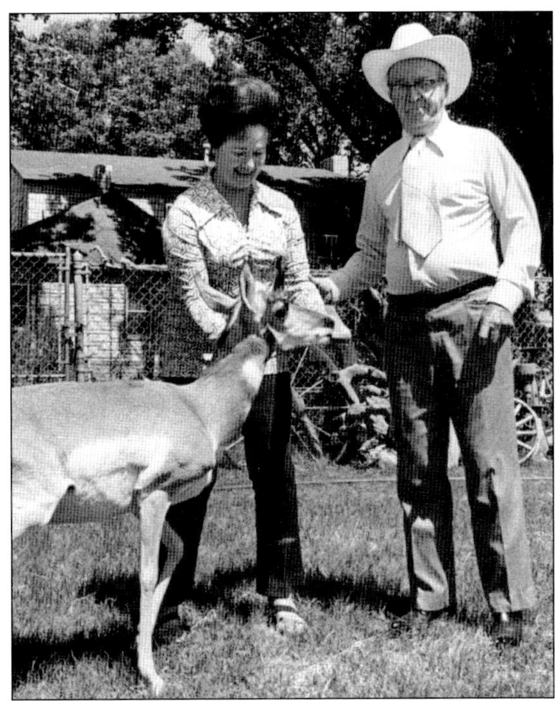

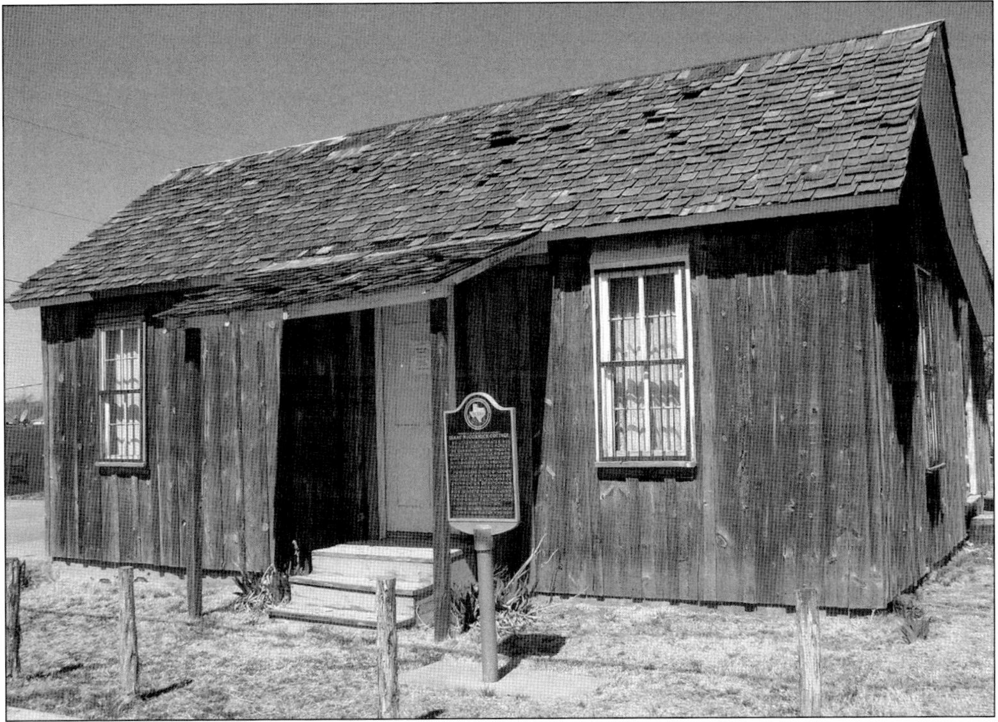

The Isaac McCormick house was moved from Edgar Britain's Lazy E Ranch to a lot on Main Street in Stinnett in 1928. It was later relocated to a site north of the Hutchinson County courthouse, where it remains today. The cottage was donated to Stinnett in 1964 and later deeded to Hutchinson County. A Texas historical marker was placed at the house in 1967. (Photograph by Clay Renick.)

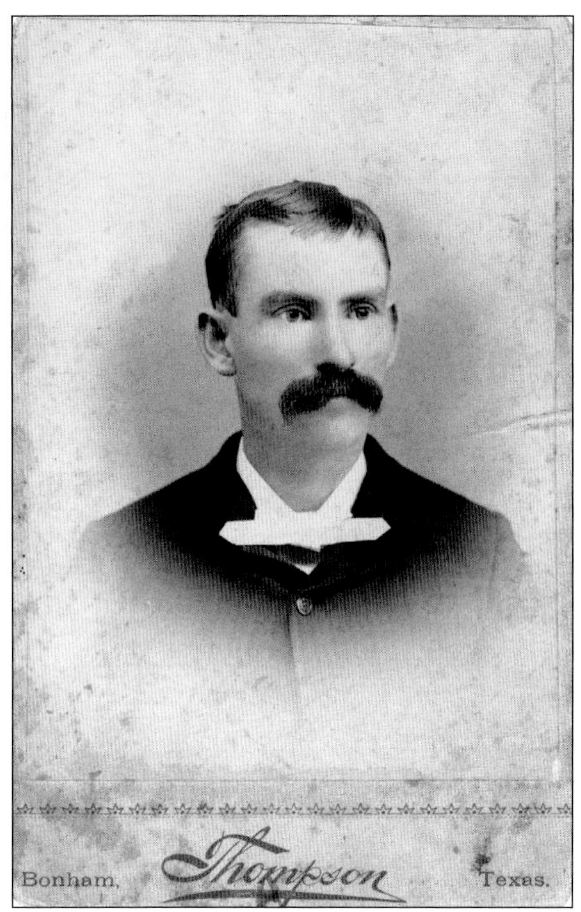

Wyndham Robinson Harvey was born in 1863 in Arkansas and came to the Texas Panhandle, settling near Childress, where he worked as a cowboy. Harvey, who came to be known as Bunk, was a frugal businessman and saved his money. He bought two sections of land in southeast Hutchinson County, south of the Canadian River near Spring Creek, in 1901. He steadily bought land over the years with the profits he earned through hard work and tenacity. From his original purchase of 1,320 acres, he built a ranching empire of 33,600 acres in 35 years. Below, carriages, cars, and cattle illustrate the changing times at the Harvey Ranch.

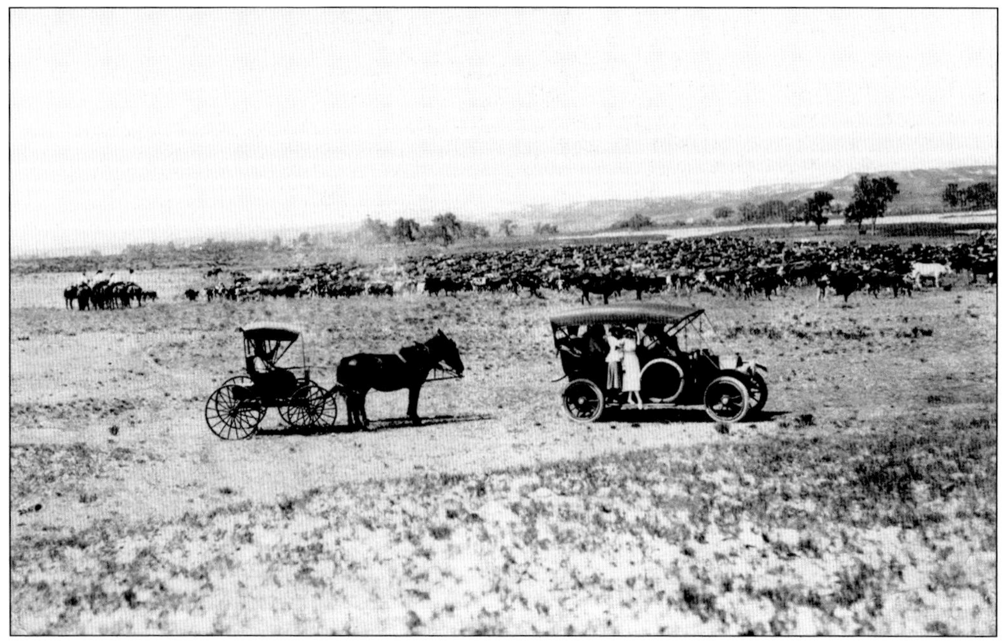

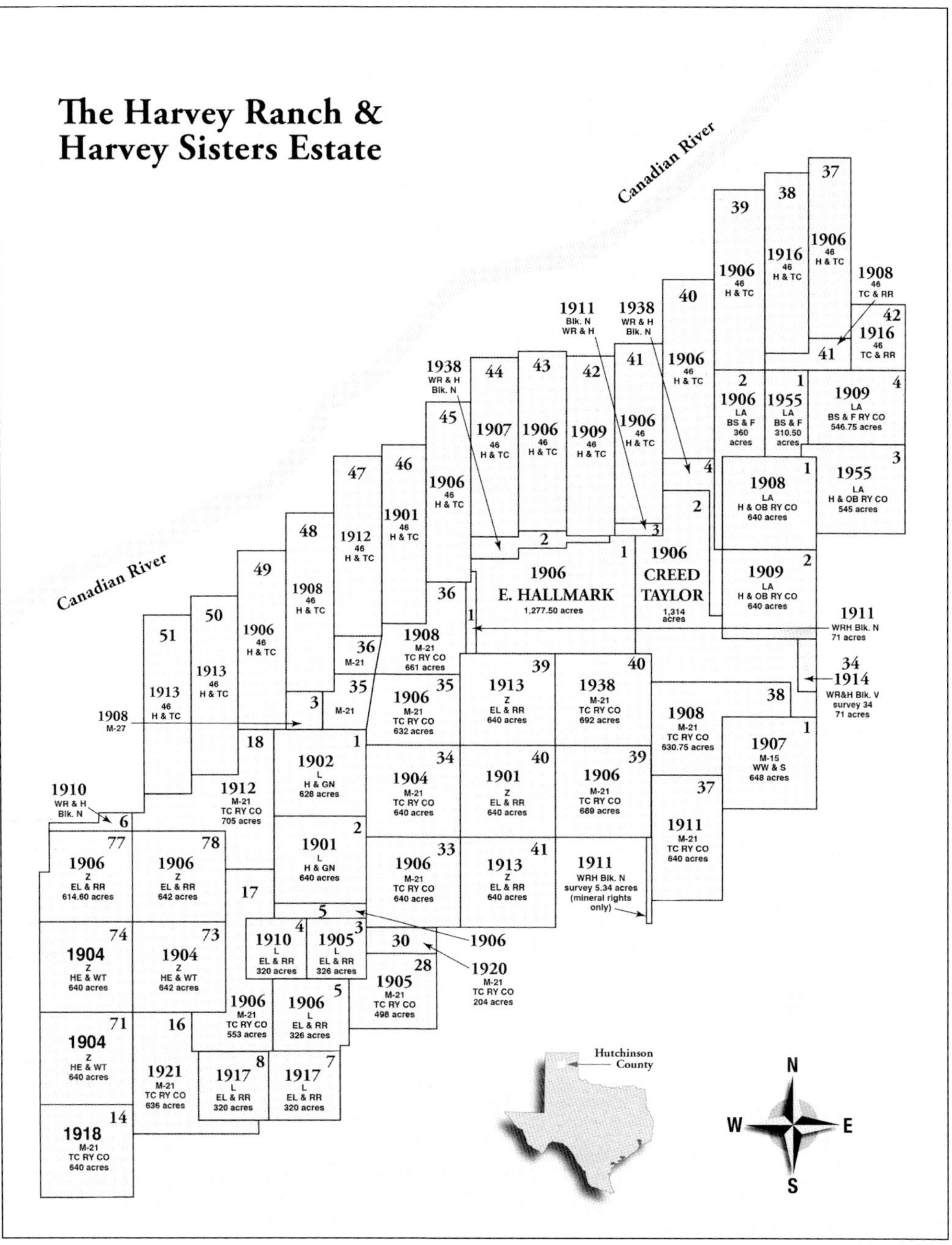

Bunk Harvey founded the Harvey Ranch in 1901 and increased its size from its original two sections to 52.5 sections—a total of 33,600 acres. Harvey died in 1935, and his will specified that the ranch could not be divided until 35 years after his death. In 1970, on the 35th anniversary of his death, his three daughters—Gladys, Bonnie, and Rachel—divided the ranch equally to establish ranches of their own. In 2021, approximately two-thirds of the ranch land is still owned by descendants of Bunk Harvey. This map of the Harvey Ranch was drawn with reference to an extensive collection of historical documents provided by Harvey family members. (Illustration by Clay Renick.)

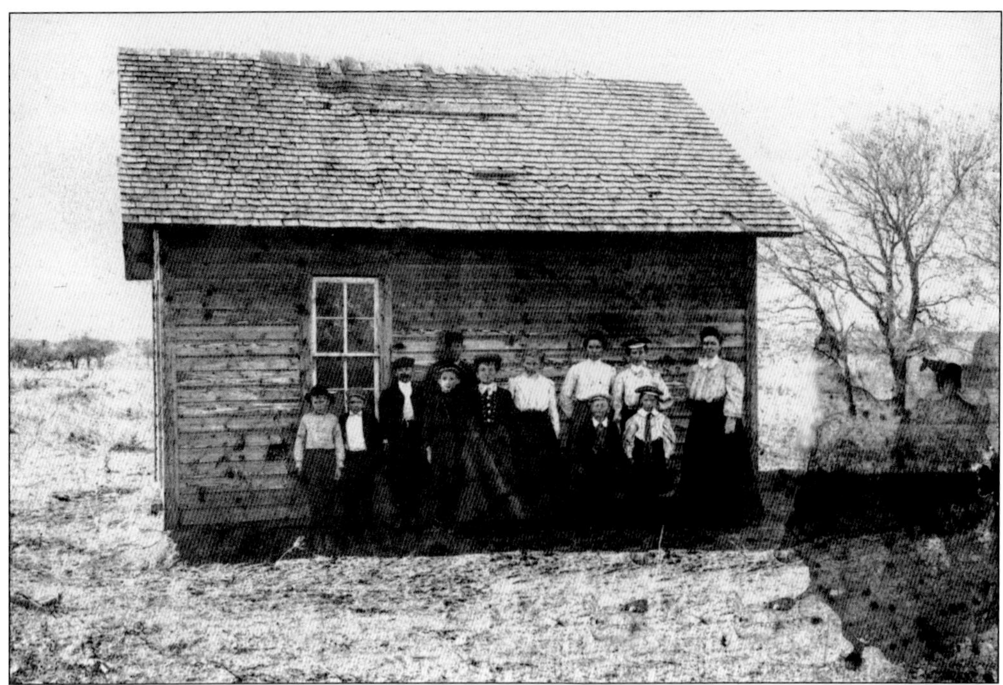

The first schoolhouse at Spring Creek is shown above around 1910. Bunk Harvey paid for the building and the first teacher's salary so that his children could be educated. Pictured below are Miss Osbourne, the first teacher at Spring Creek School, and six of her pupils. From left to right on the horse are Clay Bennet, Rachel, Gladys, and Bonnie Harvey, and Ray and Roy Bennet.

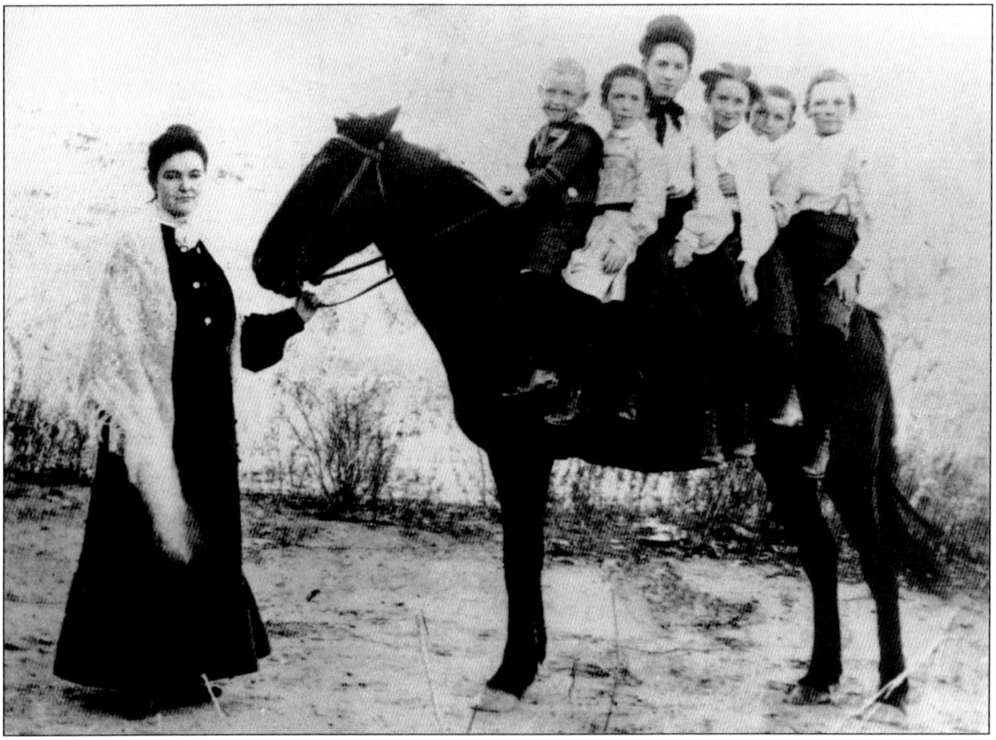

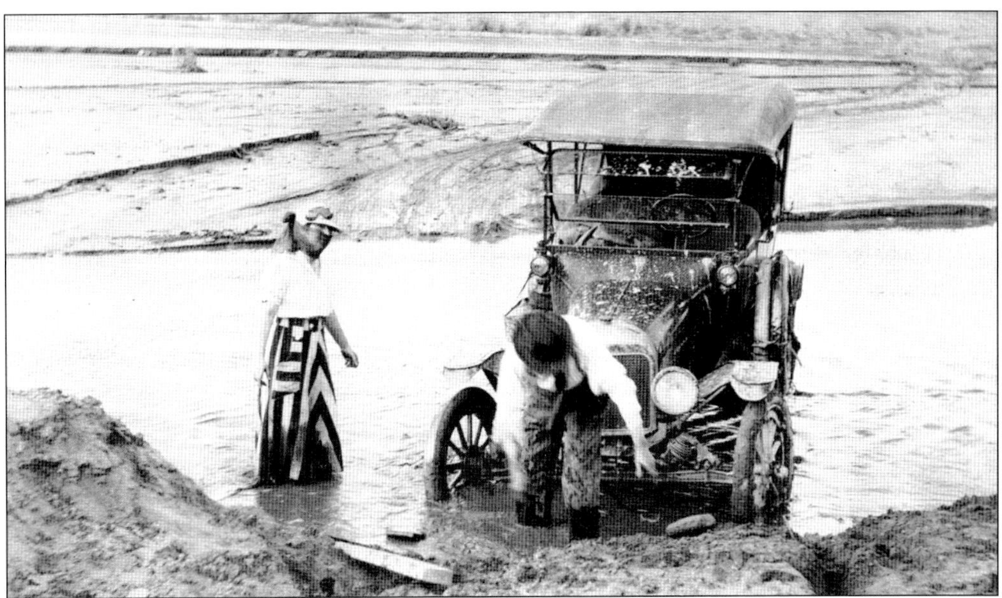

Spring Creek flowed year-round north-to-south through the center of the Harvey Ranch. Crossing any of the sandy creeks or the Canadian River often resulted in people, animals, and vehicles getting stuck, as shown here. Often, springs in the creek itself created quicksand bogs that could quickly swallow up any traveler who was unfortunate enough to wander into them.

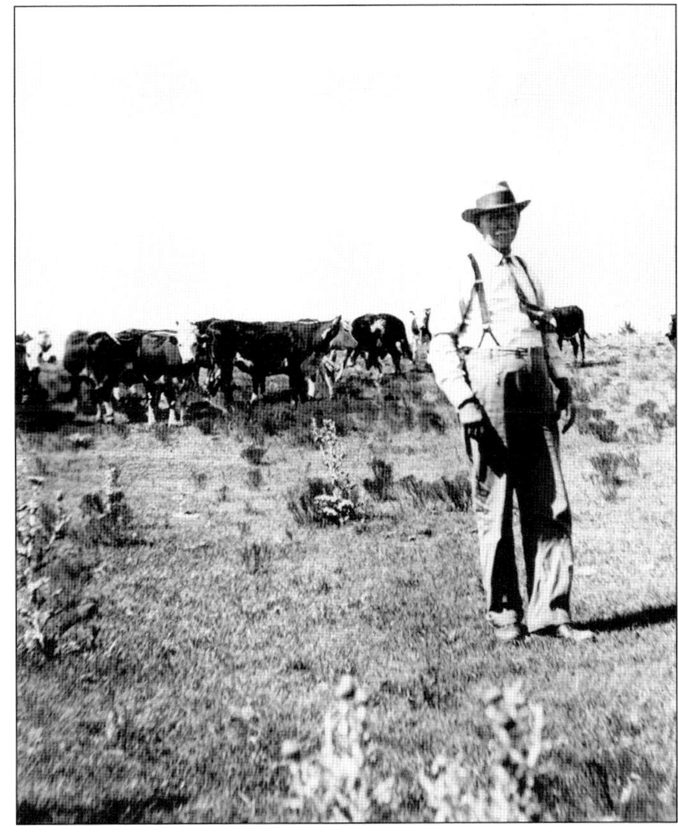

Bunk Harvey was a smart, successful rancher and businessman. Years after he established his Hutchinson County ranch, his family moved to California due to the declining health of his wife, Lucy. He started another ranch in New Mexico and managed both of his ranches from there.

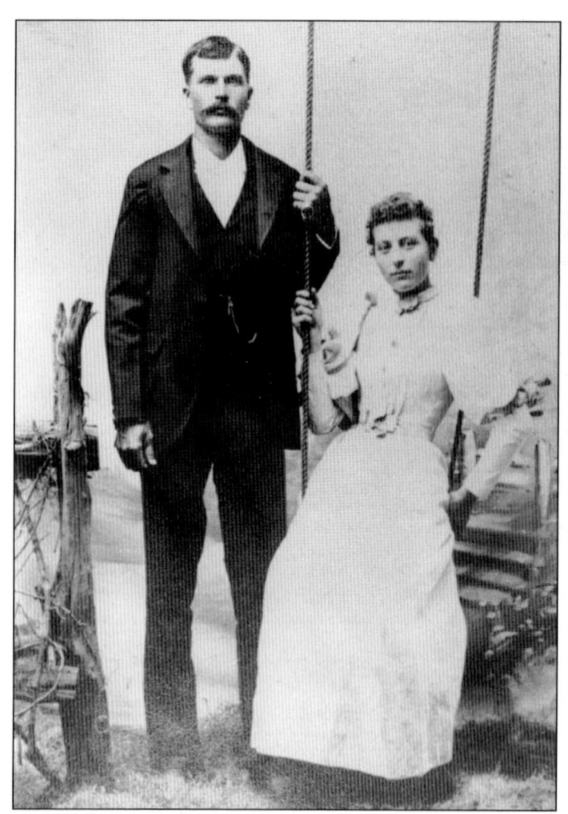

John and Maggie Weatherly came by wagon to the Panhandle in 1898. They claimed four sections of land in Hutchinson County, which was yet to be organized at the time. They called their new settlement Granada, and other pioneer settlers soon moved nearby. They established a post office and a store in their ranch house. Maggie later changed the name of the town to Isom, which was the name of her hometown in West Virginia. A school was established in 1907. In October 1919 the Isom post office closed, and mail was directed to Plemons. They moved to the nearby town of Panhandle in 1923 but wisely retained ownership of their Isom townsite. Soon after oil was discovered, Missouri businessman Ace Borger bought 240 acres of their land and founded his namesake town in 1926. John and Maggie are seen at left below, standing in front of the dugout where they lived while John built their new house, which is in the background.

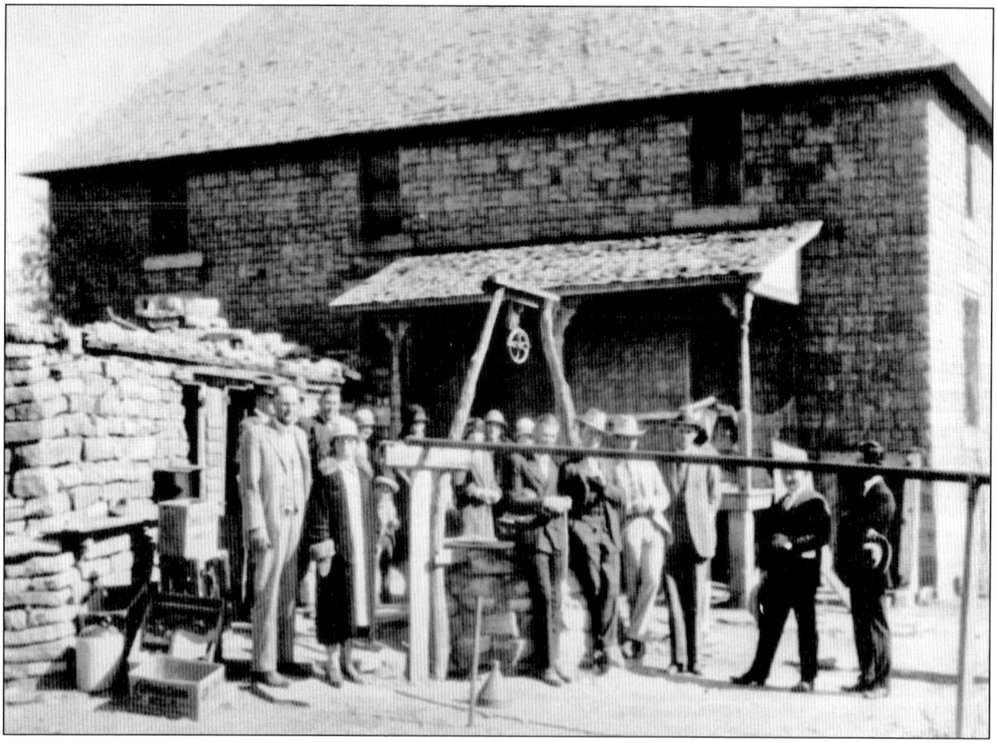

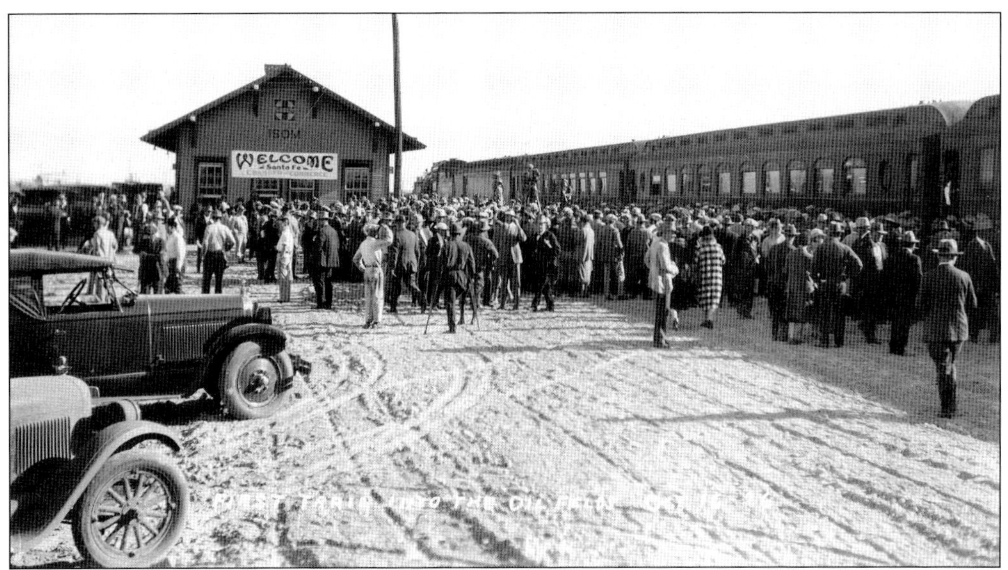

John and Maggie Weatherly watched from their home in nearby Panhandle, Texas, as Ace Borger found success building his new town. They regained interest in their Isom townsite and relocated it near the Santa Fe Railway branch that had been built just south of Borger in May 1926. Adjacent to Borger, First Street became the dividing line. All lots south of First Street were in Isom, and all lots north of First Street were in Borger. From June to December 1926, the towns competed to become the capital of the new oilfields. John Weatherly persuaded the Santa Fe Railway to build a branch terminal in Isom, believing that doing so would allow him to claim the new town's name. Borger convinced the US Post Office to open a branch north of First Street with the knowledge that if they did, he would claim the new town's name. Although Isom had a railroad depot, several oil-well supply warehouses, and no shortage of citizens, 1,200 residents signed a petition in early December 1926 to merge Isom with Borger. In 1927, the consolidation of the Isom school with the Borger Independent School District made the merger complete, and Isom faded into history. John and Maggie continued to live in Panhandle until their deaths; he died in 1944, and she in 1968. Below is a replica of the Weatherly dugout on the campus of Frank Phillips College.

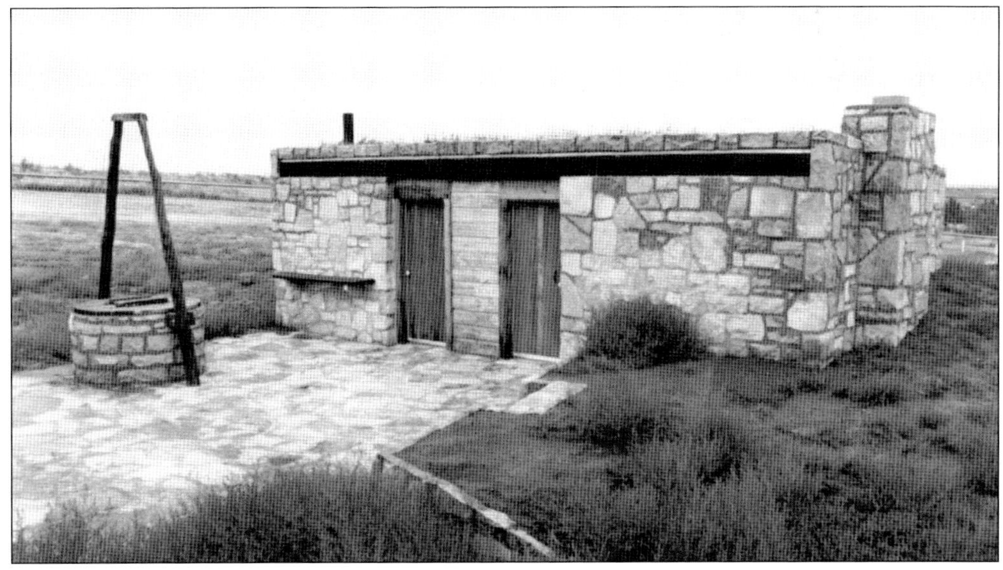

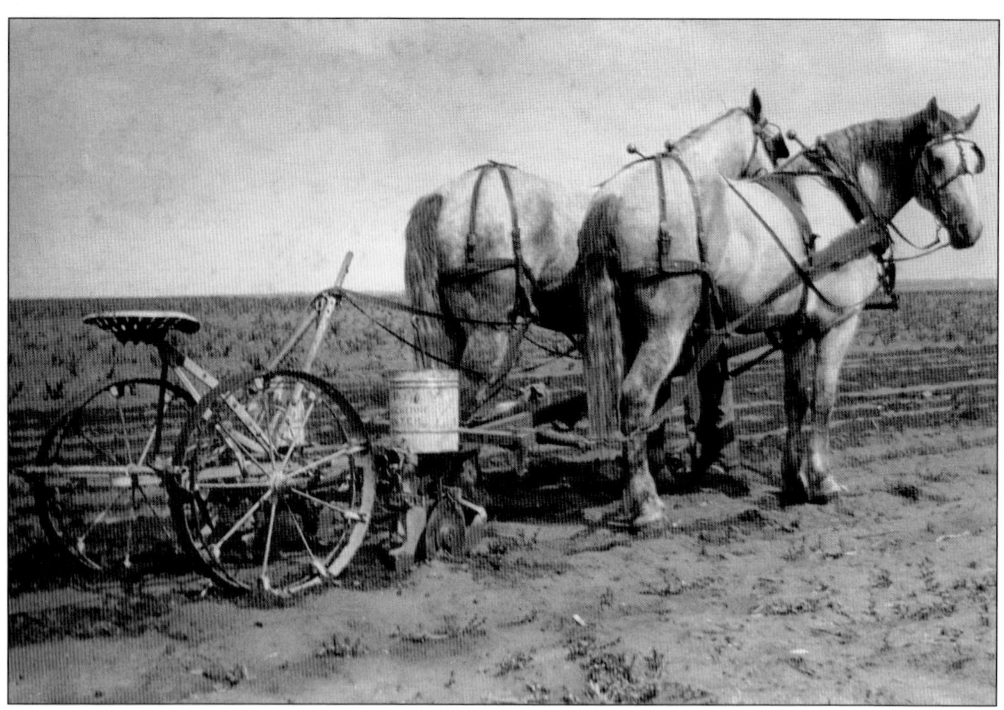

When pioneer farmers came to Hutchinson County, two horses were usually all they had to get work done, as shown above. Plowing, planting speed, and efficiency greatly improved when tractors became more common. The first tractors were powered by steam, as shown below. Although at first they were complicated, difficult to operate, and underpowered, tractors represented a paradigm shift in terms of speed, efficiency, and crop yield.

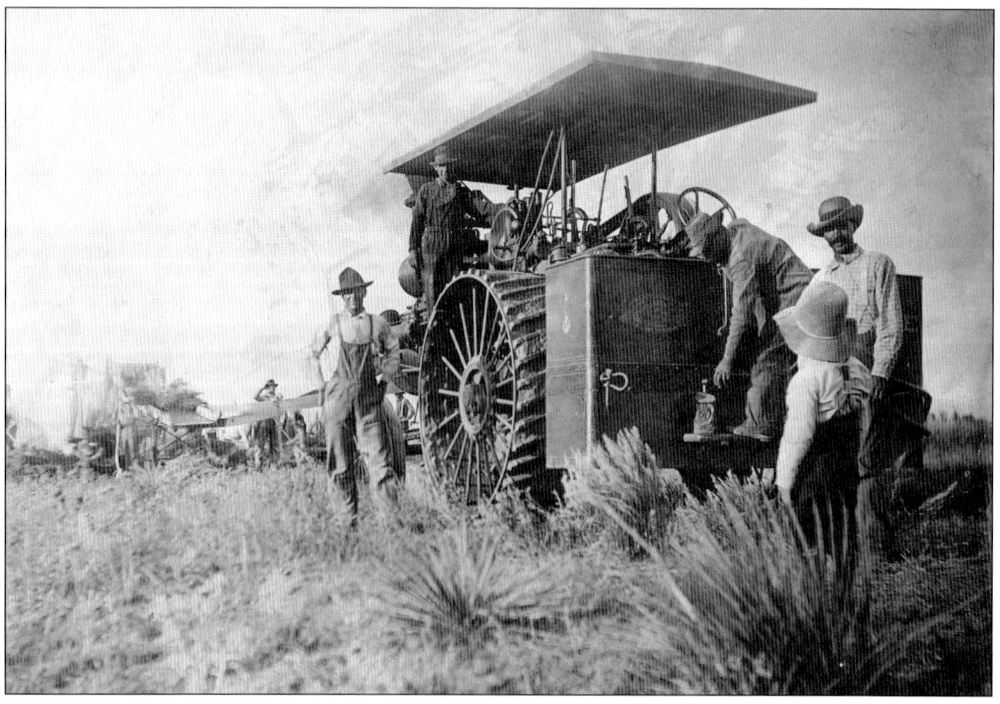

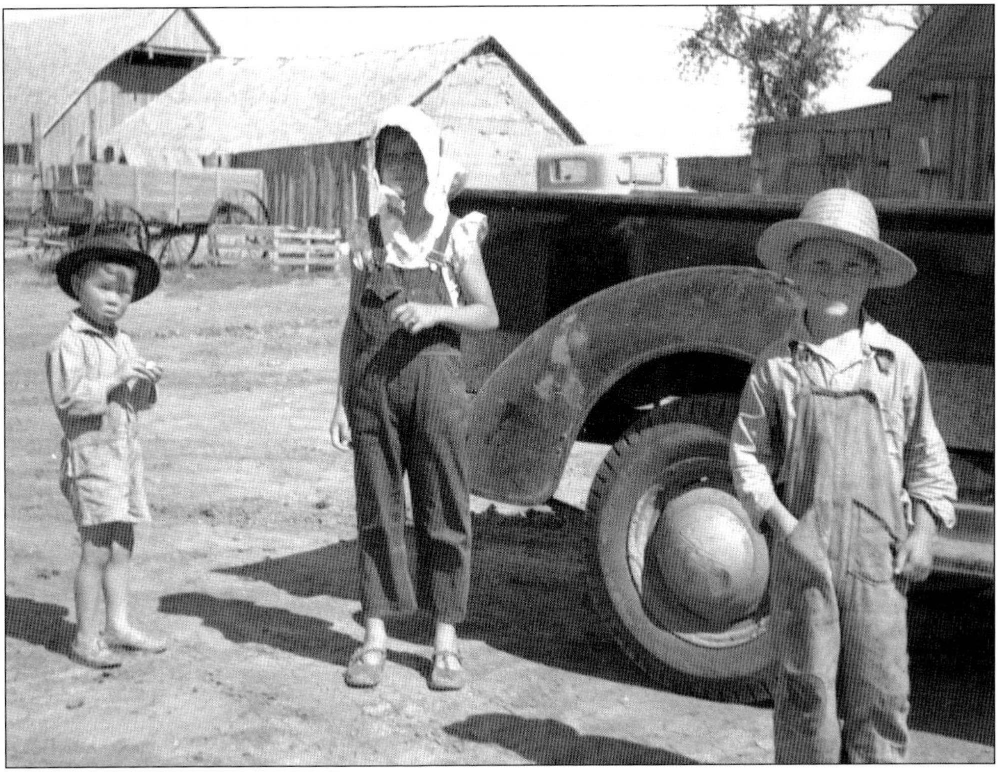

O.W. "Woody" and Effie Luginbyhl Jarvis came to Hutchinson County in 1903 and established a farm north of the Canadian River on the county's eastern side. Their grandson Tom Jarvis (left, above) is pictured with Betty (center) and Mac Luginbyhl, members of one of several families the Jarvises took in. The third generation of the Jarvis family still owned and operated the farm in 2021.

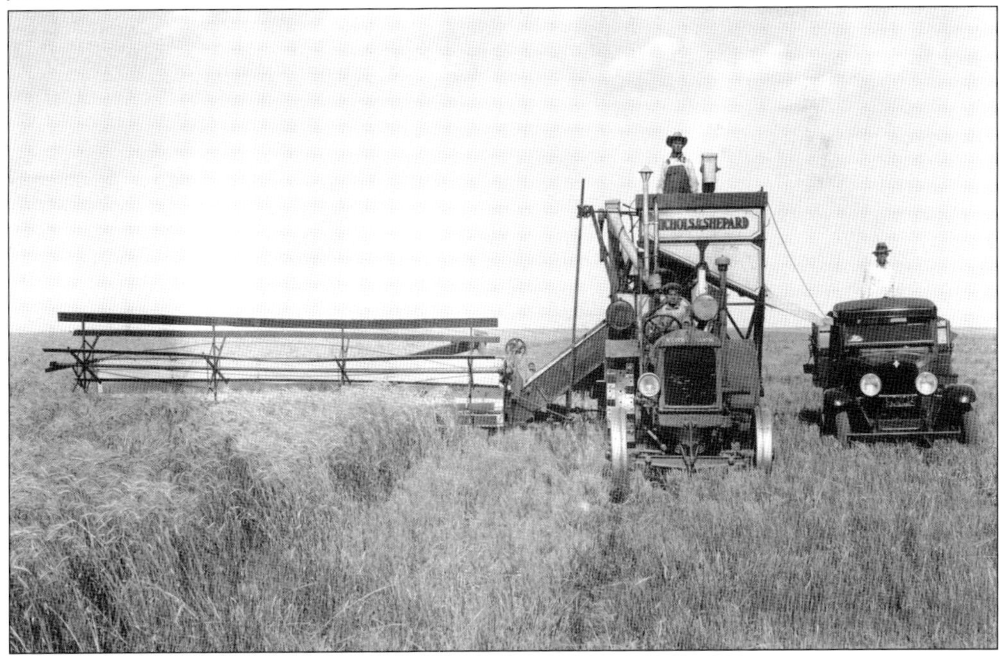

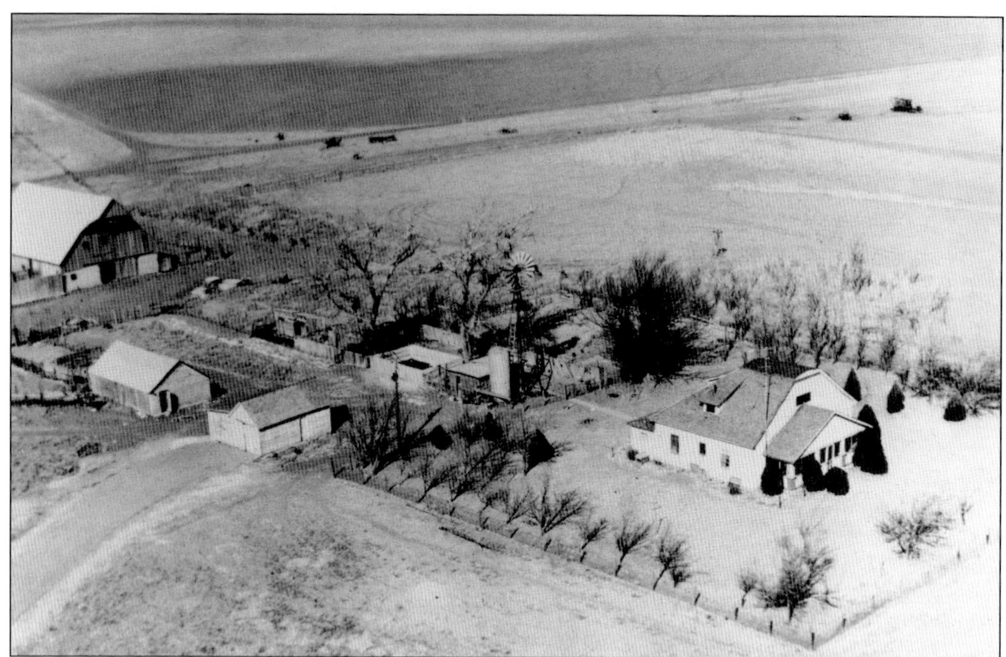

Those who came west to Hutchinson County were drawn to the area because of one thing: land. The land seemed to be available in an almost limitless supply—despite the Native Americans who resided on it and had been around for centuries—and was an irresistible attraction for farmers and ranchers in the 19th century. Ranchers came seeking the vast pasturage needed to feed cattle and other livestock. Farmers came for the flat, almost featureless plains that seemed tailor-made for the plow. They all found this part of Texas a perfect place to pursue their dreams. Above is the homestead of O.W. and Effie Jarvis in the early 1960s. Below are the wide open spaces of northern Hutchinson County.

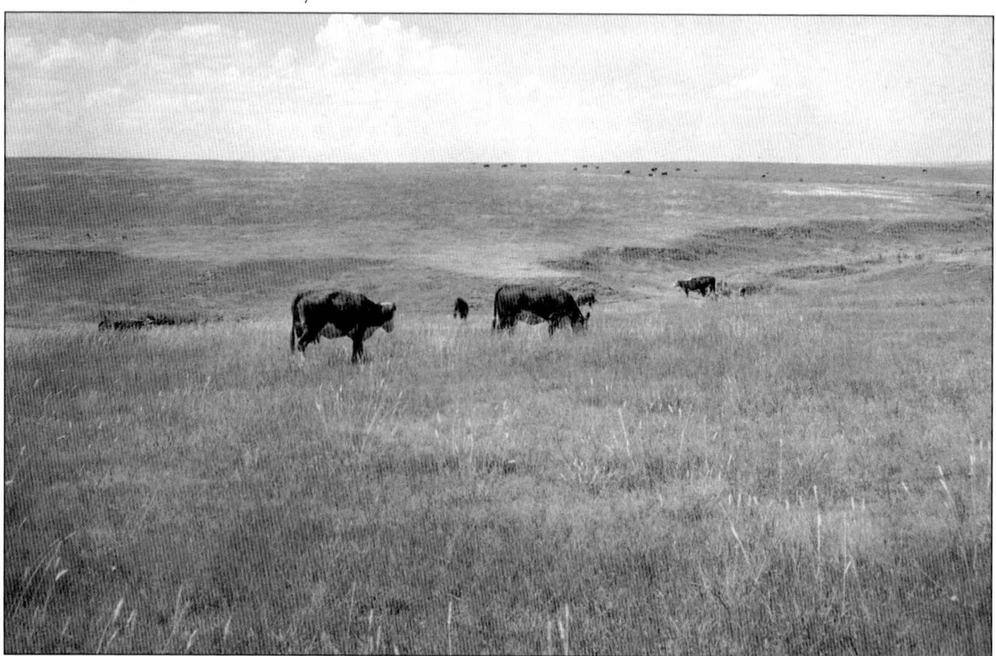

Four

The Canadian River and the First Town

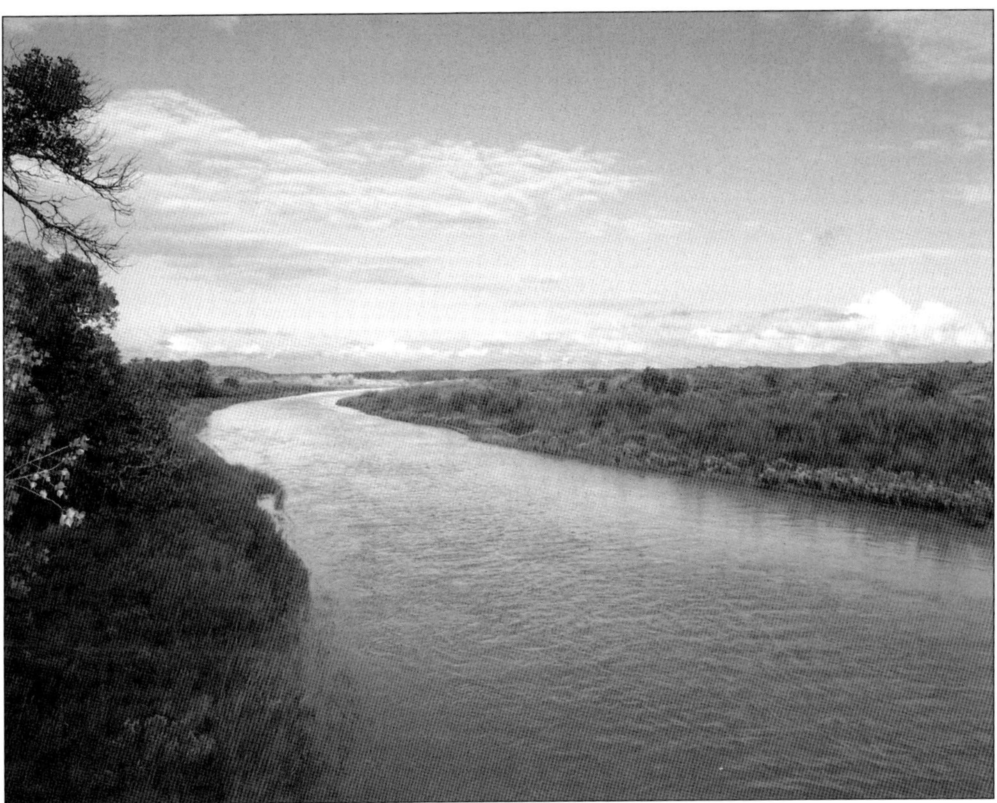

The Canadian River cuts across Hutchinson County from the southwest to the northeast. Its source is in the Sangre de Cristo Mountains in southern Colorado. It follows a southeasterly path through New Mexico and crosses the Texas Panhandle, flowing east and northeast through Oldham, Potter, Moore, Hutchinson, Roberts, and Hemphill Counties. Much of the river's course across the Texas Panhandle passes through a gorge 500 to 800 feet below the plateau. Patches of quicksand in the riverbed, plus the depth of the gorge, made the river difficult to cross or bridge. The river merges with the Northern Canadian tributary and crosses into Oklahoma and flows southeast, where it merges with the Arkansas River in Oklahoma. The total length of the river is about 760 miles, 190 of which are in Texas. This photograph was taken in Moore County west of Hutchinson County during a period of flooding in 2015. (Photograph by Clay Renick.)

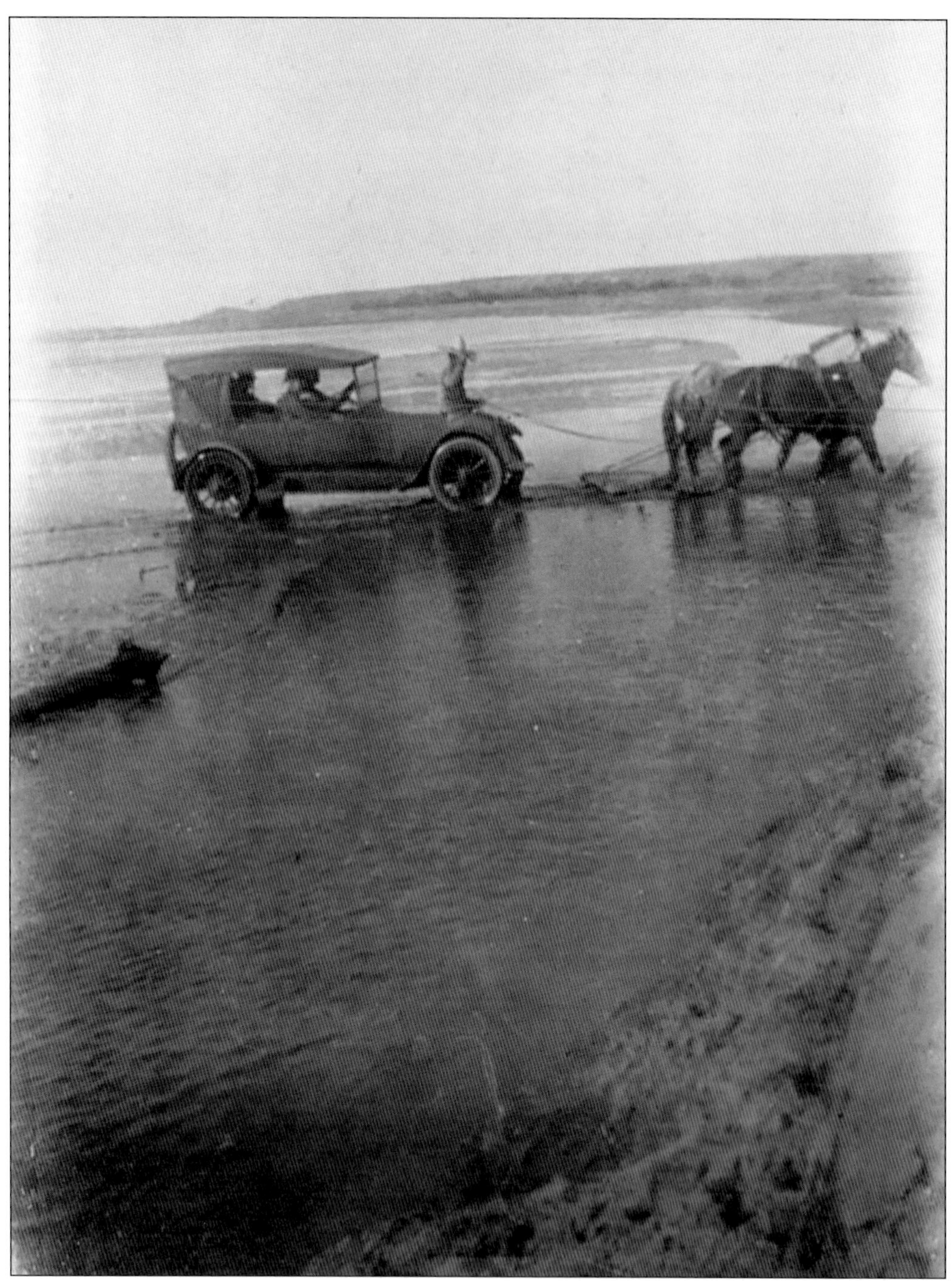

Crossing the Canadian River was often dangerous and sometimes fatal, as the river was full of quicksand bogs that could swallow a man, a horse, or even a wagon in a matter of minutes. Barney Plemons discovered that his horse had the uncanny ability to recognize quicksand traps in the river and was able to find his way around them. Seeing an opportunity, Plemons started a business guiding people across the river, and the site became known as Plemons Crossing. The village of Plemons prospered on the banks of the river, and when the county was organized in the spring of 1901, Plemons was chosen as the county seat.

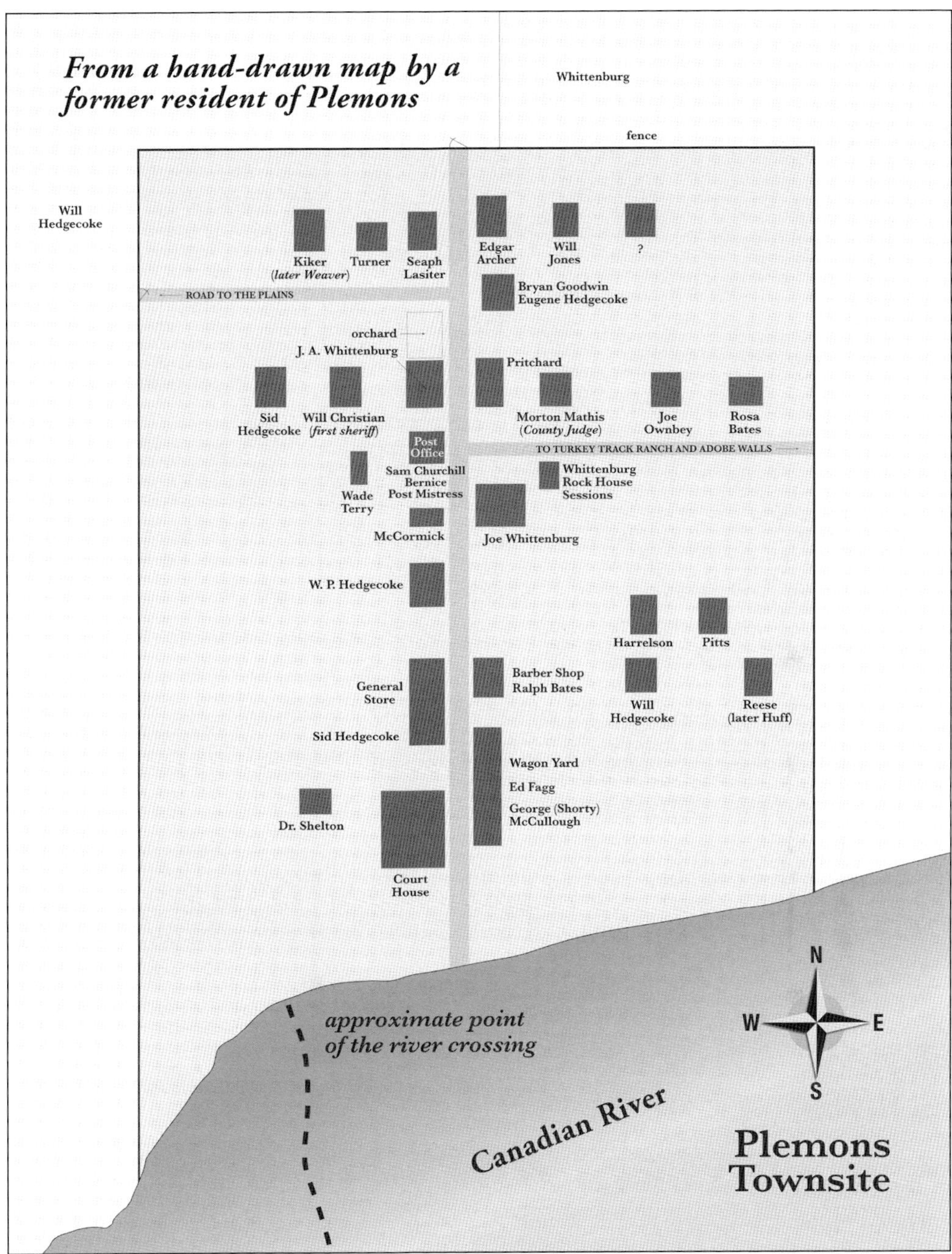

Today, all that remains of Plemons, the first town in Hutchinson County, is its small cemetery. Pioneer rancher James A. Whittenburg built a dugout into a hill overlooking a bend in the Canadian River, and the town came into existence about 1893 when Barney Plemons, the son of Amarillo judge and state legislator William Buford Plemons, filed for 80 acres on either side of the same bend in the river where Whittenburg built his dugout. Barney Plemons started a business leading travelers across the river. This illustration was created by referencing a hand-drawn map that belonged to a former resident of Plemons. (Illustration by Clay Renick.)

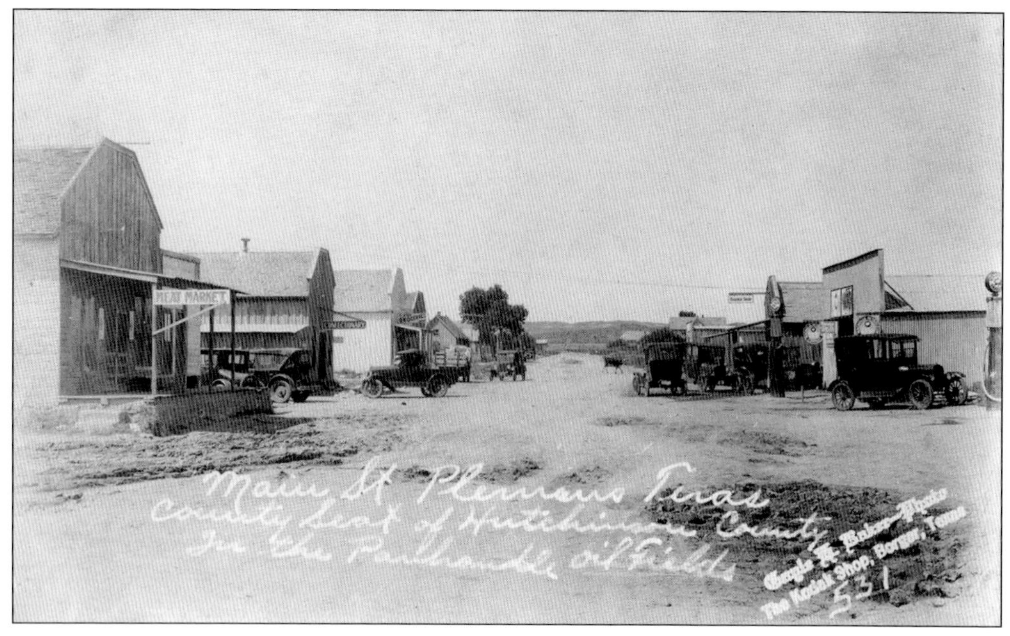

In 2015, an elderly woman came to the Hutchinson County Historical Museum with a suitcase full of photographs her son had found in an old building in Plemons many years before. Her son had purchased the building to recycle the wood it contained and discovered the suitcase in the attic before he demolished it. Until that time, the museum had no images of early Plemons. These two photographs are from the collection in the suitcase. Above is a view looking north on Main Street in Plemons. The below image looks south on Main Street toward the river from approximately the same position as above.

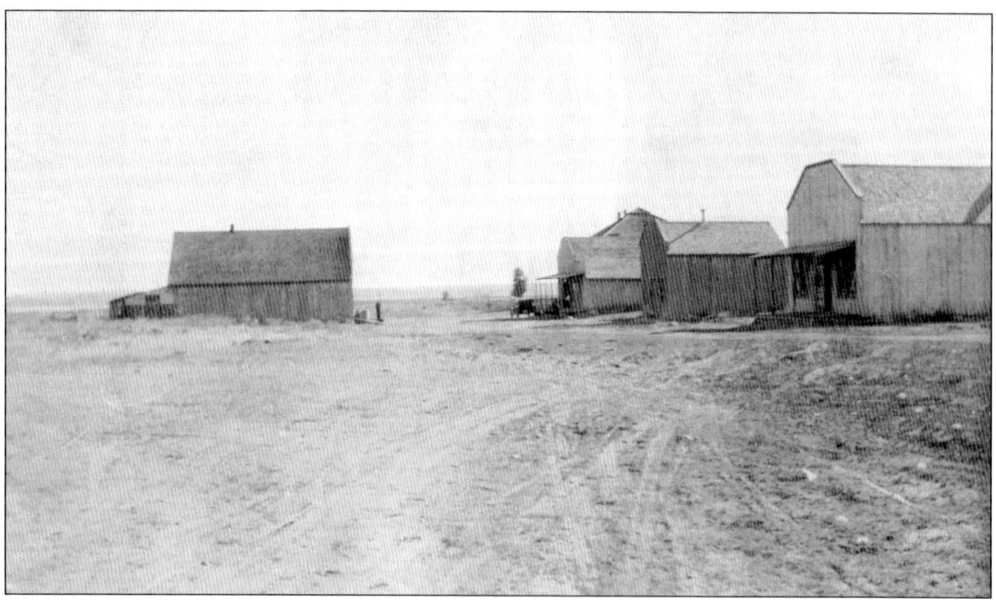

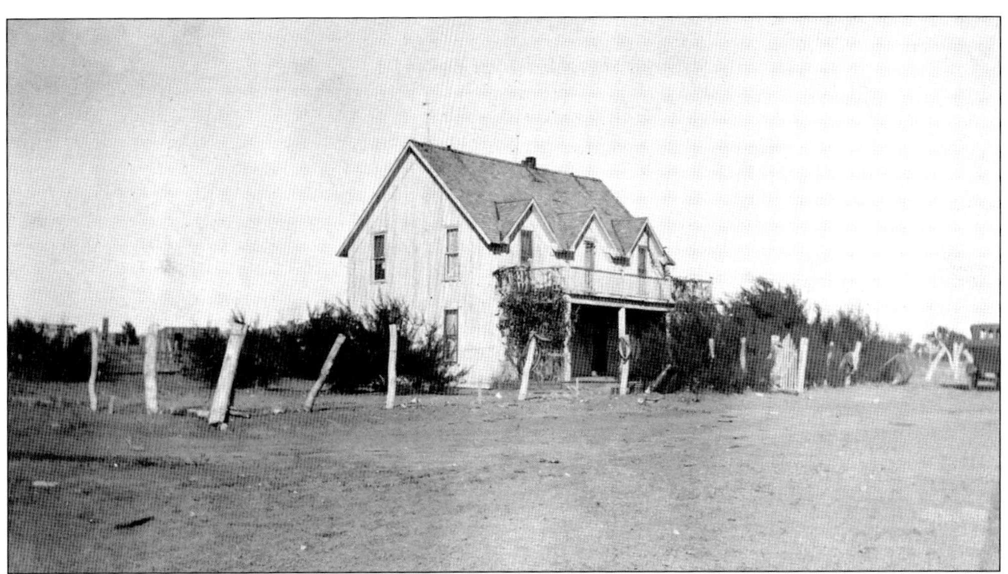

Pioneer rancher J.A. Whittenburg's hotel in Plemons is pictured above. In 1898, Whittenburg built a dugout into the cliff near the bend in the river where Plemons would soon be established. He later became the owner of the Turkey Track Ranch, which is still one of the largest ranches in Texas. The Turkey Track Ranch's southern border is just north of where Plemons once stood. Below, a group of children sit in front of the Plemons post office, where Adobe Walls hero Billy Dixon once served as postmaster.

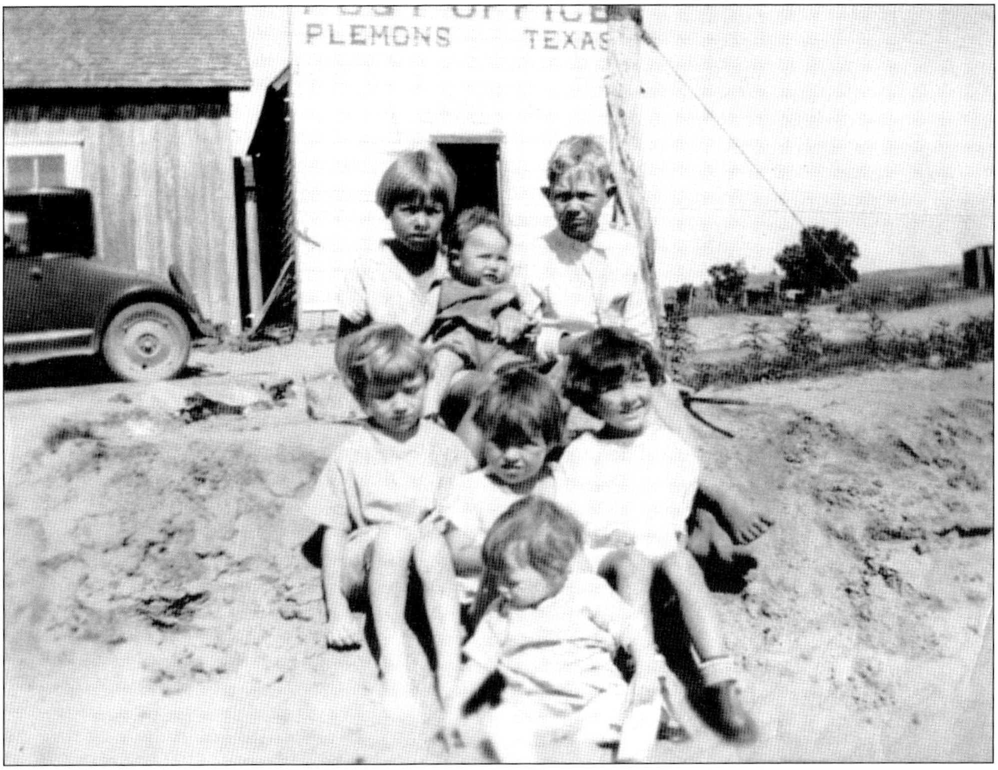

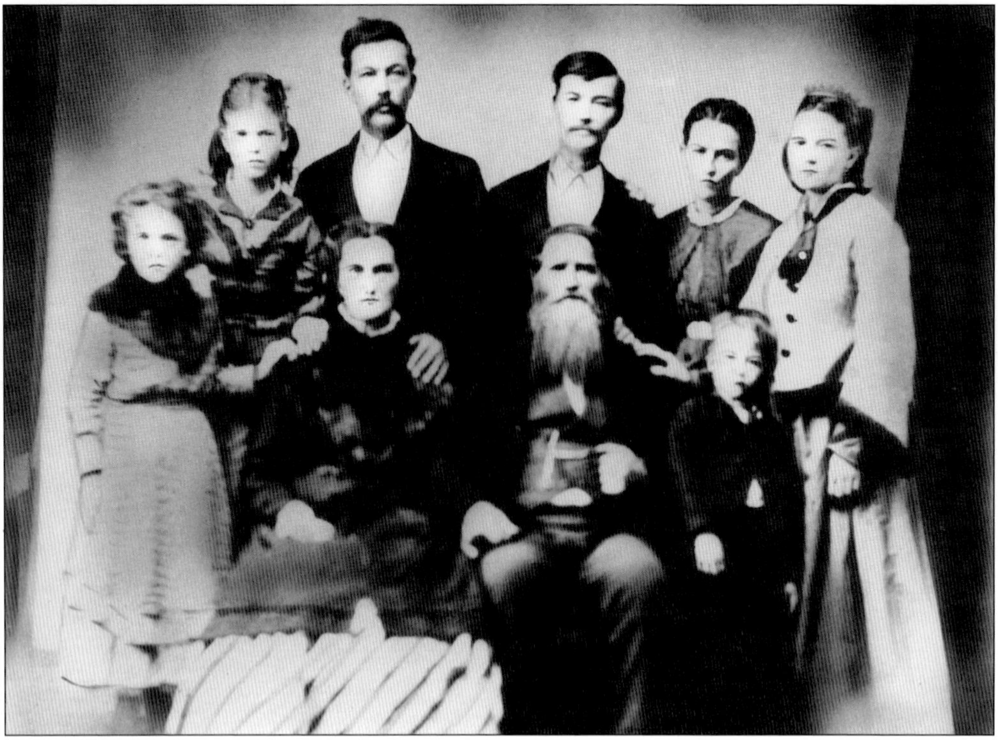

The Hedgecoke family was one of the pioneer families of Hutchinson County and Plemons. From left to right above are (first row) Rose Lee (1865–1937), Elizabeth TeLitha (1825–1892), Minter (1817–1883), and Samuel Minter (1869–1936); (second row) Lou (1861–1939), unidentified, John Monroe (1848–1930), Mara Angeline (1845–1912), and Annie Laura (1856–1908). Below is the family of Hutchinson County's second sheriff, S.J. Board: his wife Lola, (center) with daughters Eunice (left) and Sally. Board served as sheriff from 1905 to 1910.

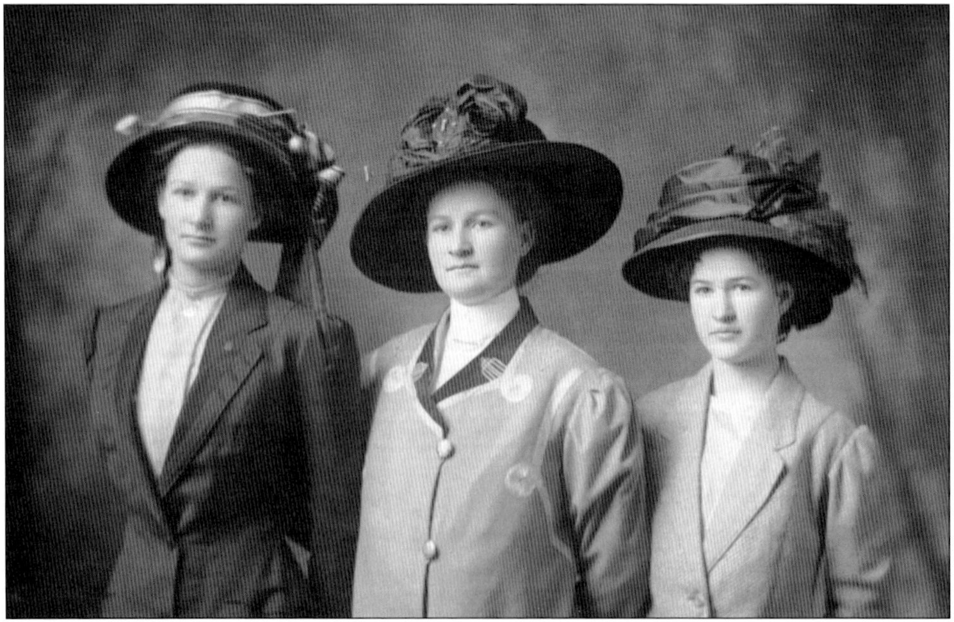

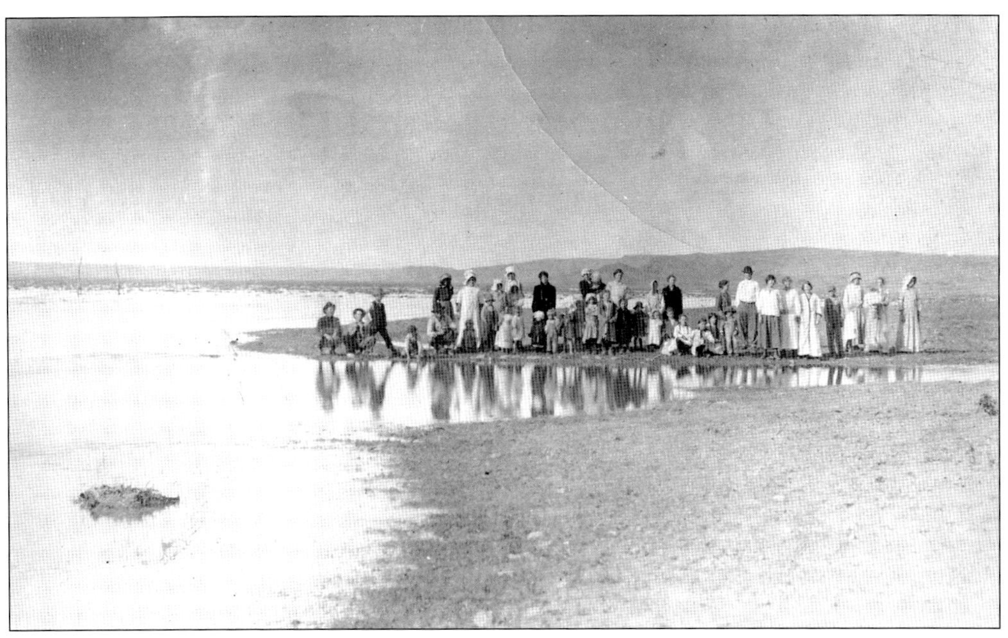

Citizens of Plemons are seen above during the Canadian River flood of 1907. Among those pictured are Wayne Hedgecoke, Jim Pollock, Sam Churchill, Mrs. J.B. Ownbey, Eula Jennings, Mrs. Jennings, and Mrs. Christian. Main Street in Plemons started just to the right of where the people are standing. Hutchinson County's second courthouse is seen below during the same flood.

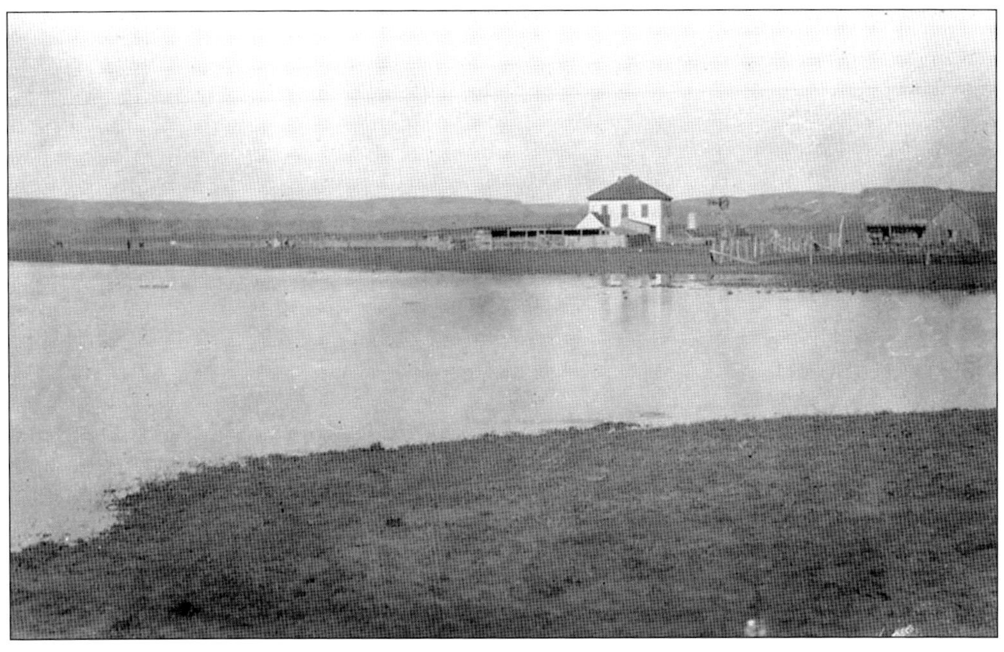

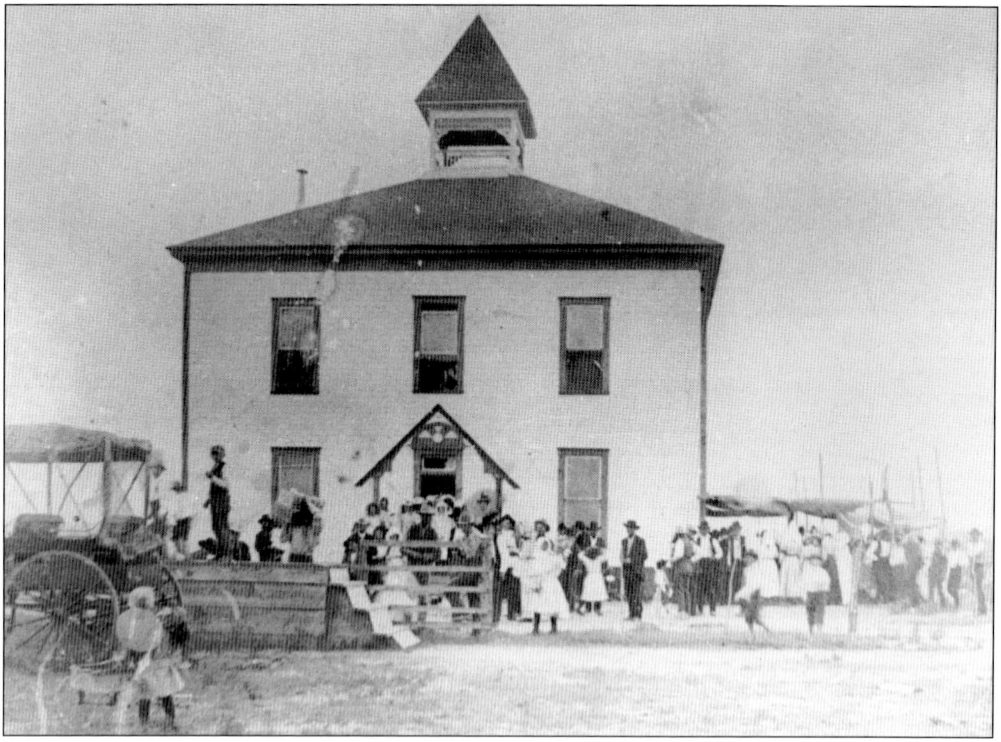

On May 13, 1901, Hutchinson County was officially organized, and the river village of Plemons was named county seat. A temporary courthouse was built to serve until a more permanent structure (pictured) was built. The Panhandle oilfield was discovered in the 1920s and brought money, jobs, and prosperity to the area.

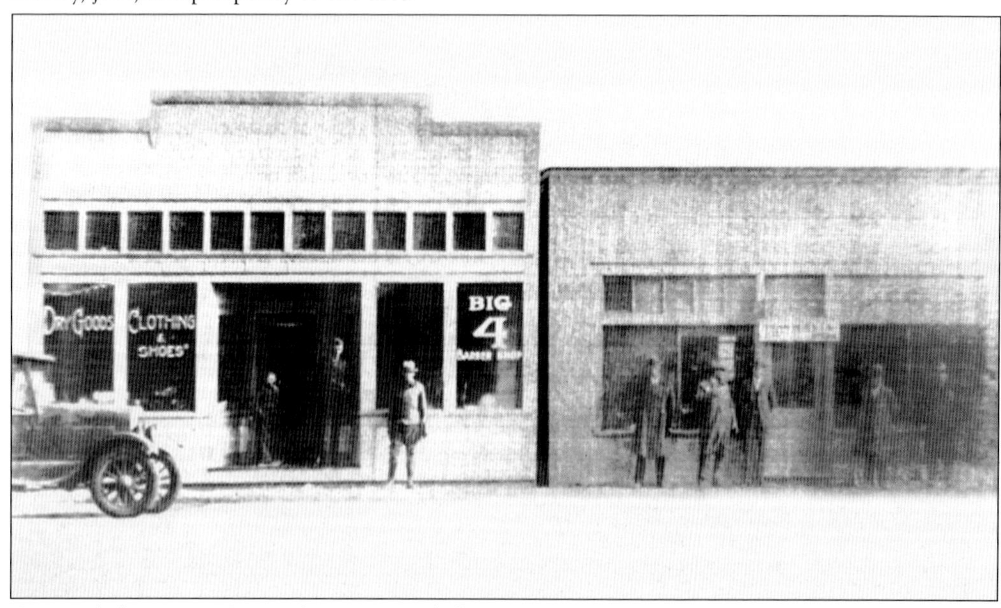

A special election on September 18, 1926, led to Stinnett being named the new seat of Hutchinson County. County offices were in an office building in Stinnett until construction could begin on the new courthouse on Main Street in 1927.

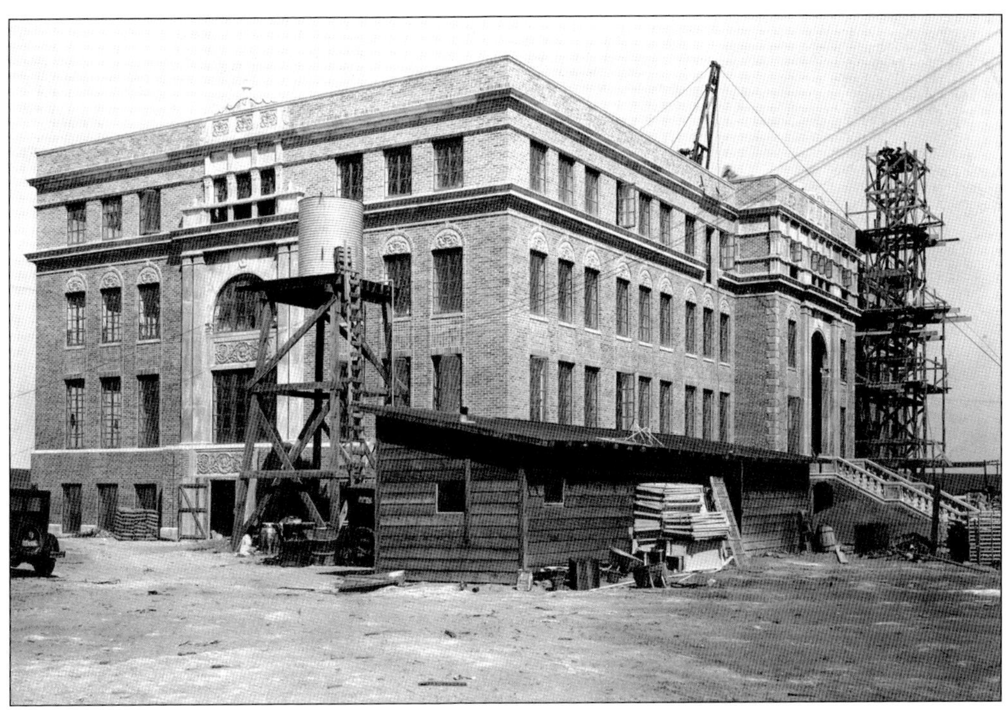

Hutchinson County's fourth and current courthouse, shown above while still under construction, was designed by architect William C. Townes in the Texas Renaissance style. It was completed and dedicated on December 15, 1928, at a cost of $506,000—an astronomical sum at the time. Seen below after completion, it has been meticulously maintained and updated and continues to be a significant architectural landmark in the Texas Panhandle.

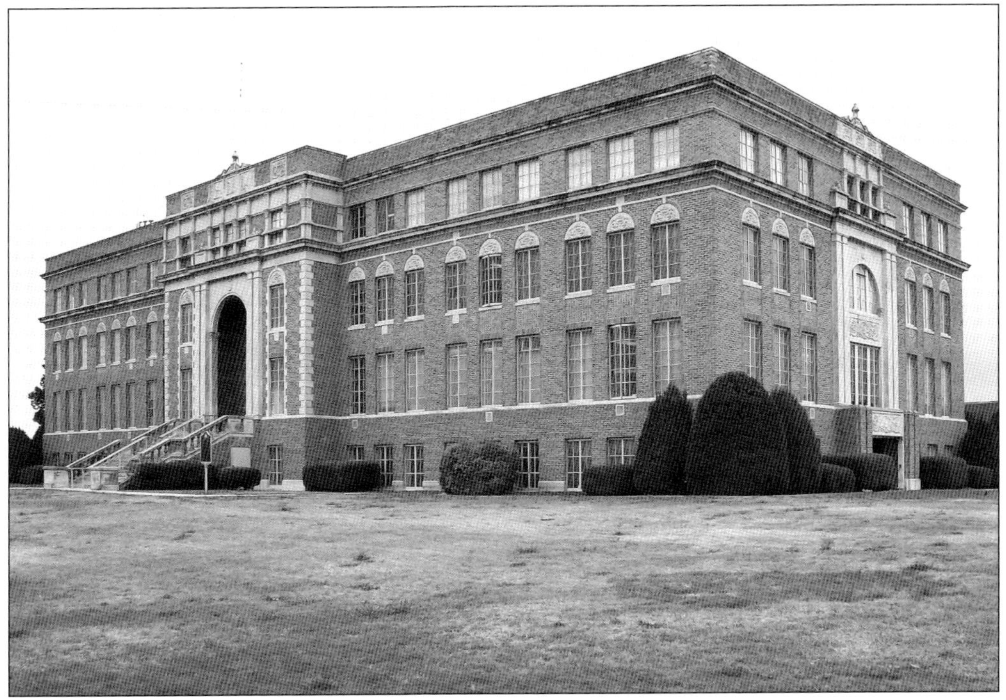

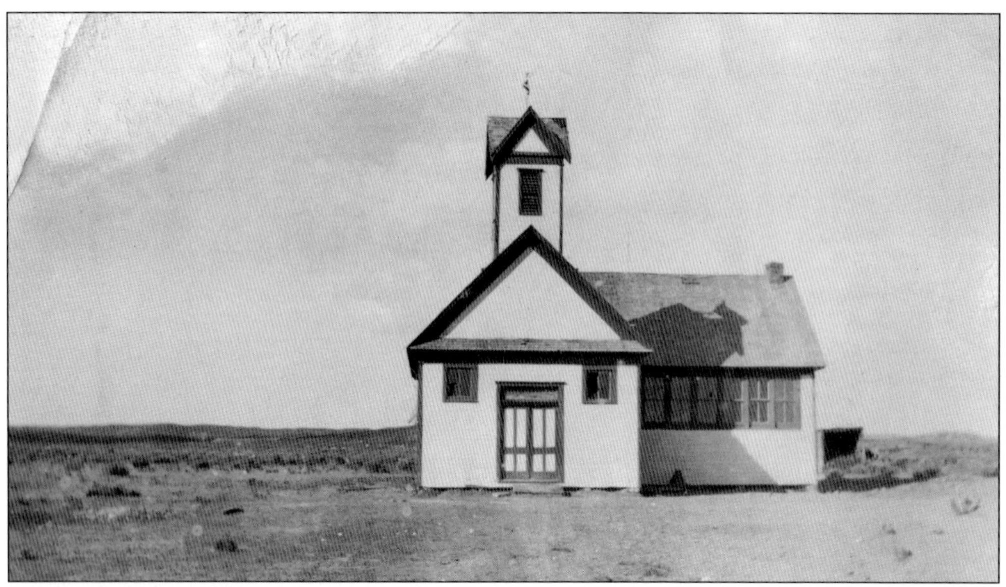

The citizens of Plemons established a school and a post office soon after the town was named the county seat. Plemons grew slowly as a river crossing, but between 1902 and 1905, a doctor's office, drugstore, wagon yard, barbershop, and mercantile store were established. As many as 15 families made Plemons their home at that time. A permanent church building was never constructed, but a parsonage was built, and services were held at the school or the courthouse.

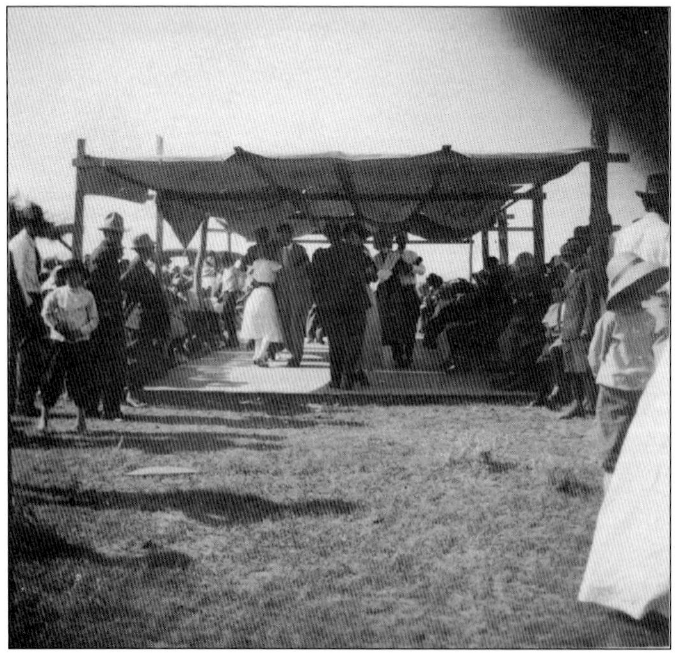

The community also became noted for its string band, which is shown here playing for a dance and picnic in 1913. By 1940, Plemons had only three businesses and about 100 people. By the 1950s, even more residents had moved to other communities. The Plemons post office closed in June 1952. Today, only the cemetery stands as a reminder of the time when Plemons existed.

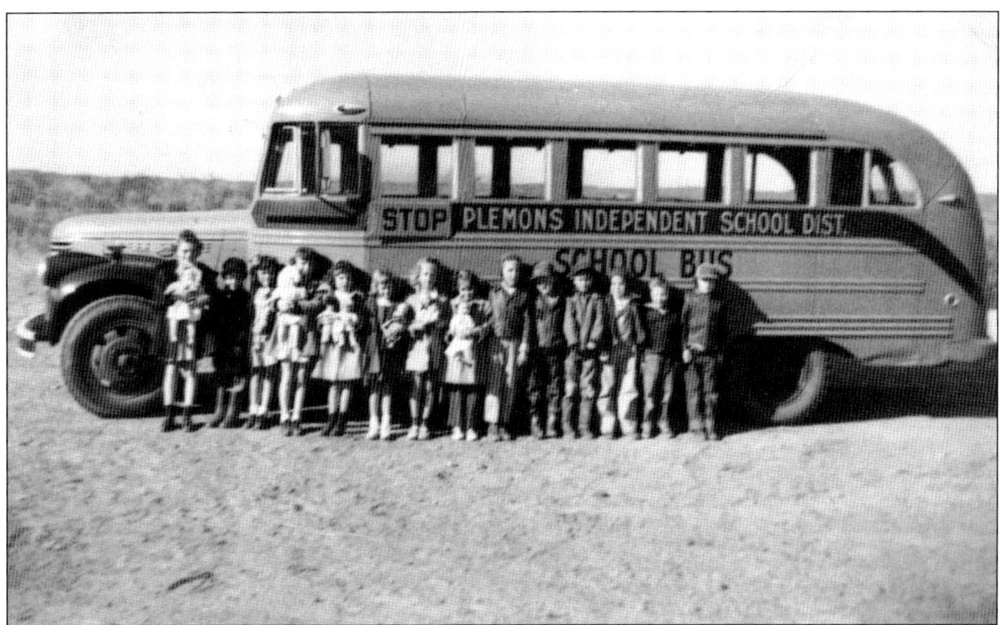

Mrs. Clarence Hamilton's first and second graders are pictured with the school bus in 1949. This photograph was taken just after Christmas, when the girls had new dolls and were allowed to take them to school.

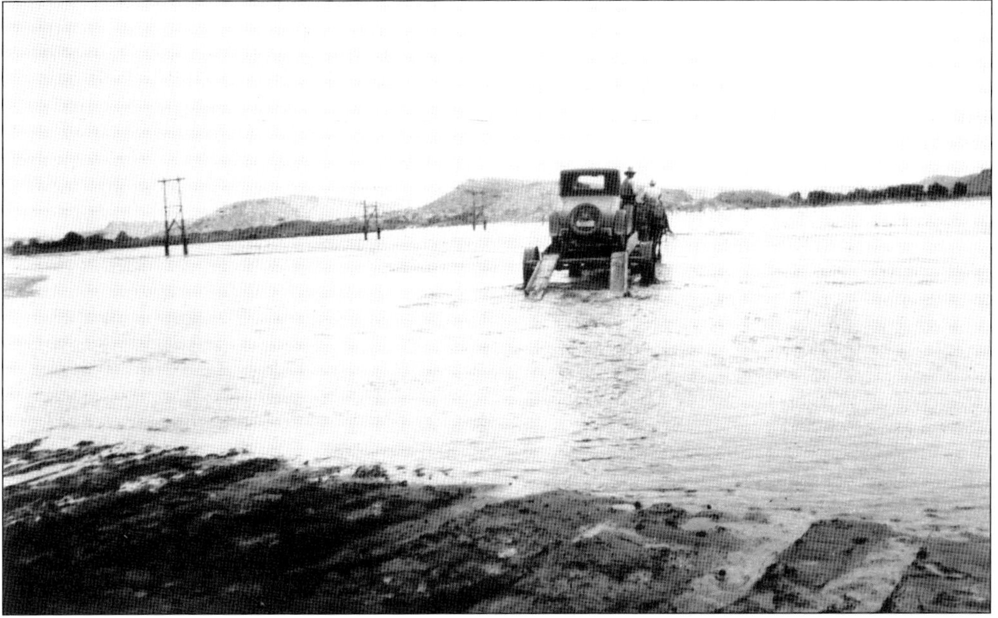

The Canadian River was a formidable barrier for anyone traveling north or south before modern dams were built to control snow melt and rain runoff in Colorado and New Mexico. Rain in New Mexico and west Texas could turn the river into a raging torrent within minutes. Early settlers often faced the river's wrath for days at a time. When the river flooded, travel across it stopped until the high water subsided. As seen here, residents improvised as needed to move themselves and their heavy loads across the river. The river was an inconvenient hazard until 1927, when the first bridge was built at Plemons.

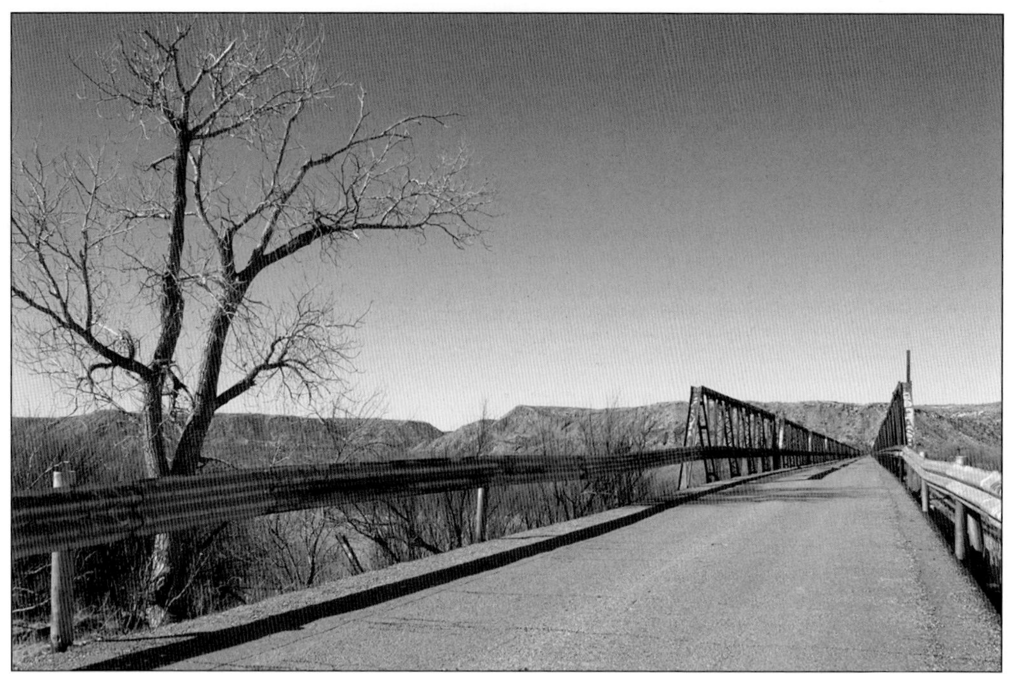

After the discovery of oil on the Dial Ranch in 1926, this one-way bridge, measuring five eighths of a mile, was built across the Canadian River west of Plemons by the Austin Bridge Company at a cost of $135,000. The Plemons bridge was the first to span the Canadian River in Hutchinson County. It was a major achievement that allowed the county's oil, ranching, and farming businesses to grow. (Photograph by Clay Renick.)

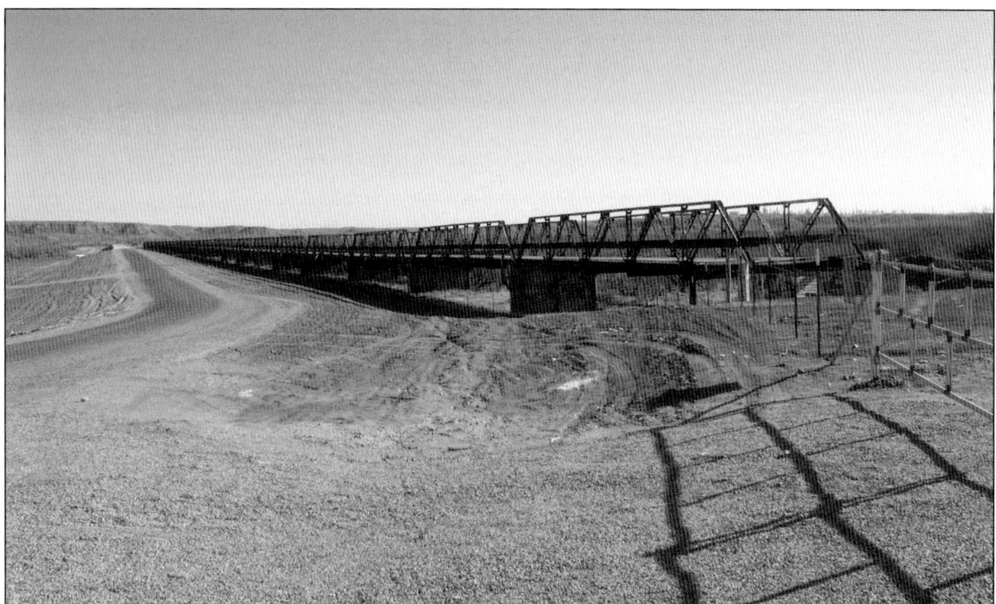

In 2011, the original Plemons Bridge (at right) was removed from service, and the new bridge was built adjacent to it. The Sanford Dam was built across the Canadian River between 1962 and 1965, and the "Mighty Canaj'un" was no more. After it was dammed, the river was reduced to barely more than a creek on its course through Hutchinson County. (Photograph by Clay Renick.)

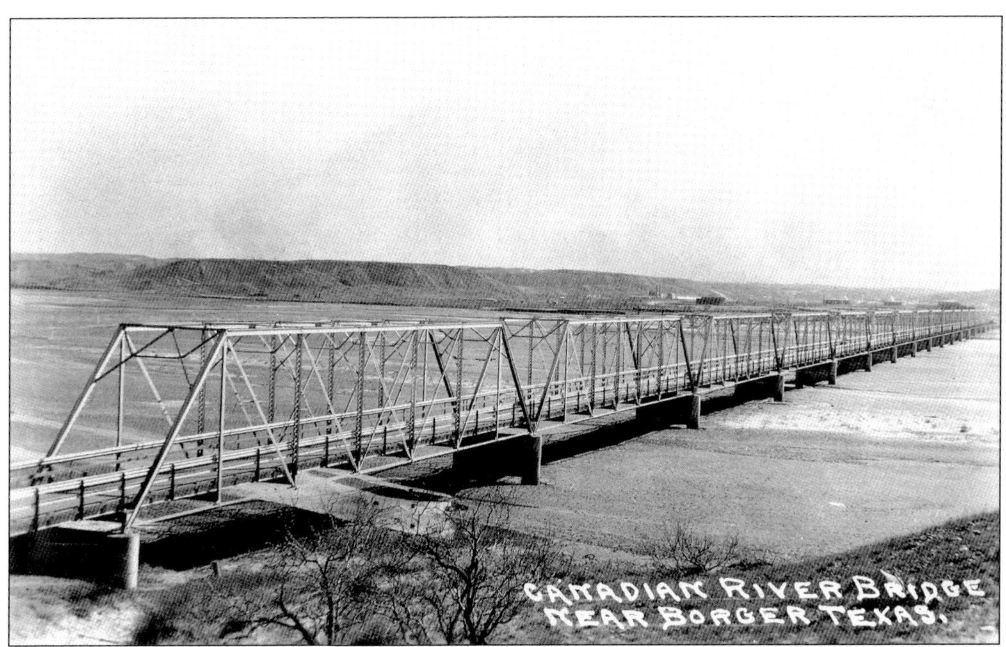

As the county grew, traffic did too. The Plemons bridge was built in 1926, and was followed by another built in 1927 north of Borger on Highway 136. These two bridges eliminated the dangerous barrier of the river for travelers. Several newer bridges have been built in the same location over the years. Today's travelers are unaware of the hardships people once faced when crossing the river. The original two-lane bridge was built in the late 1940s. The photograph below shows the two additional lanes that were added in 1974–1975. The four-lane bridge was named in honor of local senator Fritz Thompson and dedicated in 1975. Senator Thompson was the husband of Ace Borger's sister Helen. (Below, photograph by Clay Renick.)

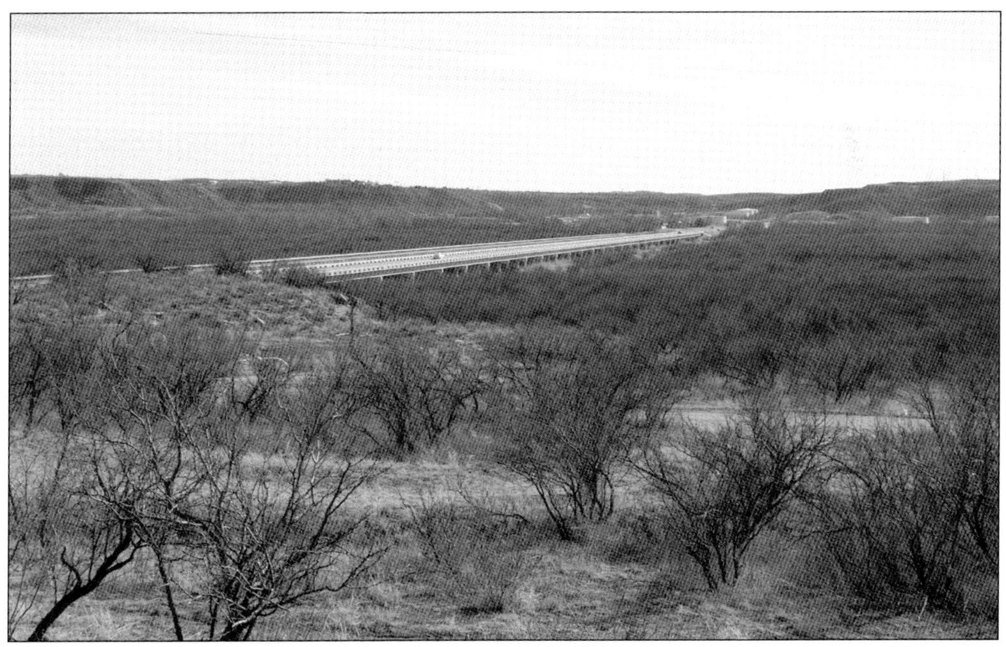

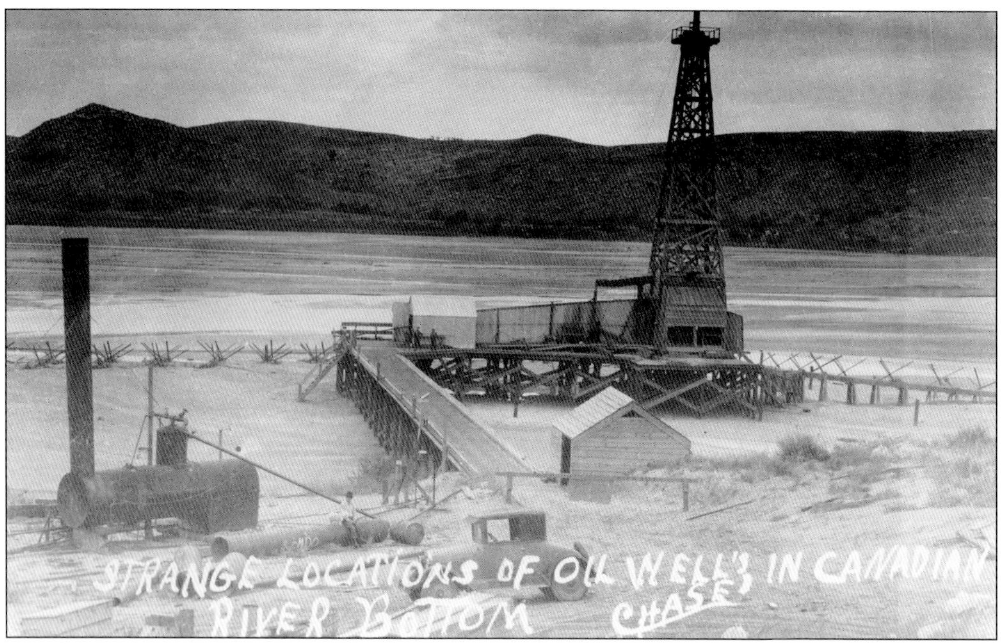

Hutchinson County's rough terrain and the Canadian River presented many challenges to all who worked in the early Borger oilfields. They adapted to almost any situation—because they had no choice. From putting up drilling rigs on shifting sand to moving large loads across small bridges, "awlmen" did what they had to do to get the job done.

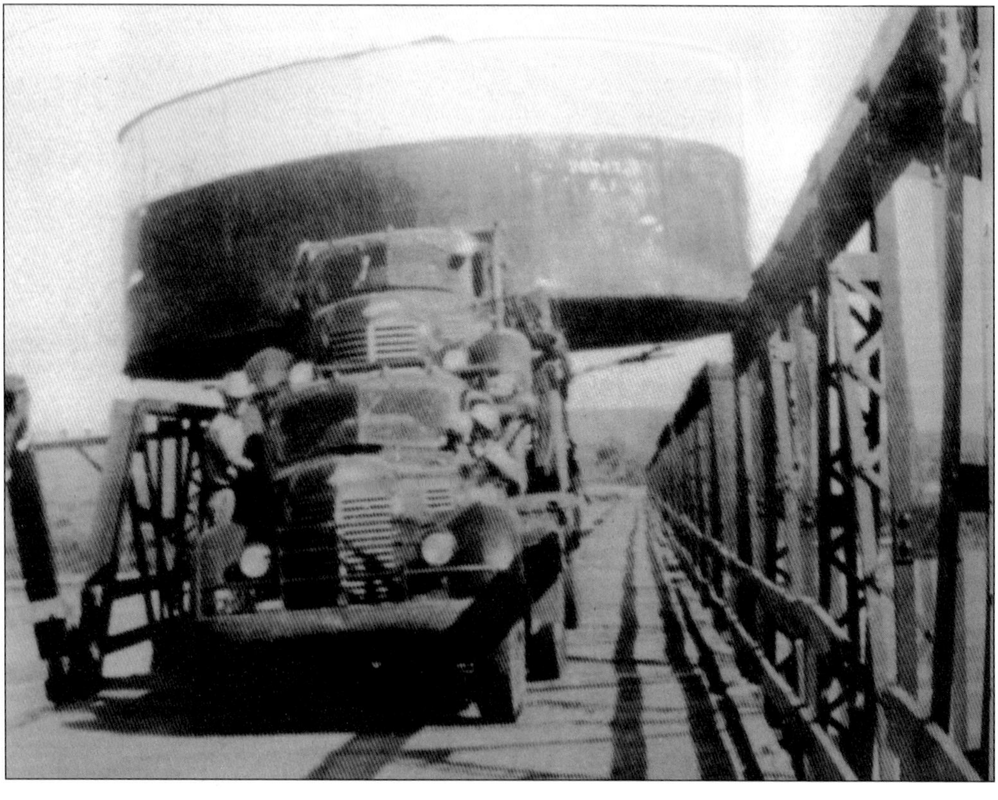

Five

The Oil Boom

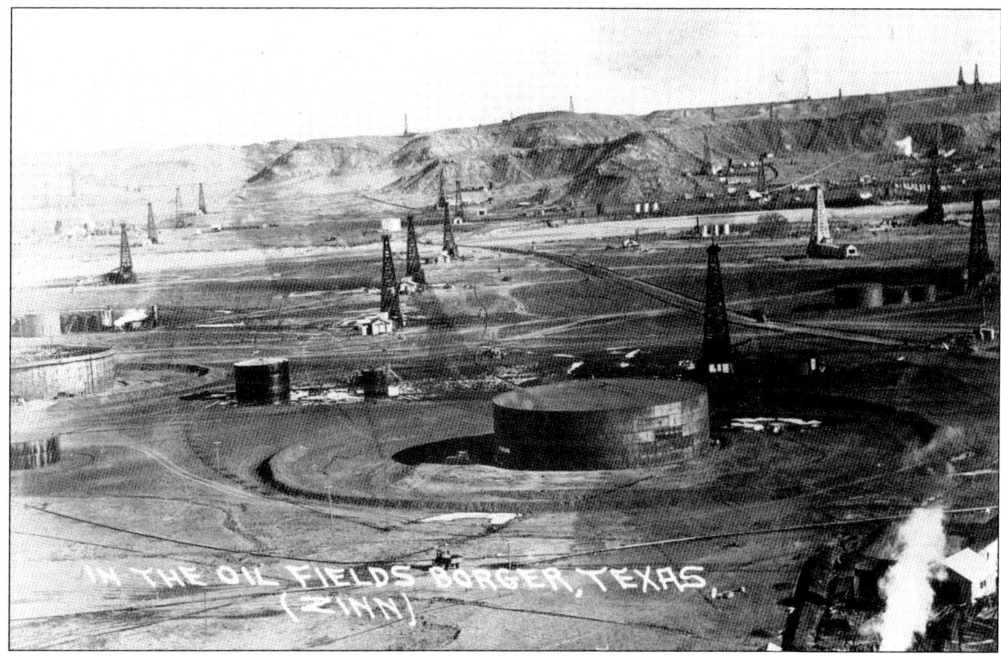

In the 1920s, the quiet, routine life of the cowboys and farmers who had lived in Hutchinson County for half a century was forever changed by the frenzied, chaotic activities of oil speculators, drillers, roughnecks, suppliers, and con men. Oil industry work was difficult, dangerous, and never-ending, and the men who worked with livestock and agriculture soon realized that they had much in common with those who arrived during the oil boom. The work ethic in Hutchinson County remains strong to this day.

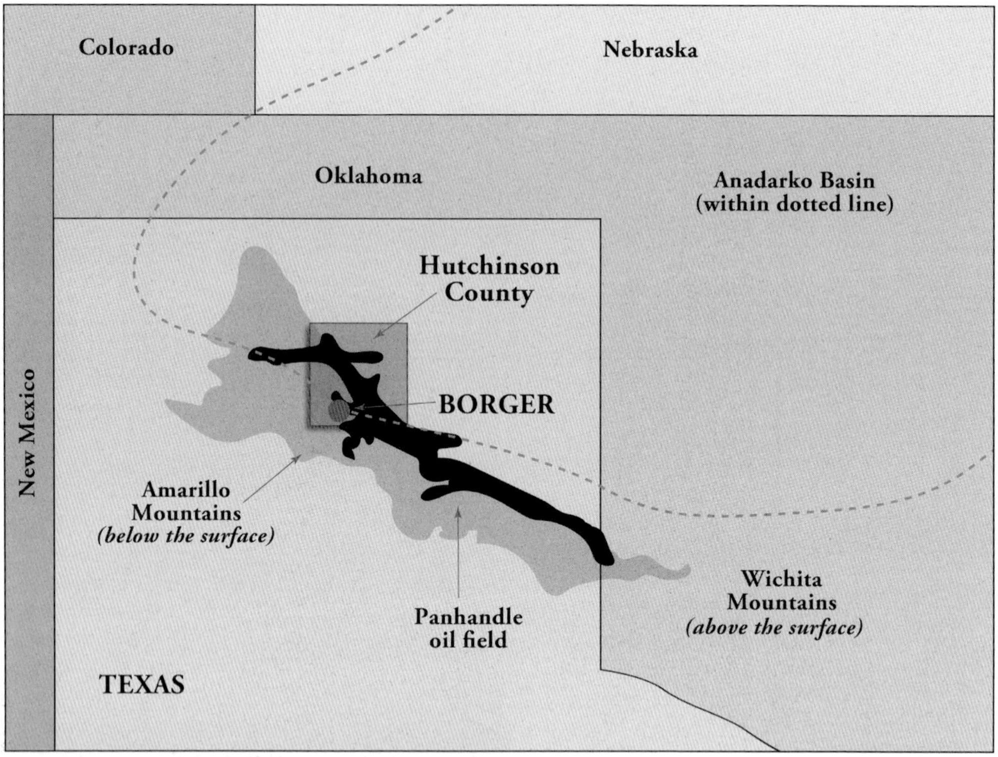

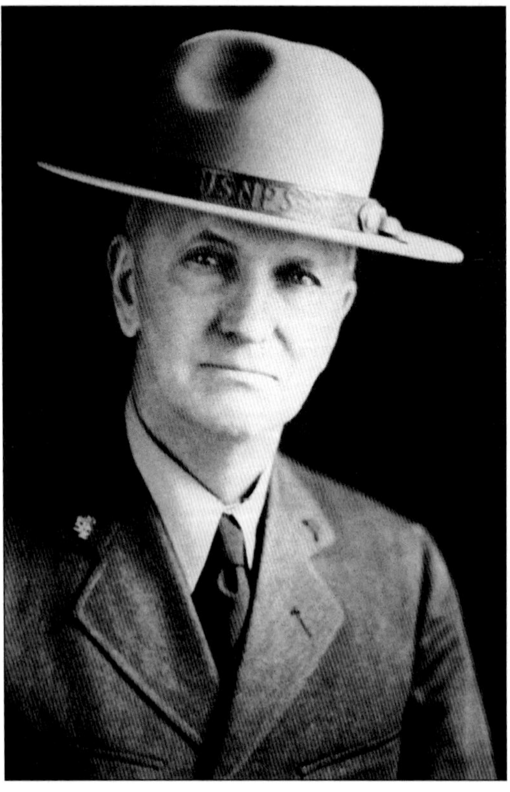

Charles Newton Gould was a geology professor at the University of Oklahoma in the early 1900s. Pres. Theodore Roosevelt commissioned him to study the Canadian River drainage area between 1903 and 1905 and map its water sources. While working in Potter and Hutchinson Counties, Gould noted a geological structure that led him to believe that oil and gas could be found below the surface. In 1918, he was hired by Amarillo businessmen to locate a test well on the Masterson Ranch in northern Potter County. Upon completion, the Masterson No. 1 became one of the largest gas wells ever drilled. This proved Gould's theory and set in motion a period of wildcat petroleum exploration in the Texas Panhandle. The Gulf Production Company discovered gas and oil on the 6666 Ranch in Carson County in 1921. Later that year, the company reported its first strike in Hutchinson County. Gould's observations, made years earlier, had led to the discovery of one of the world's largest oil and gas fields. Gould later served as a geologist for the National Park Service. (Above, illustration by Clay Renick.)

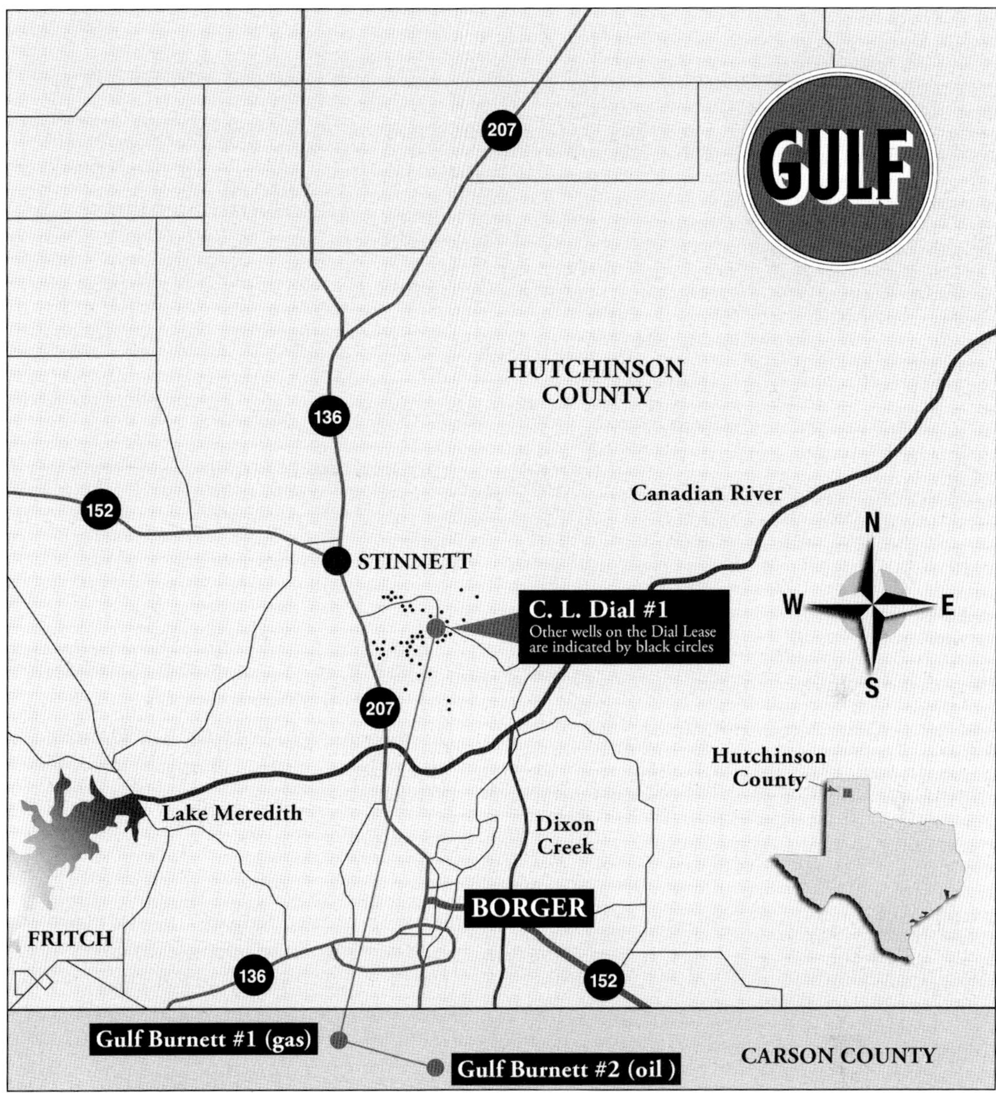

The C.L. Dial No. 1 was the third oil well drilled in the Texas Panhandle and the first drilled in Hutchinson County by Gulf Oil Company. The Burnett No. 1 was drilled on Capt. Burk Burnett's 6666 Ranch in Carson County in 1921. It was known as a gasser, because it produced natural gas but little or no oil; however, it provided the gas needed to fuel the boiler to power the drilling engine that was used to drill the Gulf Burnett No. 2 a few miles east, which struck oil. Gulf then moved north. The company built a 13-mile pipeline from the Burnett No. 1 across the Canadian River to another lease on the C.L. Dial ranch—the first oil lease in Hutchinson County. The pipeline passed directly across the land where the boomtown of Borger would later spring up in 1926. Natural gas from the Burnett No. 1 fueled the rig that drilled the Dial No. 1, which was spudded on November 10, 1921, and completed in May 1922. Though not a gusher, the Dial No. 1 was the well that proved oil could be found in Hutchinson County. It was further proof of Charles Gould's theory, and it provided the spark that set off the oil boom of 1926. (Illustration by Clay Renick.)

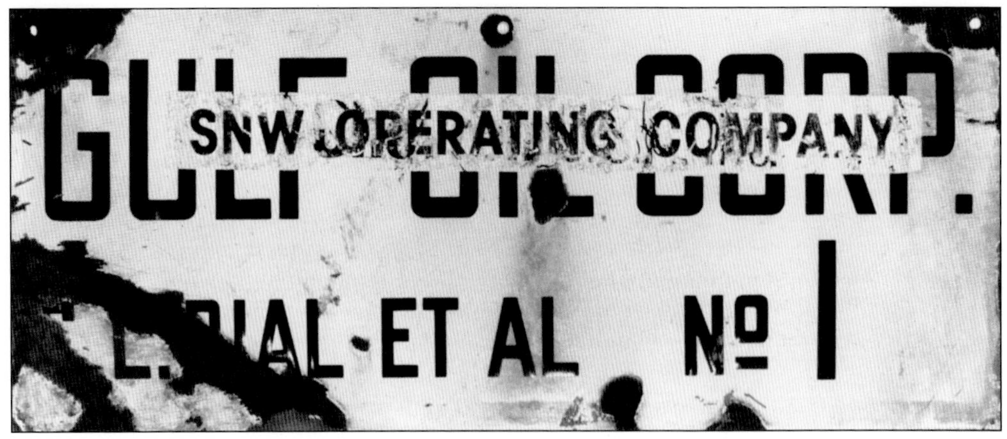

This is the original lease sign for the C.L. Dial No. 1 oil well, which was completed in 1922. Each well and each lease had unique signage that listed the owner of the lease, the number of the well, and the order in which it was drilled. The signs are made of thick, porcelain-coated steel, which was virtually impervious to the elements. This sign was donated to the Hutchinson County Historical Museum by the SNW Operating Company, which owns the lease; the company's name appears on the sticker attached to the original sign. Below is all that remained of the C.L. Dial No. 1 in 2005. (Below, photograph by Clay Renick.)

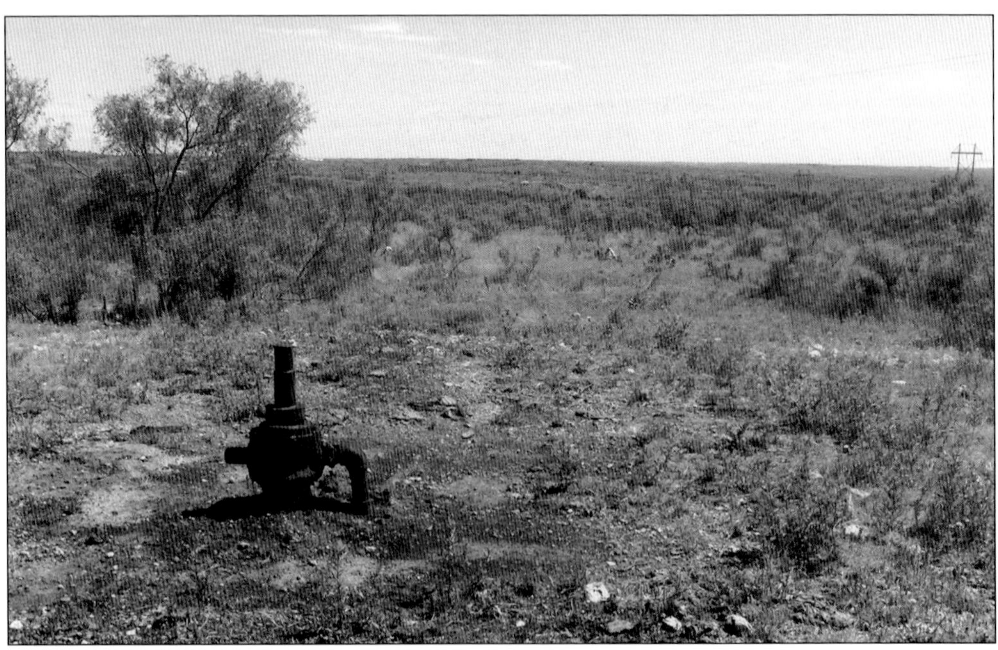

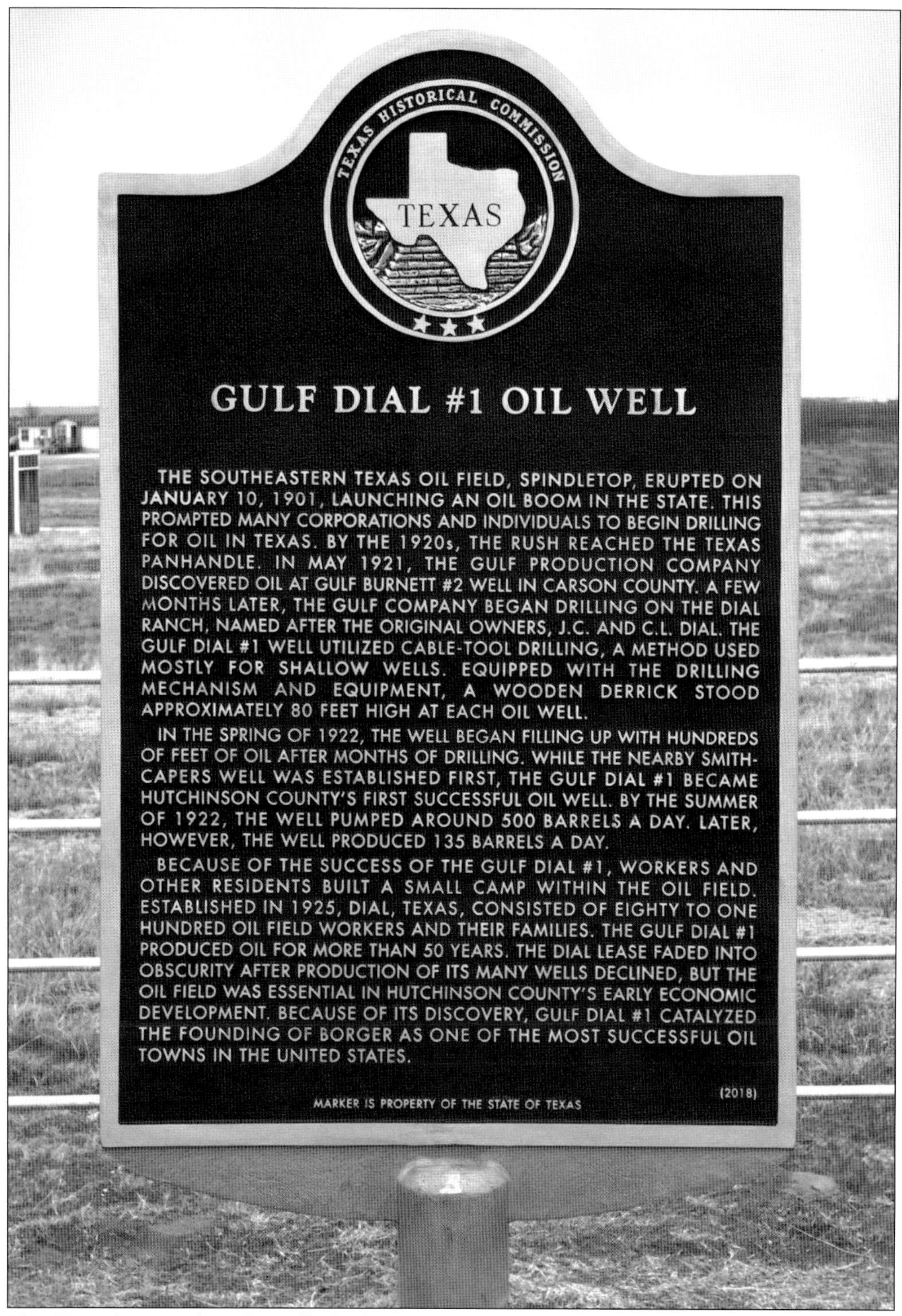

This Texas historical marker tells the history of the first oil well drilled in Hutchinson County. It was drilled about three and a half miles east of and behind where the sign was installed south of Stinnett on Highway 136 in 2018. (Photograph by Clay Renick.)

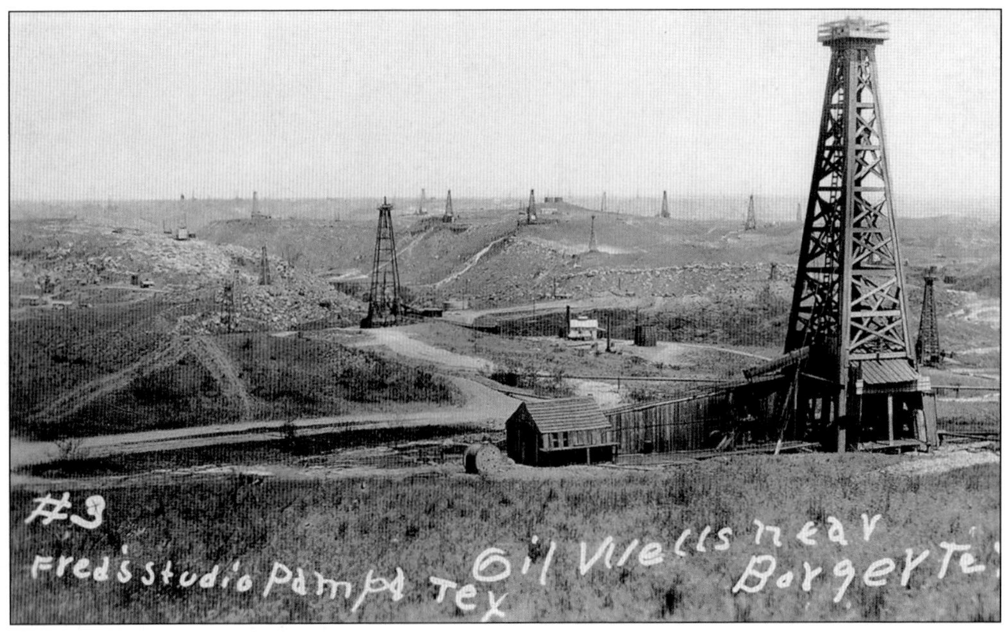

These images show drilling rigs that were erected between Borger and Pampa in the early days of the oil boom. Today, many regulations control the spacing of wells and the number of wells that can be drilled on a specific piece of land. At the time of the 1926 oil boom, there were no such rules. This lack of regulation often led to chaos and violence. Dixon Creek, southeast of Borger, is where the strike occurred that started the oil boom in 1926.

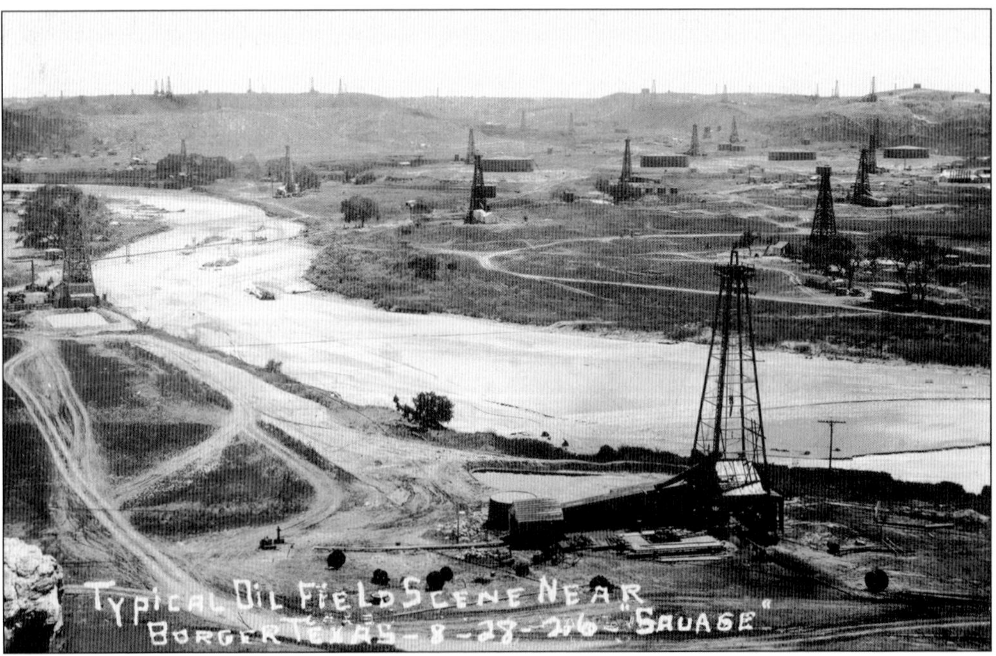

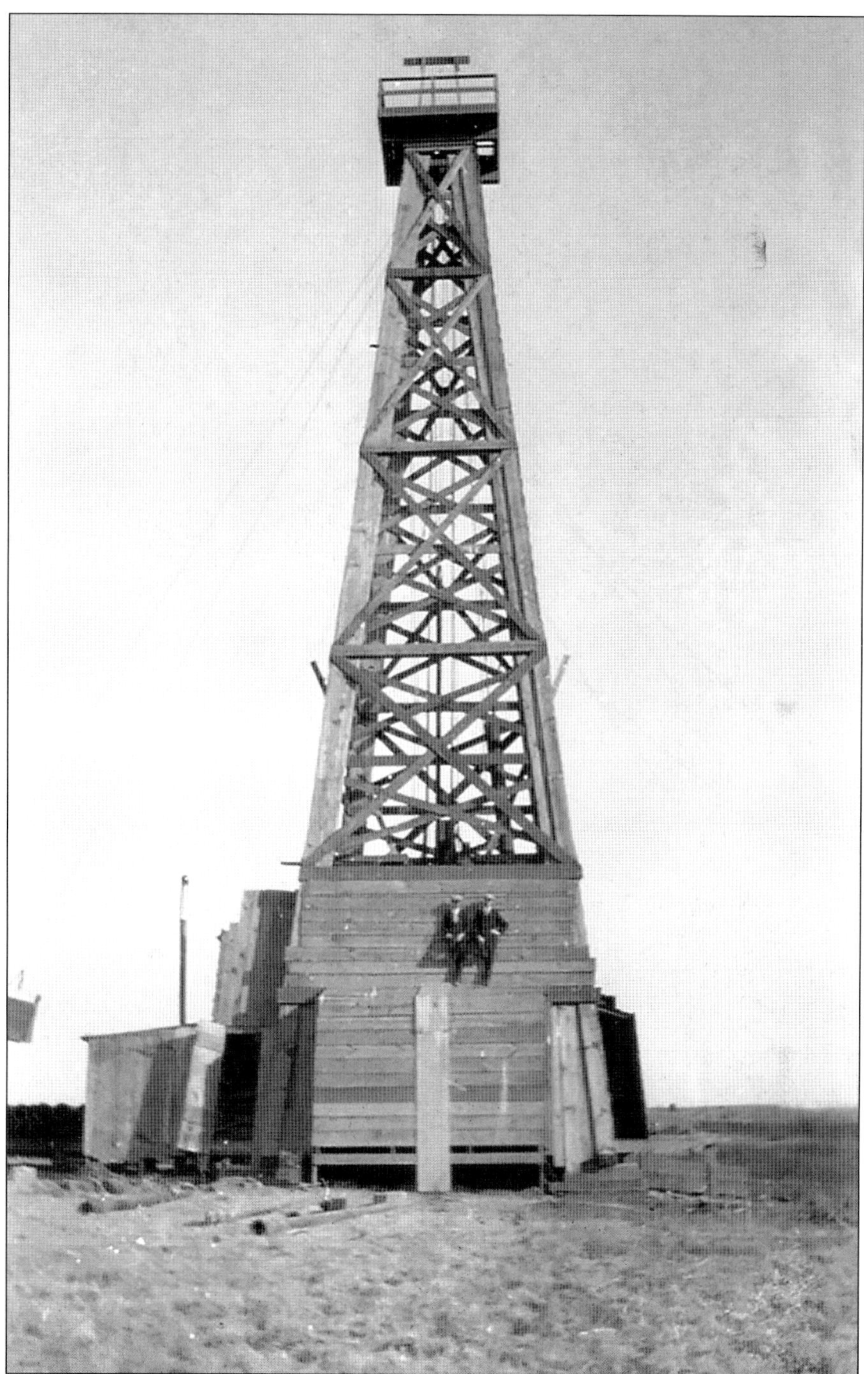

An experienced four-man crew could build a wooden drilling rig like the one shown here in five to seven days. Wooden rigs were erected on concrete piers and were about 90 feet tall. Natural gas or wood-fired boilers powered steam engines that repeatedly raised and lowered the massive steel drill bits that were suspended on cables. The rigs pounded holes into the ground that ranged from 2,500 to 3,500 feet deep. Drilling was conducted around the clock, often for weeks or months. More expensive steel rigs were also used; these could be disassembled and moved to drill additional wells.

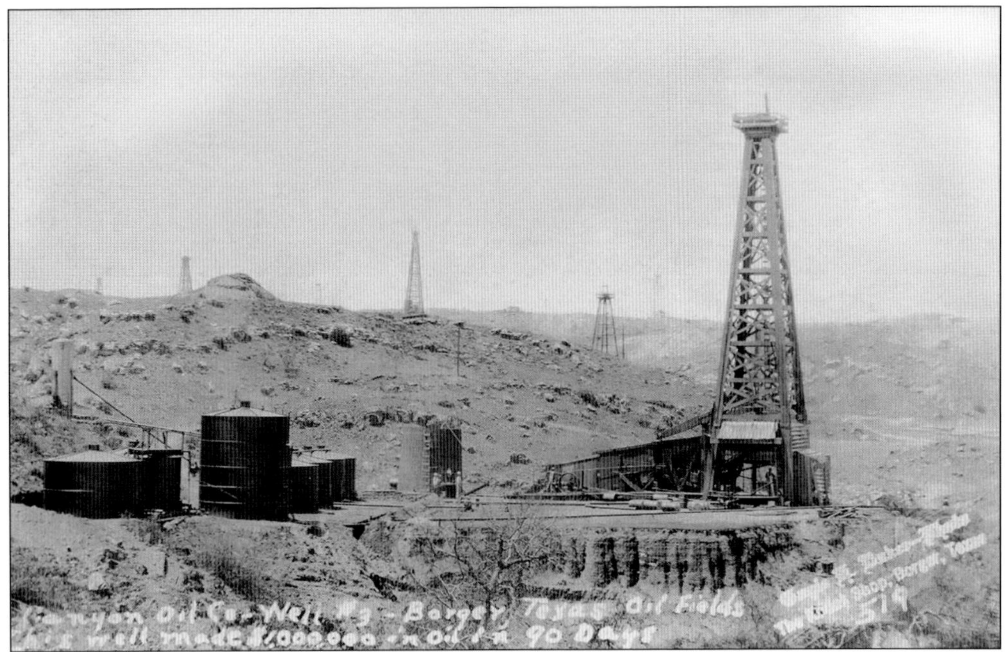

Rough terrain in the canyons near the river often meant a great deal of "dirt work" had to be done before rig construction or drilling could begin. Roads had to be built so that needed materials and machinery could be transported to the site. Because there was no railroad service in Hutchinson County until October 1926, to move the oil to market, storage tanks were built near the wells to hold oil until it could be transported by truck to the nearest railhead in Panhandle, 25 miles away. There were no highways in the county at that time, and the roads were often muddy quagmires that were both difficult and dangerous to travel on. Many of the wells were drilled in the canyons on both sides of the Canadian River, often in the riverbed. Quicksand, flooding, and mud made prospecting for oil in the Borger field a dangerous occupation.

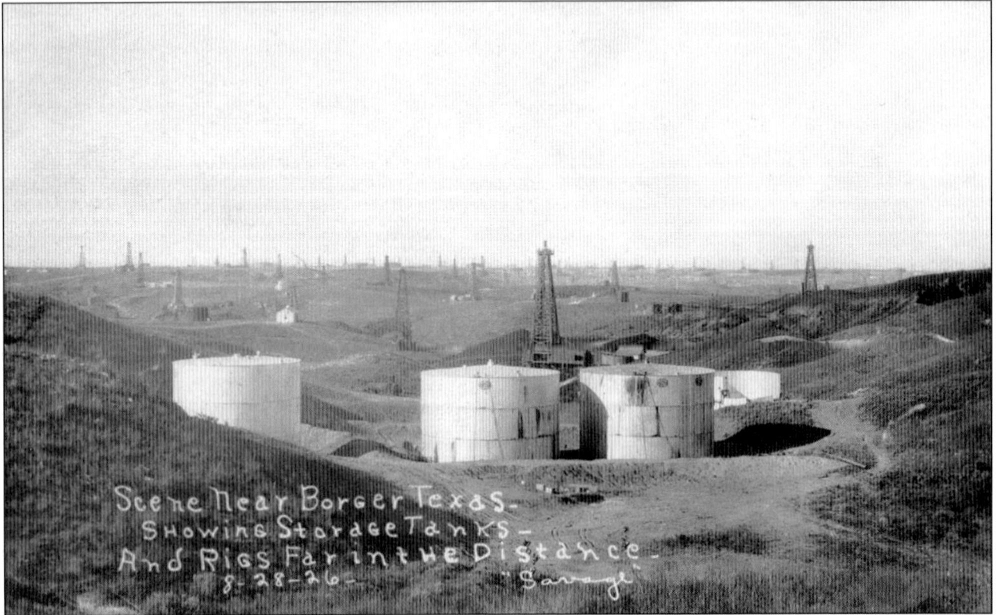

Six

Oil Camps and Ghost Towns

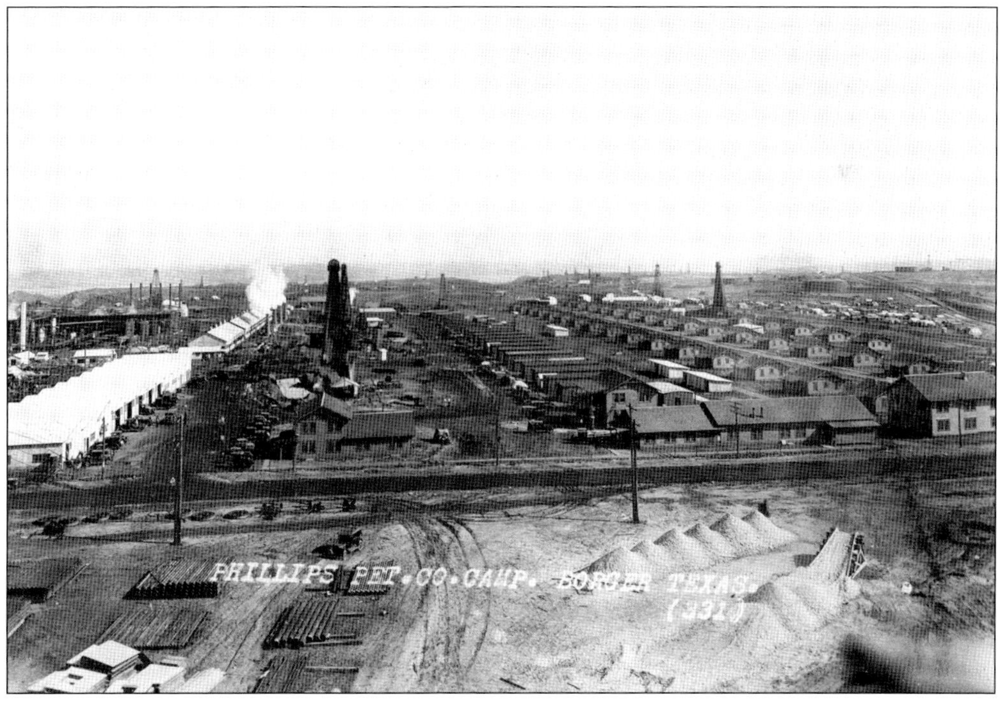

Early in 1926, after oil was discovered in Hutchinson County, rancher James A. Whittenburg sought to cash in on the boom by founding a town on his land three miles northeast of the new town of Borger in south central Hutchinson County. He named his new town Whittenburg. The Phillips Petroleum Company, also seeking to cash in, built its first refinery adjacent to Whittenburg in the Texas Panhandle. The Alamo Refinery was completed at Pantex in 1927. Shortly after, the village of Pantex was renamed Phillips. As the company developed, the boomtown shanties and rooming houses gave way to more permanent housing. As the town's population grew, additional facilities were built to house employees and their families. A hospital, several churches, and a progressive school system soon followed. In 1935, a $77,000 school building replaced an earlier structure. The villages of Pantex and Whittenburg competed for naming rights. In 1938, Pantex and Whittenburg voted to merge under the name of Phillips.

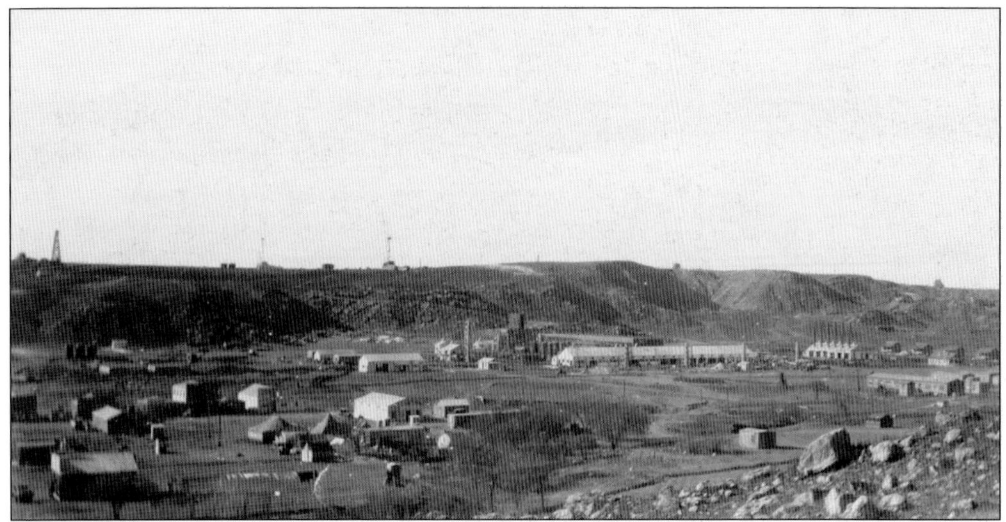

Electricity came to Hutchinson County in 1926 with the oil boom. The Riverview Power Plant, which became known as Electric City, was the county's first electricity-generating station. Construction of the plant began on the south side of the Canadian River in south-central Hutchinson County in July and continued around the clock—24 hours a day, seven days a week—until the plant began operating in November. A camp grew around the facility, and plant employees and oil field workers formed a sizable settlement nearby. With the improvement of local highways and transportation, employees no longer found it necessary to live close to the plant, and by the early 1960s, Electric City was no more.

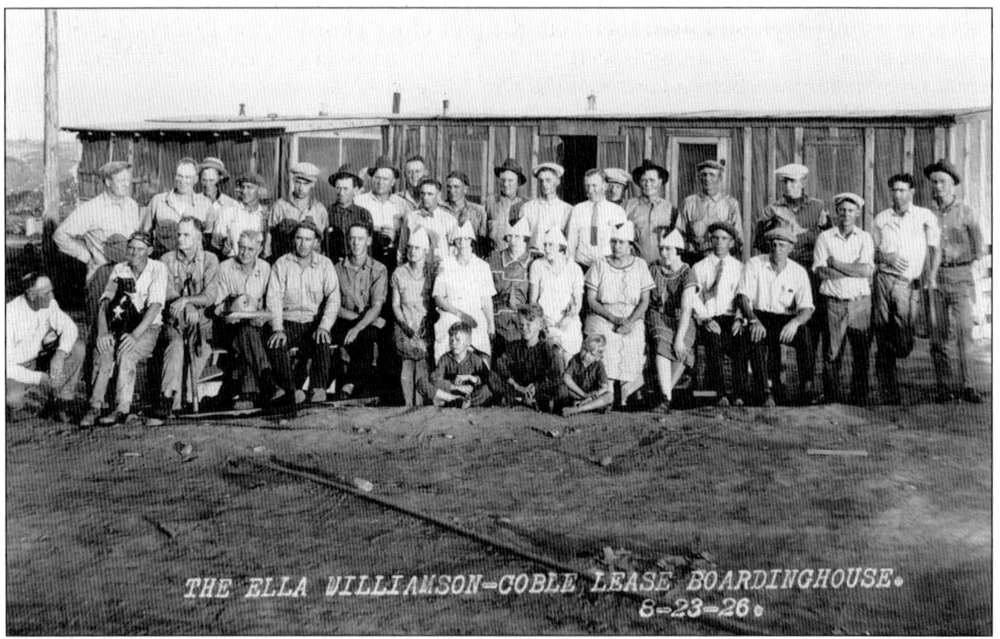

Until camps could be built, workers often lived in boardinghouses located on the leases. Leases were often named for the landowner, but this lease included the names of both the drilling/production company and the landowner. Members of the Coble family became pioneers of ranching in Hutchinson County and had significant landholdings. They shared the bounty of oil when it was discovered on their ranch.

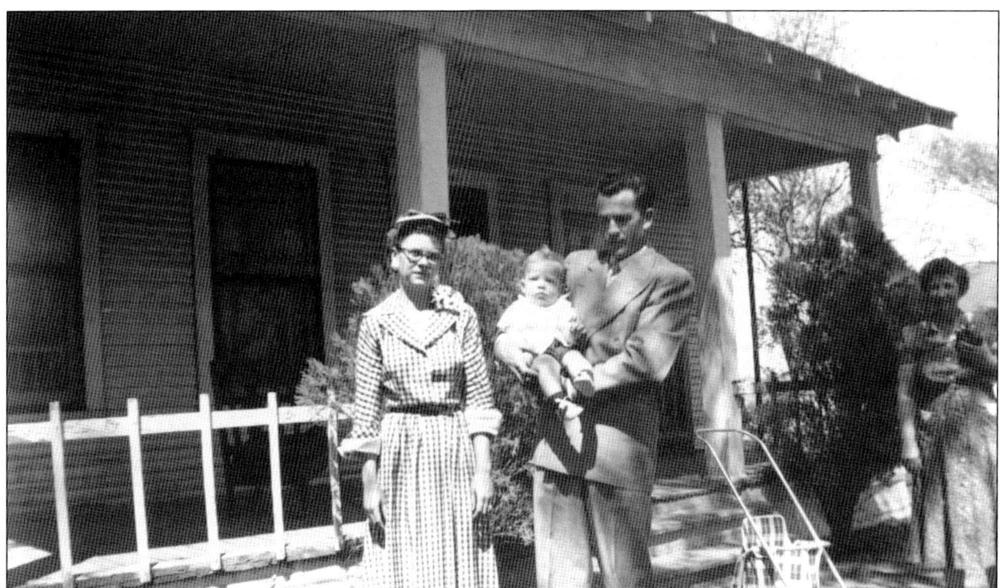

In 1918, Gulf Oil Company established an oil lease on land owned by rancher C.L. Dial, just north of the Canadian River in central Hutchinson County. Drilling began in 1921 on the county's first oil well, the Dial No. 1. The company struck oil there in 1922. A Gulf employee camp soon came to life on the lease on what is now Farm Road 2277 southeast of Stinnett. The Dial Camp had a post office, grocery store, and gas station, and by 1926 was flourishing. Over the years, as highways improved, the population of the oil camps declined, including the Dial camp. In the 1960s, about 80 people still lived there, but the post office closed in the 1970s and Dial soon became a ghost town. The author is seen here with his parents, Hester and Charles Renick, and maternal grandmother, Bertha Fowler, at the Dial camp in 1954.

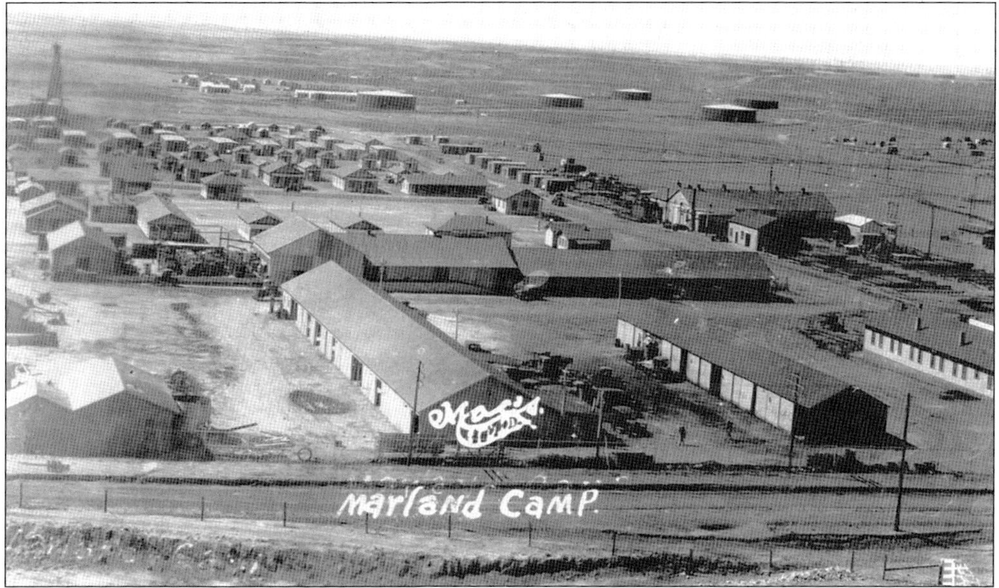

The Marland Oil Company, which existed from 1921 until 1928, had a legendary reputation in Oklahoma and surrounding states. This was the company camp of the Marland Oil Company, which later was absorbed by J.P. Morgan's Continental Oil Company (now Conoco).

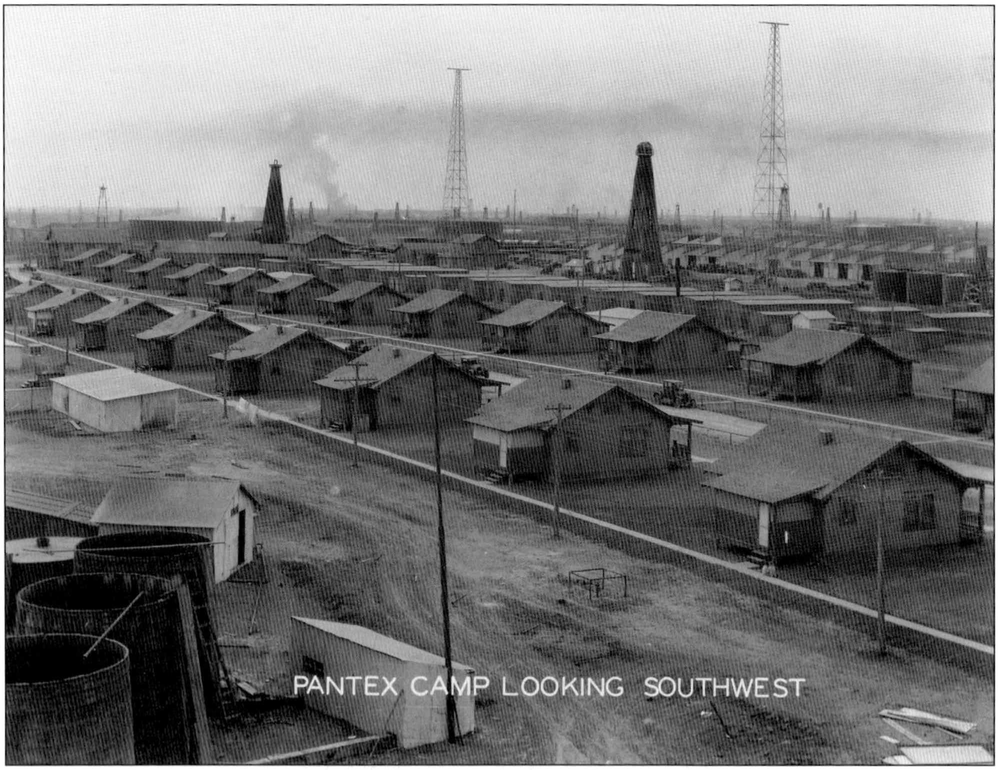

PANTEX CAMP LOOKING SOUTHWEST

This is Phillips company housing at the Pantex camp near the Alamo refinery. Employees owned their houses, but not the land on which they were built. The company leased the land at low rates.

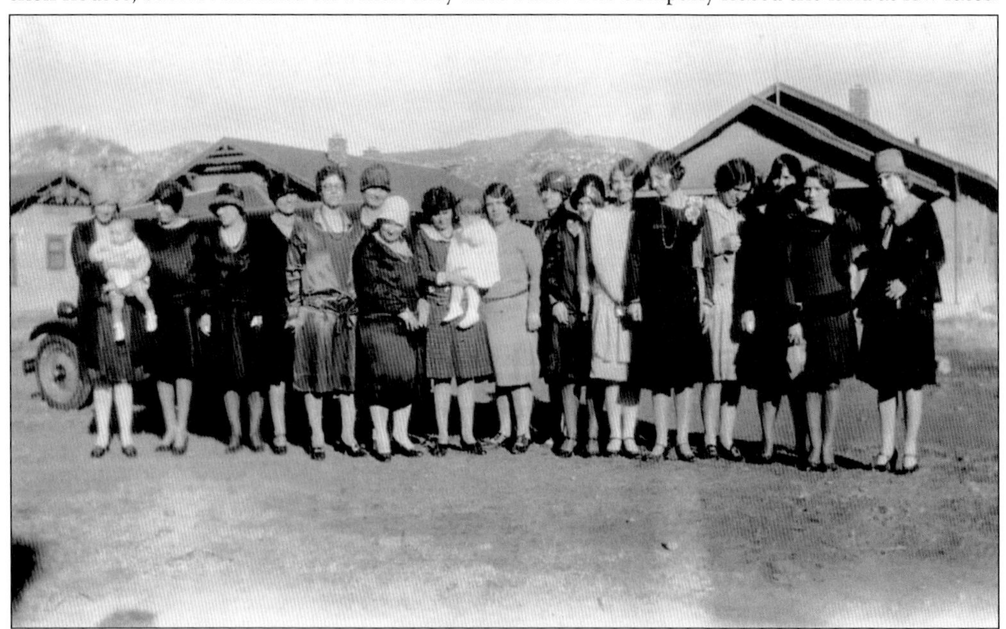

Members of the Twentieth Century Club are pictured in 1928. This chapter's efforts to establish a county library in Stinnett in 1937 resulted in the construction of an authentic adobe brick library in Borger by the WPA in 1938. The new Hutchinson County Library was dedicated in 1940.

Seven

The City of Borger Is Born

Your Opportunity Lies In

BORGER

The New Town of the Plains

LOCATED IN THE HEART OF THE PANHANDLE OIL FIELDS, 27 MILES NORTH OF PANHANDLE TEXAS, IN SECTION 19, BLOCK Y, HUTCHINSON COUNTY.

Lot Sale Opens Mon., March 8

ALL DEEDED LOTS

Terms of Sale

30% Down

BALANCE IN 10 EQUAL PAYMENTS

FOR FULL PARTICULARS, WRITE OR WIRE

A. P. BORGER

PANHANDLE, TEXAS

The town has been surveyed and the streets are being marked off and graded and everything will be in readiness for the formal opening. The first contract for a building in Borger was for a bank building, which will be constructed of brick.

In March 1926, Ace Borger placed this advertisement in the Panhandle, Texas, newspaper to advertise lots for sale in his new town. Borger had pneumonia at the time sales began, and because of his illness, he was forced to conduct business from his room on the second floor of the historic Panhandle Inn Hotel because there were no acceptable hotels in his new town.

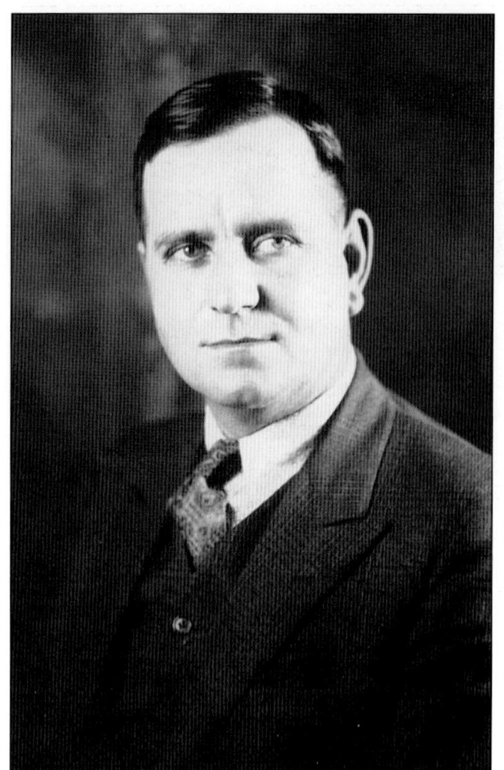

Asa Phillip "Ace" Borger (1888–1934, left) once said, "the secret to success in the oil business is being ahead of the rest of the crowd a few minutes, a few hours or a few days." Ace, his brother Pete, and his partner Johnny Miller (below right) first came to Hutchinson County in early 1926 on a tip from their brother in law Clyde C. Horton, who told them about the major oil strike he expected very soon. Horton was a job boss for Gulf Oil Company in Carson County on the 6666 Ranch. Oil was discovered in Hutchinson County in 1921. Wildcat drilling and prospecting were underway until 1926, when a big strike near Dixon Creek set off the oil boom that put the new city of Borger on the map. Ace was ahead of the crowd when he bought 240 acres from John and Maggie Weatherly for $50 an acre. He and his partners became very wealthy very quickly! They and C.C. Horton formed the Borger Townsite Company and began selling lots on March 8, 1926. They sold the company in late September that year for over $1 million, about $13 million today. Ace's wife, Elizabeth Willoughby Borger (1889–1933), is pictured at left below.

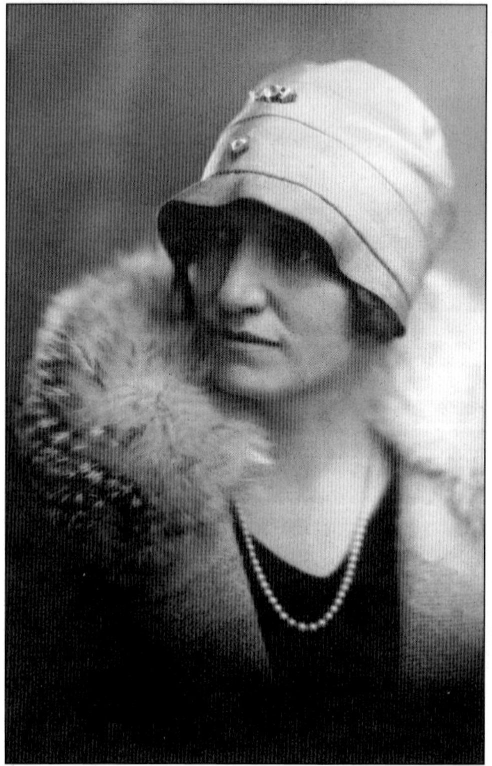

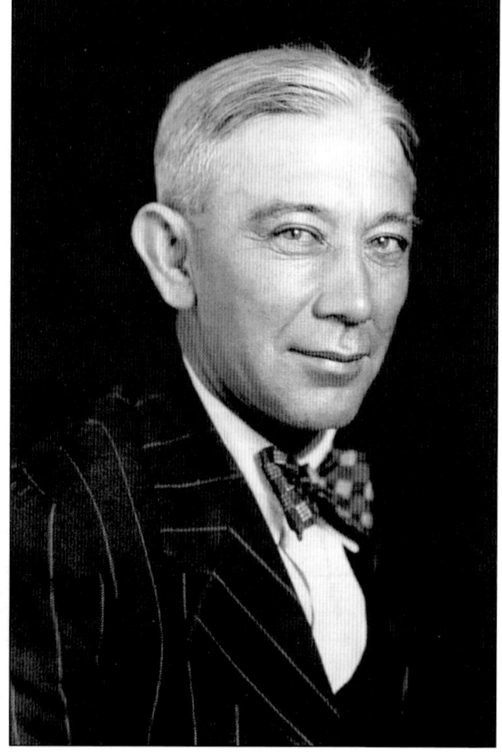

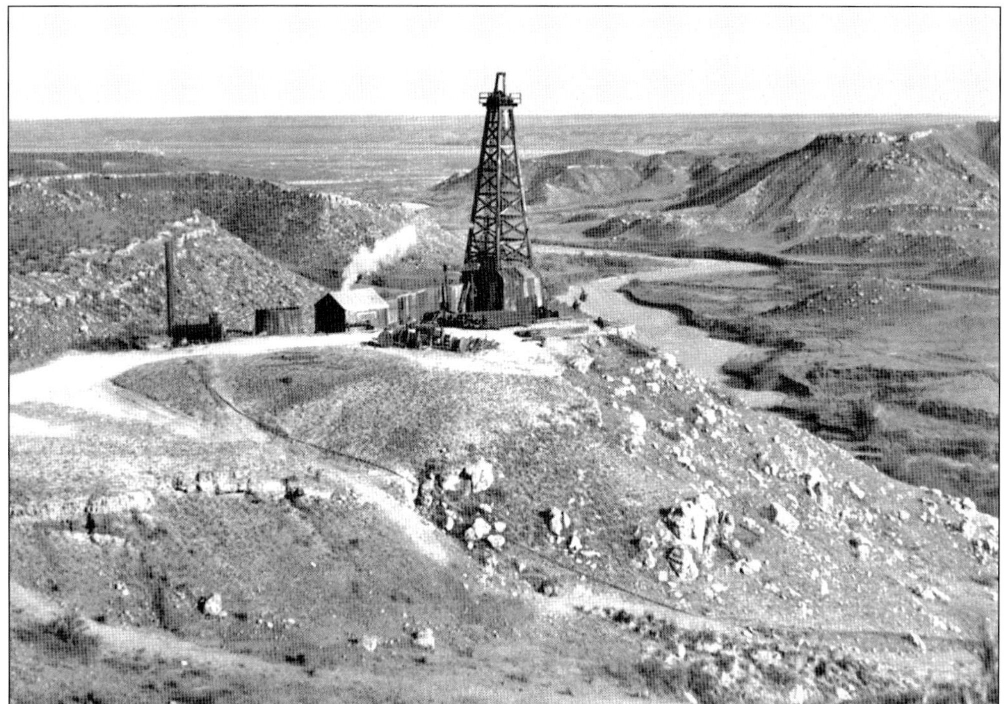

From the tops of the bluffs to the bottom of the valleys and everywhere in between, drilling for oil in Hutchinson County was a difficult business. Well sites usually had to be dramatically improved just to make it possible to move equipment and materials to the site to build a rig. Remote locations and the lack of good roads made getting to work difficult. Rig hands often lived on-site for several days at a time, because going back and forth to work was not always possible.

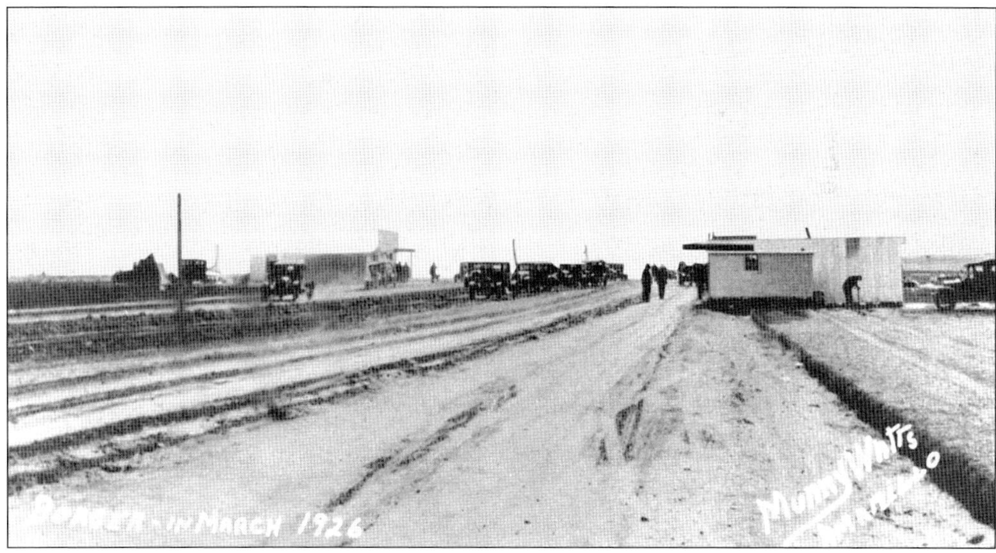

On March 8, 1926, lots went on sale in the new town of Borger. Ace Borger hired a horse team and plowed deep streets in the virgin prairie to define where the lots were located. These streets often became impossible to navigate when it rained and they turned to mud.

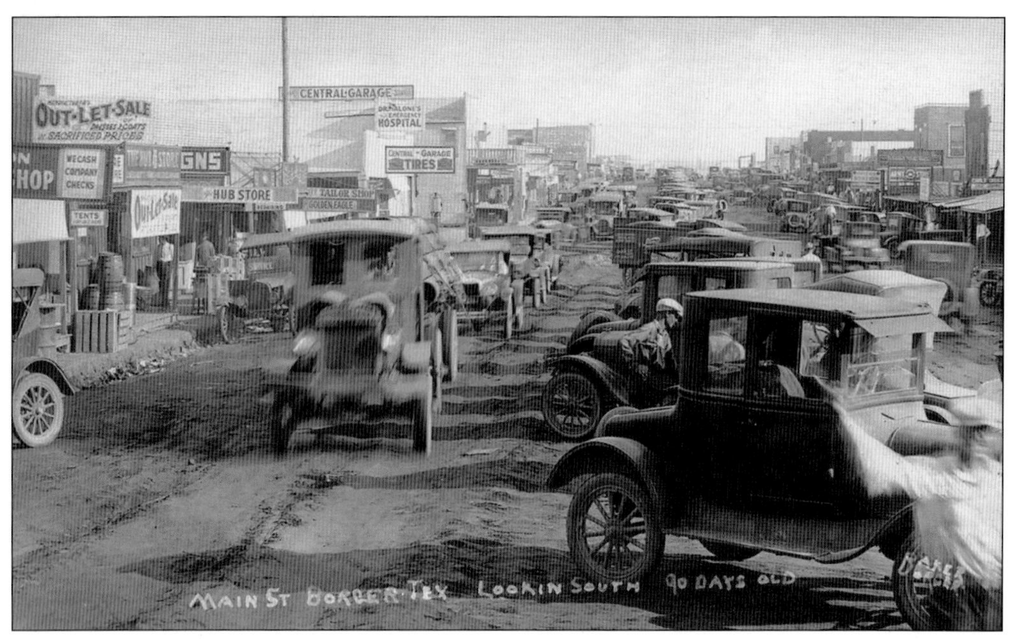

The above image, labeled by the photographer who made it, shows the amazing growth of Borger. Just 90 days earlier, this land was virgin prairie. At the time of this photograph, Ace Borger owned the only lumberyard in his new town. Below, Borger is in his element as he walks among construction materials on a jobsite in his new town.

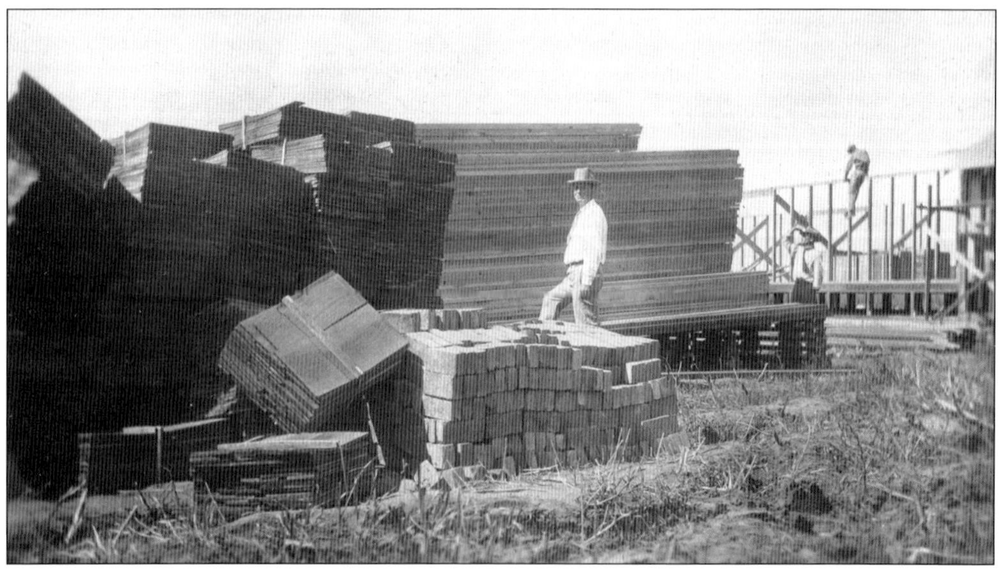

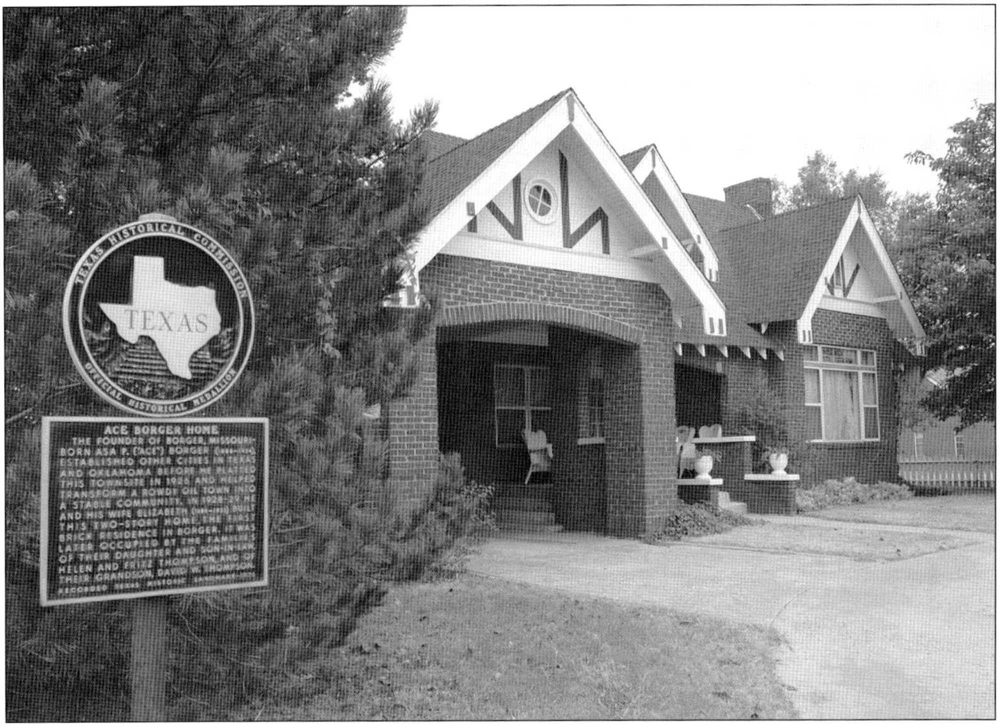

Above is Ace and Elizabeth Borger's home as it appears today; it is still owned by their descendants. The Texas historical marker was placed on the site through the work of the Hutchinson County Historical Committee in conjunction with the Texas Historical Commission. At right, the Borger home is shown in an earlier photograph.

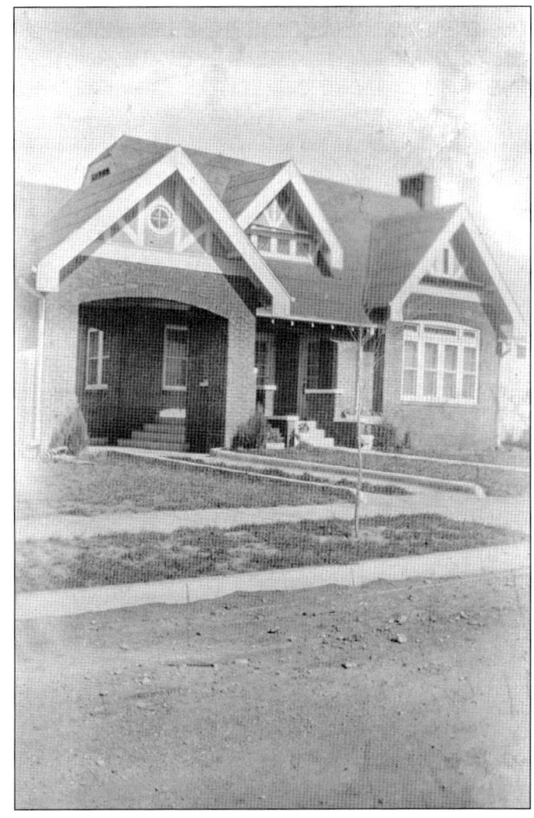

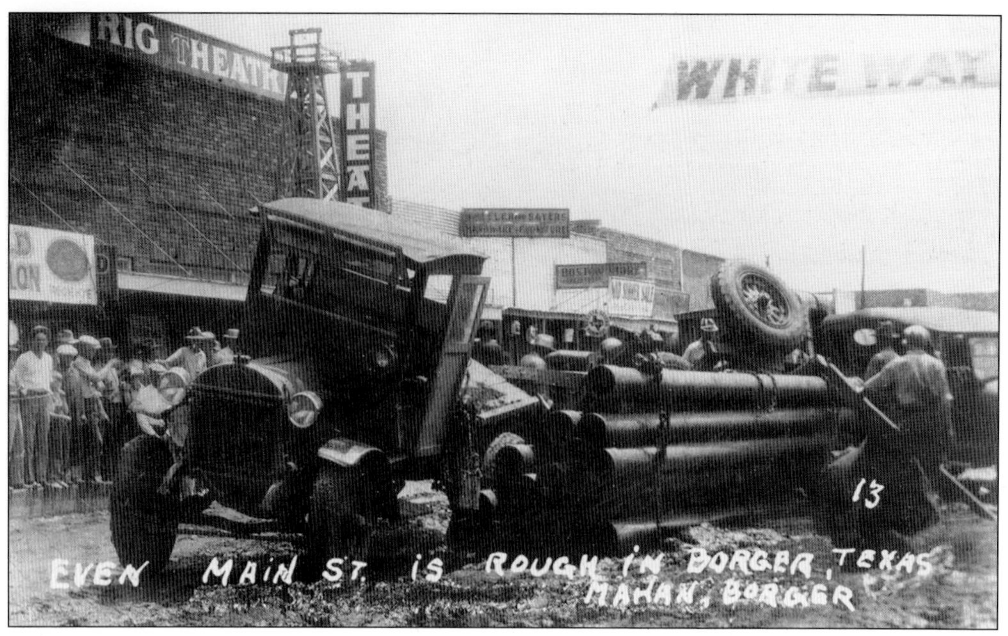

Ace Borger used a horse-drawn grader to create the streets for his new town. When it rained, the streets became muddy ruts that made driving difficult and greatly increased the likelihood of getting stuck. The combination of oil trucks hauling heavy loads and hundreds of cars pounded the streets into muddy, water-filled tracks that often took weeks to dry out.

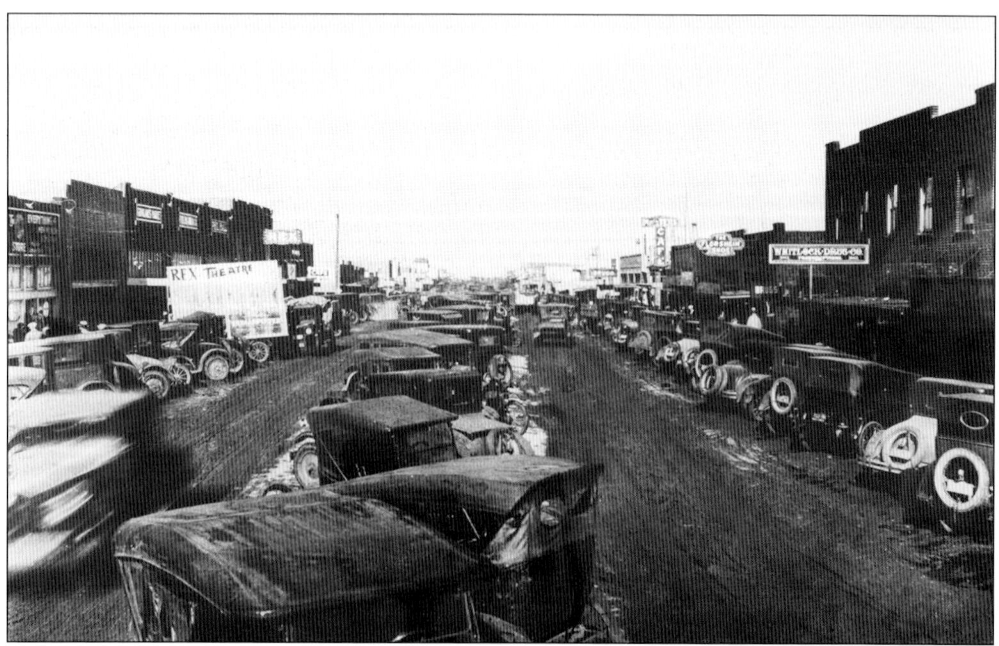

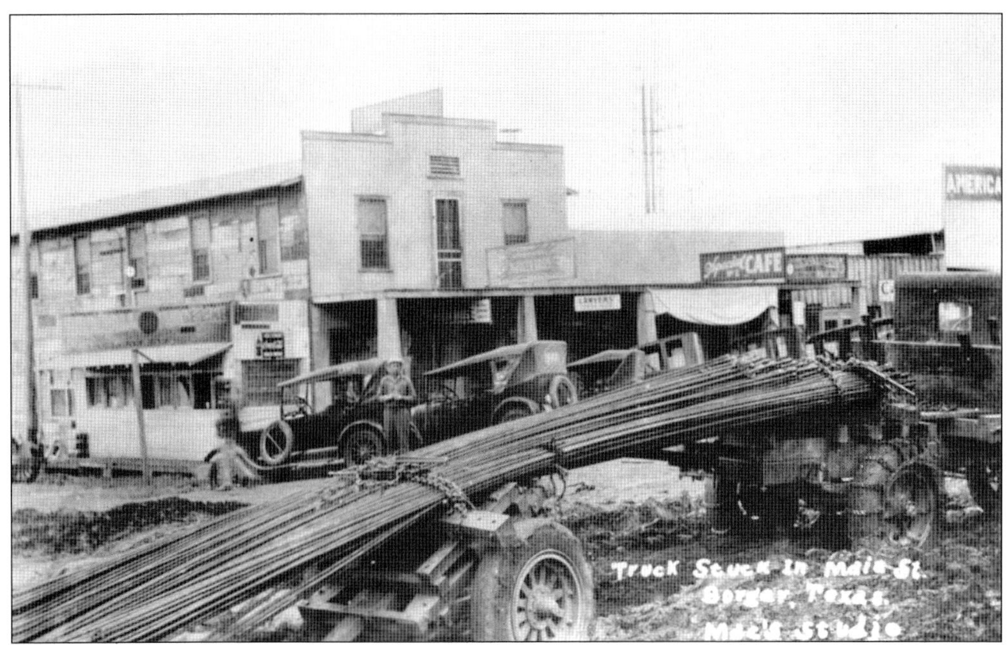

The mud did not stop business owners who wanted to reap the rewards of the boom, because the lots on Main Street sold quickly. The lots on both sides of the street, from Fourth Street to Seventh Street, had requirements in their titles that stipulated that a two-story brick building had to be constructed on the land within one year from the date of sale, or ownership of the land reverted to the seller. The lots were sold, the brick buildings were erected, and business boomed.

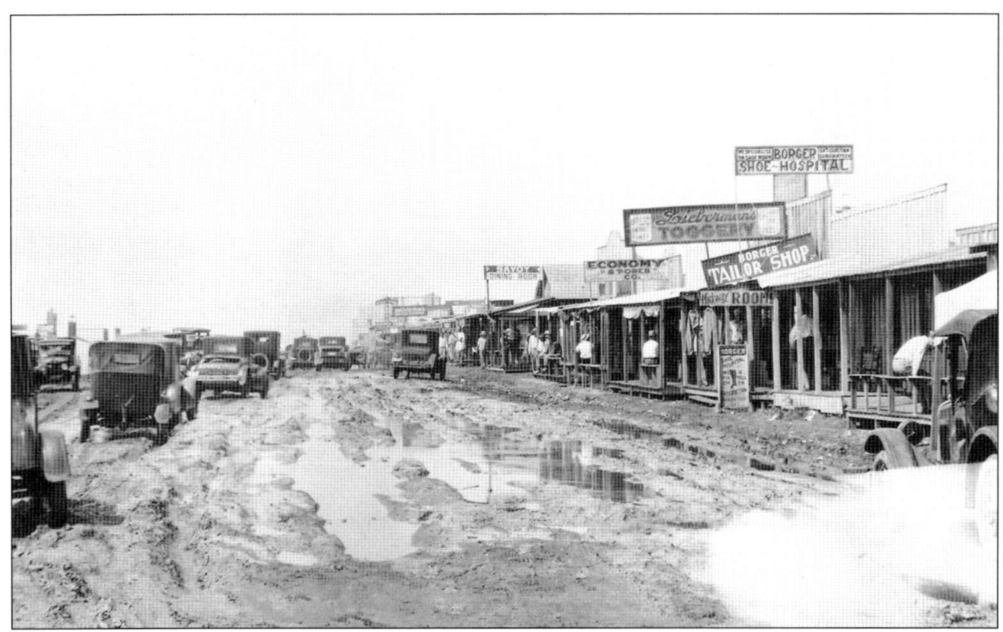

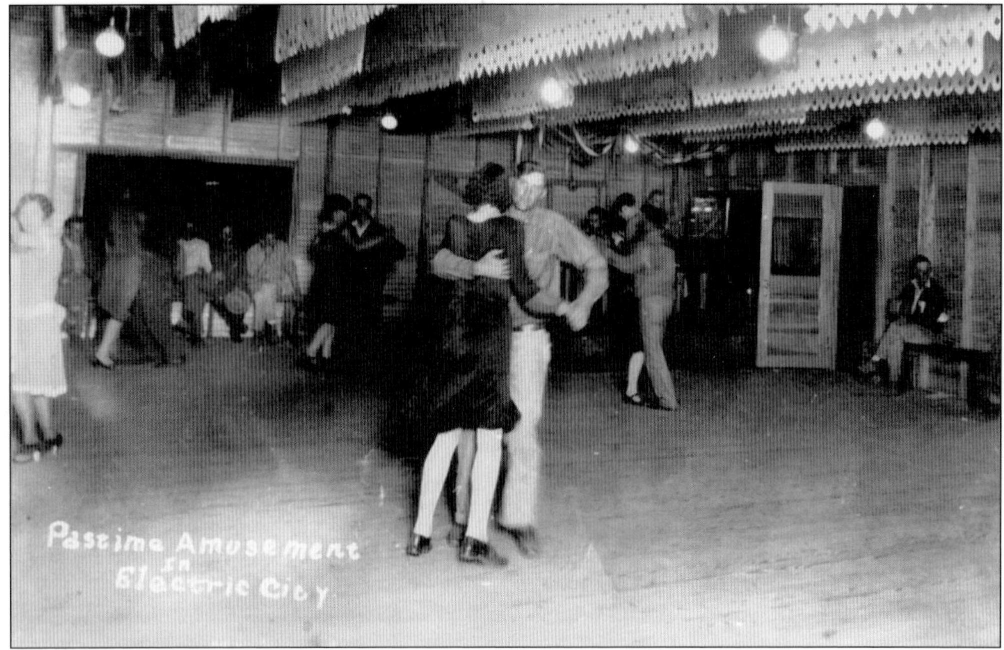

In its early years, the newly created boomtown was known as Borger by day and "Booger Town" by night. Abundant jobs and steady work meant oil workers had plenty of money. Workers who were single—and even those men with families who came to the area to work—had money in their pockets and were looking for fun when the work was done. Moonshine, gambling halls, corrupt officials and law officers, illegal narcotics, and a bounty of brothels made Borger a good place to find trouble. Oilmen, prospectors, roughnecks, panhandlers, and fortune-seekers flooded the area, and along with them came a number of shadier elements, including card sharks, bootleggers, and drug dealers. Borger had a bad reputation for a few years and attracted fugitives from the law, as well as some of the toughest hoodlums in the Southwest.

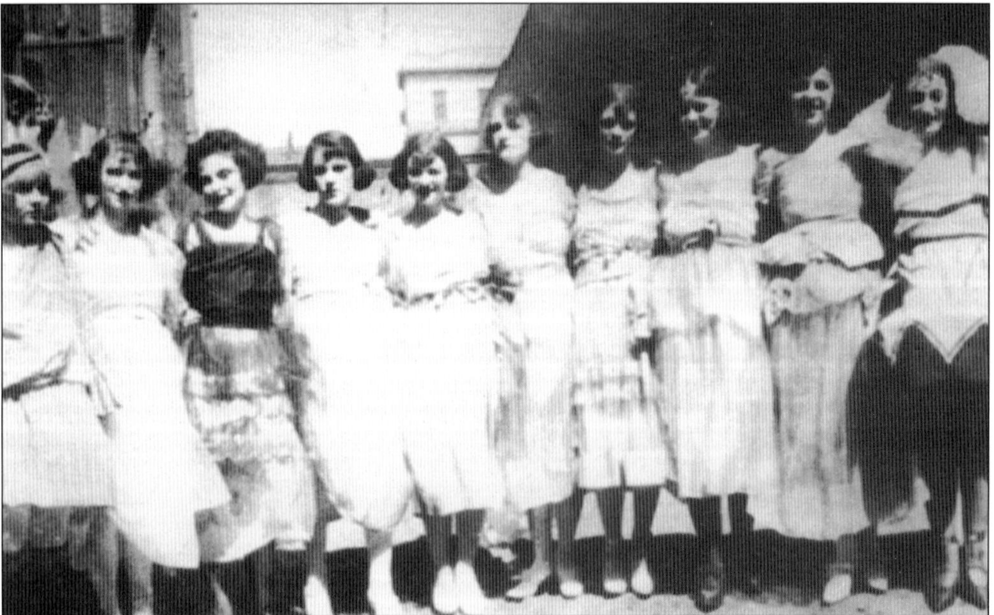

An 800 gallon still that was captured by the Texas Rangers and National Guard is seen here. The canyons surrounding Borger were filled with illegal stills, as bootleggers could make big money in Booger Town. The Texas Rangers came to clean up Borger in October 1926 and again in the spring of 1927. This photograph and the one below could be from either time.

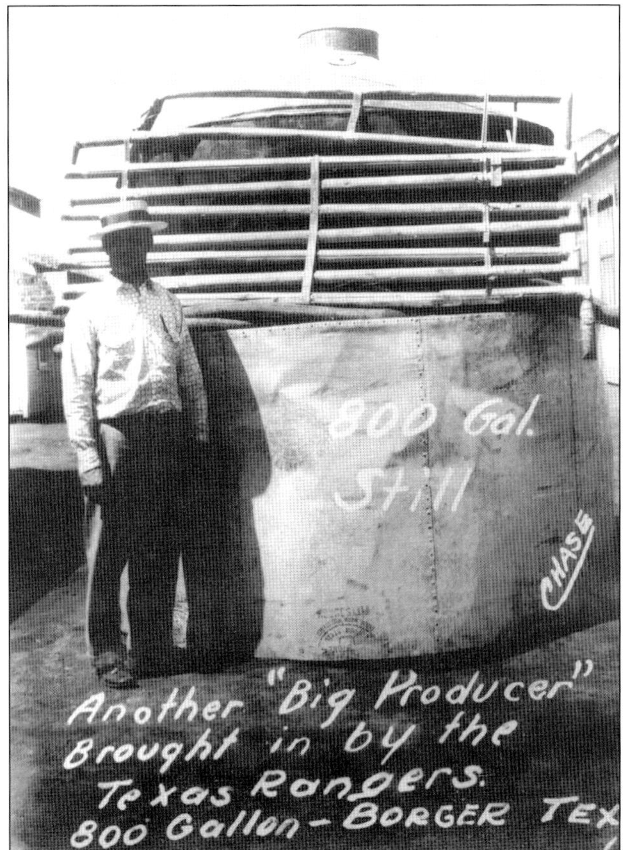

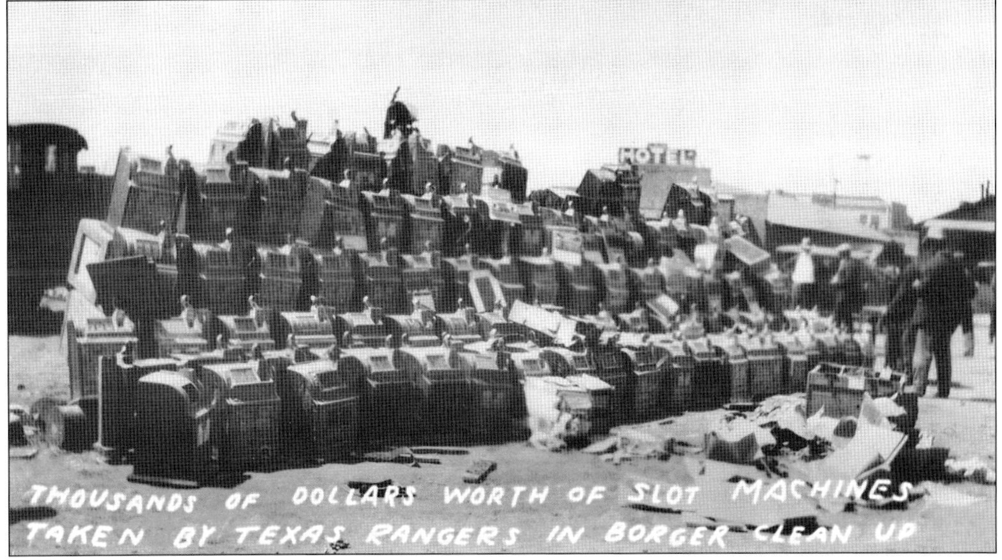

Gambling halls were common in Borger, as demonstrated by these slot machines captured by National Guard troops and the Texas Rangers. Stories have been told of National Guard soldiers and Texas Rangers giving the money from the slot machines to children who happened to be on the street near the gambling halls as they were being raided.

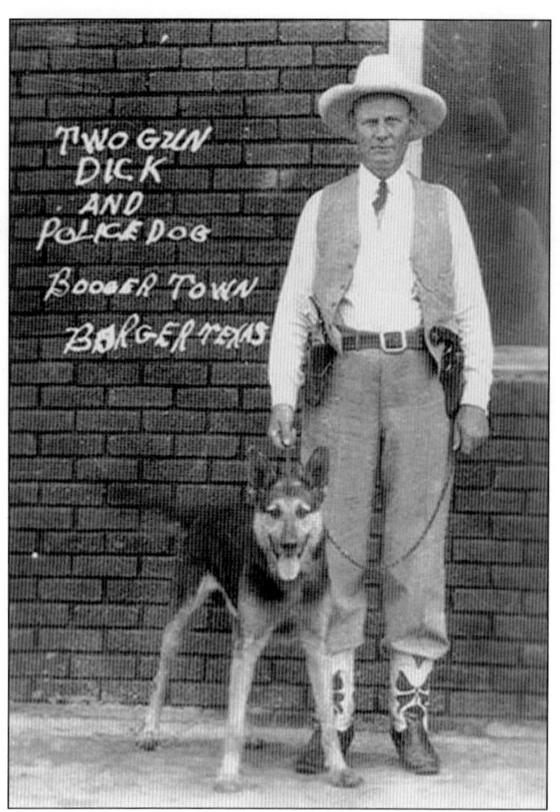

Town government in Borger fell under control of an organized crime syndicate led by Mayor John Miller's shady associate Richard "Two-Gun Dick" Herwig, who was under indictment for murder in Cromwell, Oklahoma, when he was hired by Ace Borger to be the town's chief law enforcement officer. Two-Gun Dick brought a number of his felonious friends to "police" the flourishing town. Their primary responsibility was collecting fees from bootleggers and prostitutes. Herwig and his men "supervised" saloons in defiance of Prohibition while supplying their own lines of bootlegged alcohol, beer, and narcotics to the illegal barrooms. Dixon Street (now Tenth Street) was the center of the activity, complete with brothels, dance halls, speakeasies, and gambling dens. As many as 2,000 prostitutes plied their trade, each paying a weekly fine of $18 to stay in business. Murder and robbery became common, as Herwig's force had no time for the protection of everyday citizens.

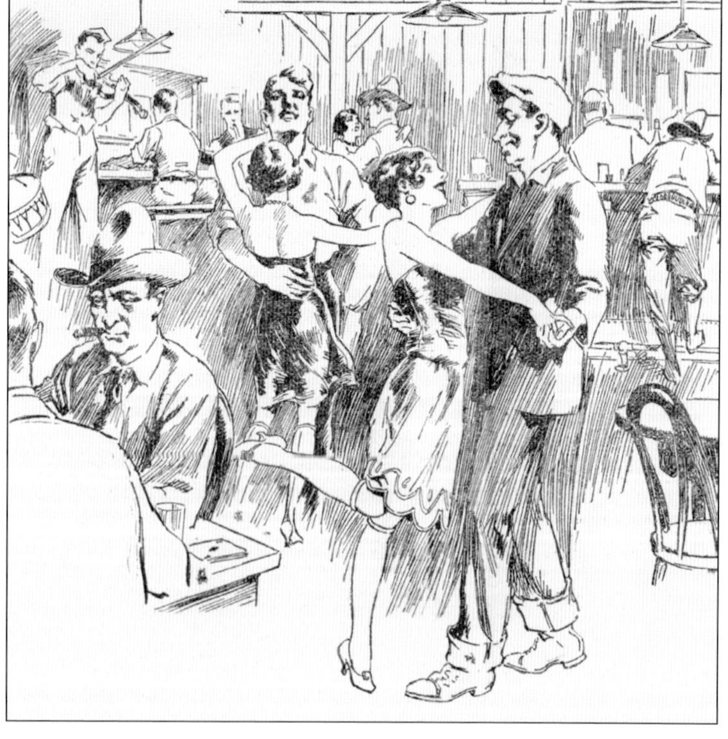

This illustration from a local newspaper at the time offers an idea of the nightlife in boomtown Borger. Thousands of men came seeking work and opportunity. They had steady, good-paying jobs, and when quitting time came, they wanted to blow off steam and have a little fun. Plenty of local businesses—and women—were ready to meet that demand.

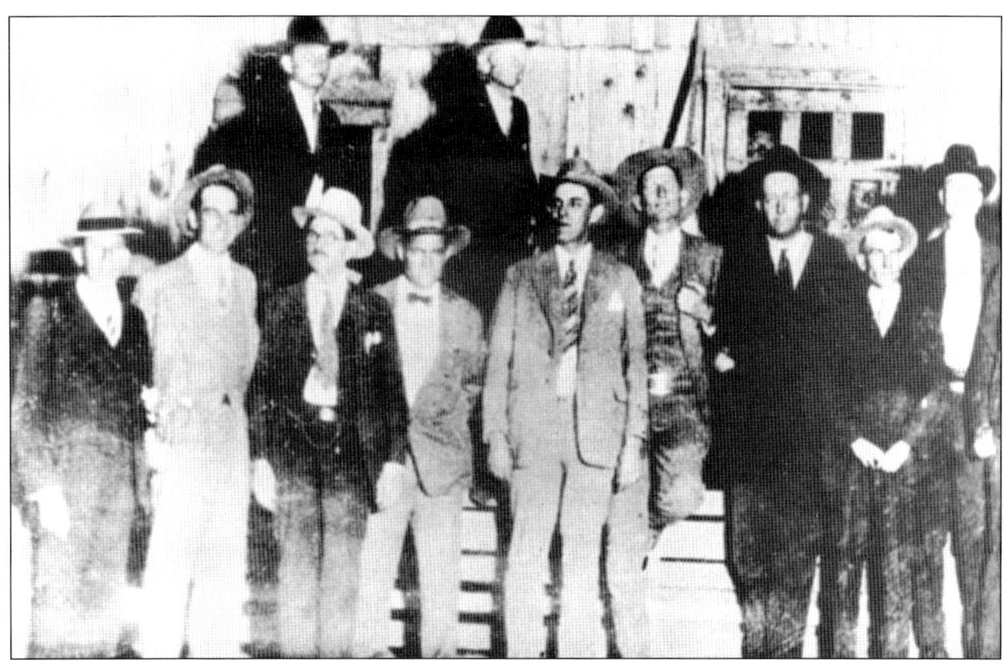

The Texas Rangers are seen here in Borger on April 17, 1927. Above are, from left to right, (first row) unidentified, Private Hickman, W.W. Taylor, A.P. Cummings, Capt. Tom Hickman, Capt. Bill Sterling, Capt. Frank Hamer, Mayor Johnny Miller of Borger, and Charles Davis; (second row) Private Purvis and unidentified. Captain Hamer went on to fame as the man who killed Bonnie and Clyde. The Texas Rangers are seen below with several prisoners.

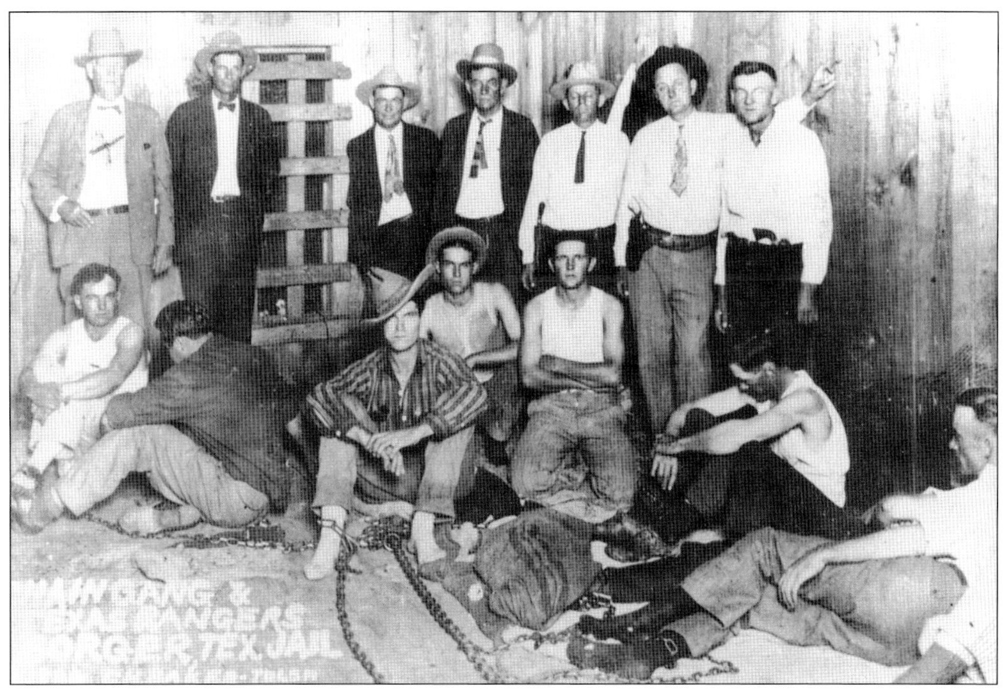

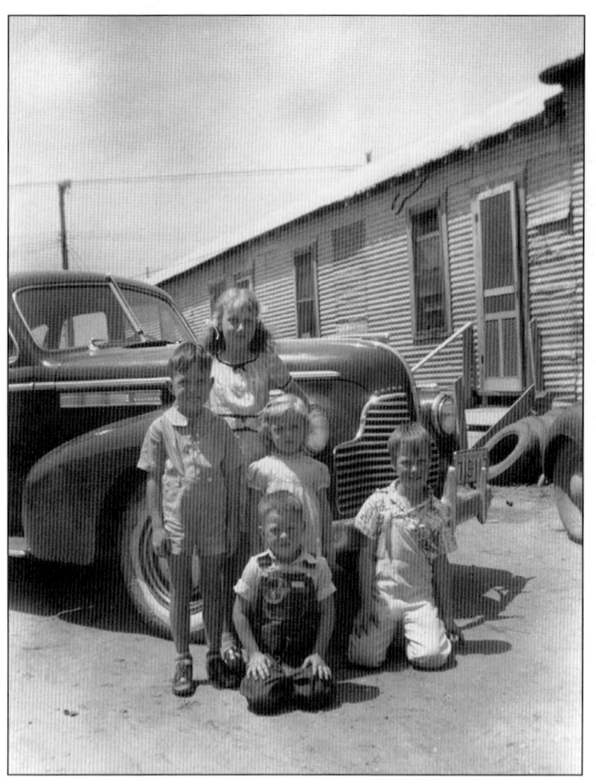

Houses that were built when the boom began were often thrown together with whatever materials could be found. Tin buildings with wooden frames and no insulation were the norm. The children were often poor, but they had freedoms unknown to kids today. These kids look like they've been playing hard!

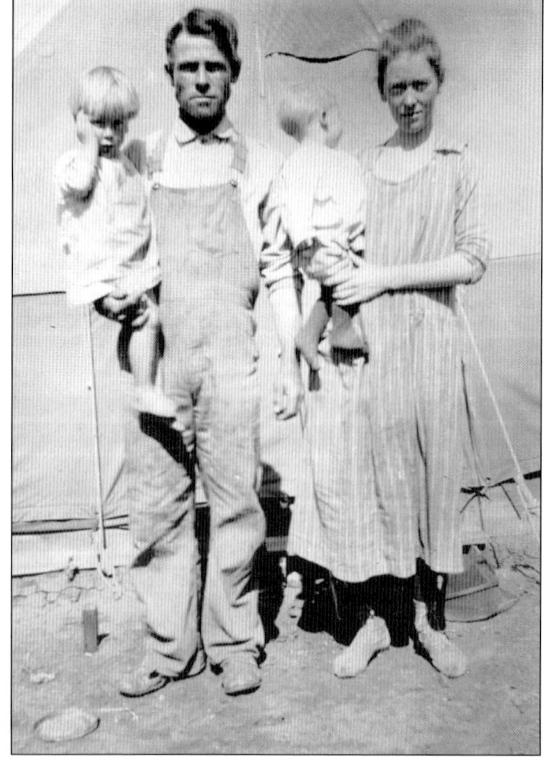

Housing was hard to find during the early years of the oil boom in Hutchinson County. Workers often bought lots and built tents on them, because lumber and other building materials were expensive and scarce—when they could be found at all. As time passed and workers settled in, the lots where they had once lived in tents became the sites where they built permanent homes.

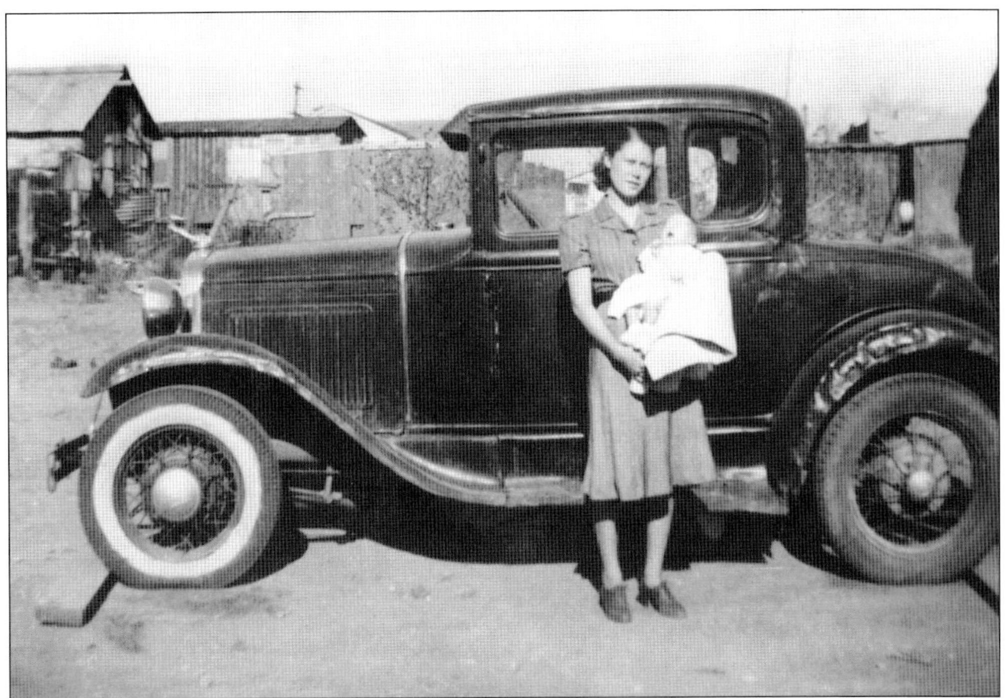

Many of the men who came to work in the early oil fields were single, but people soon realized that long-term jobs and steady work would be available in the area for many years. Men began to bring their families with them when they came to work, but housing and living conditions were less than desirable. Wives and children sometimes suffered due to the harsh environment, lack of adequate housing, and the absence of amenities such as indoor plumbing and reliable heating.

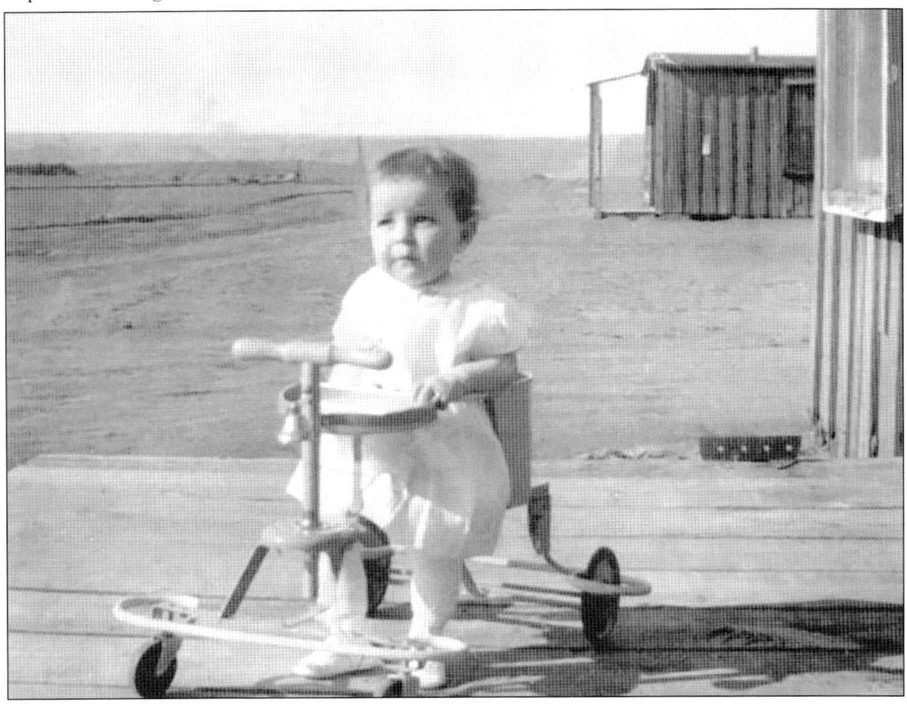

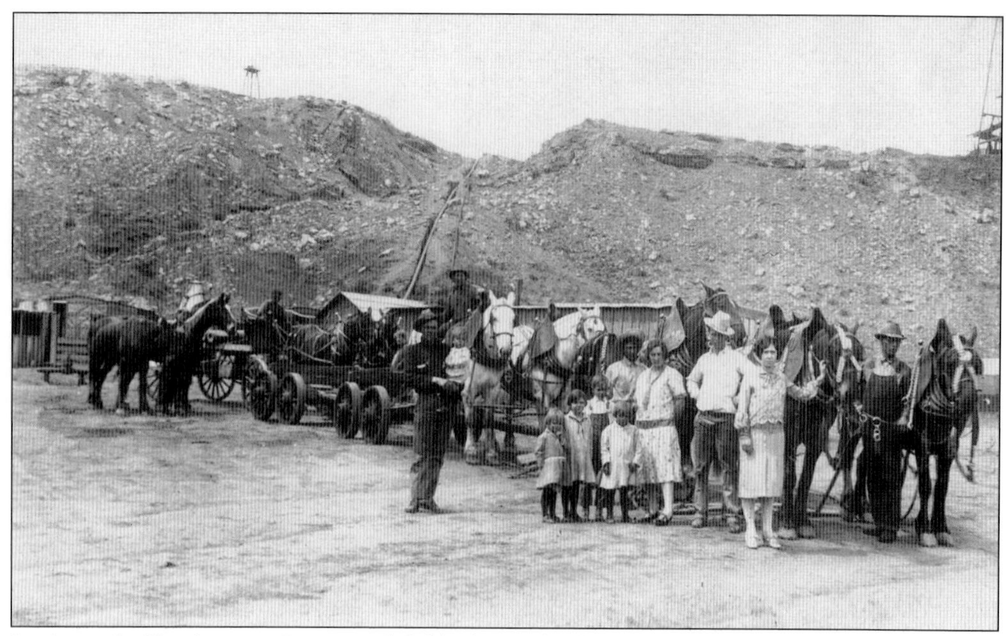

In the early Hutchinson County oil fields, heavy loads were moved by teams of horses. This photograph makes it appear as if it might have been "take your wives and children to work" day. Well sites were never far from town, and the wells were often drilled near houses, hotels, and apartments.

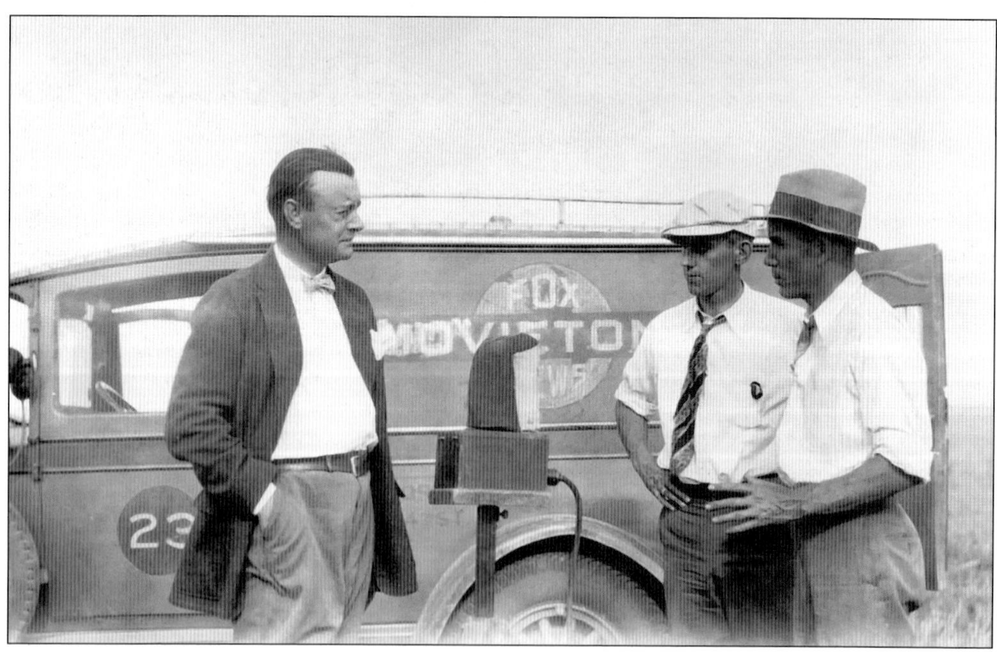

Radio and newspaper reporters came from all over the country to tell the amazing story of the Texas oil boom. Fox Movietone News produced sound newsreels from 1927 through 1963.

Eight

Schools in Hutchinson County

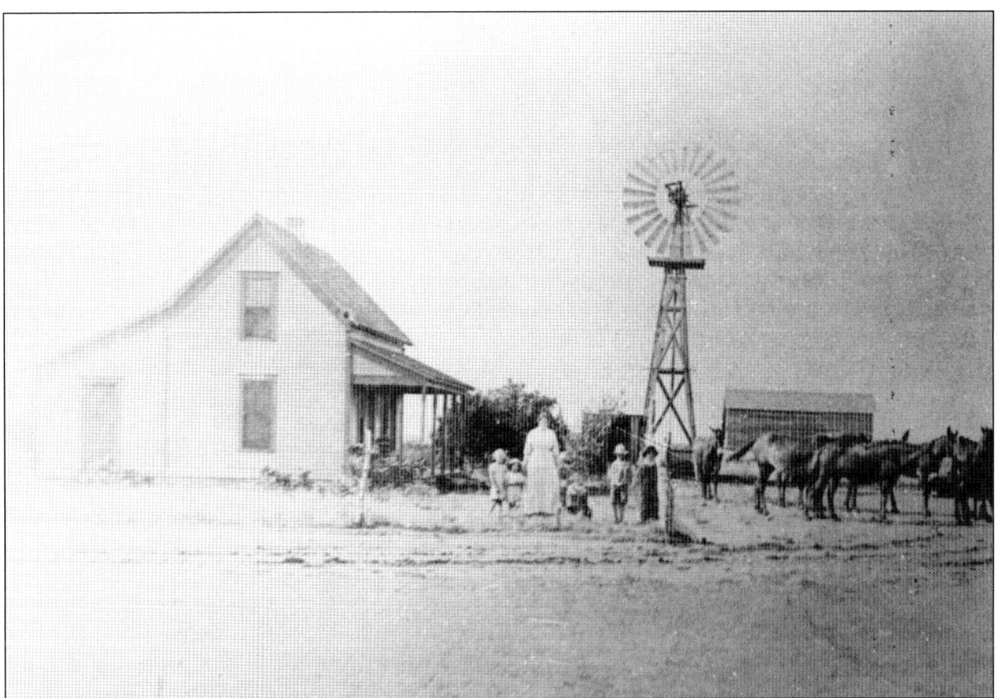

Hutchinson County was established in 1876, when 53 counties were formed from Béxar County. It was attached to Roberts County for administrative purposes until 1901. The State of Texas required 150 land purchase applications to formally establish a county seat and form the governing body needed for administration of a county. That number was reached in 1901, and Hutchinson County came into being. In 1903, early settlers Benjamin and Birda May (Kirk) Holt donated seven acres to be used as the site of a community schoolhouse and cemetery. The first person buried there was Nola Storrs, in 1909. A new schoolhouse was built there in 1916. Five acres were set aside for school purposes and two acres for the cemetery, which contained 11 gravesites. In 1948, Holt School trustees deeded the school's five acres and the vacated schoolhouse to the Holt Cemetery Association, and about an acre of this property was converted for cemetery use. The cemetery, which continues to serve the local community, contains the graves of many of the area's early settlers and of veterans of World War I, World War II, and the Korean conflict.

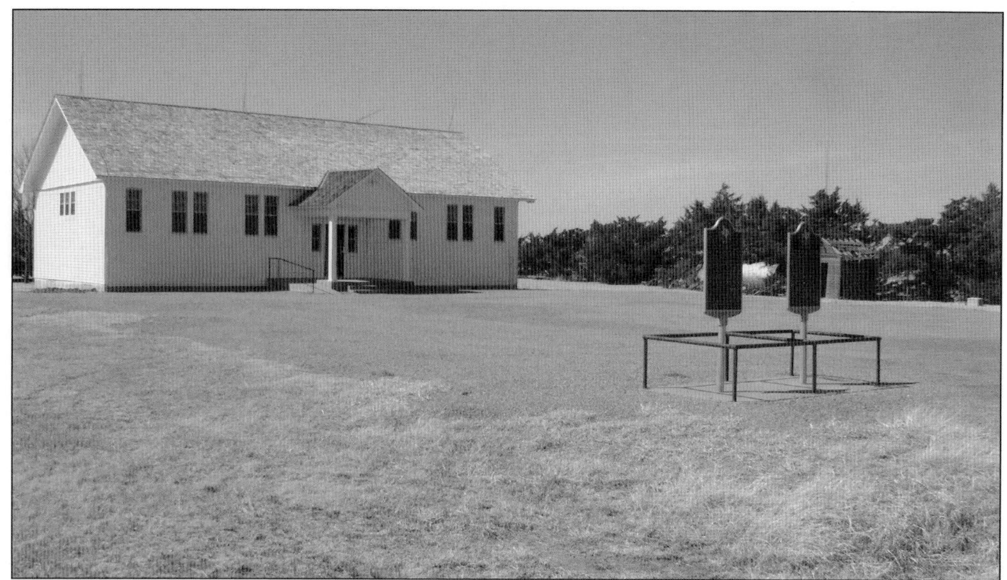

A countywide public school district was established soon after Hutchinson County was created in 1901. Common School District No. 8 was established in the northeastern corner of the county in 1902. The first schoolhouse was a one-room structure built in 1903 on land donated by Benjamin Holt. The two-room building above was constructed in 1916 with lumber hauled in from Texoma, Oklahoma. The simple wooden structure has a gabled entrance, oversized windows, and decorative wood shingles. Regular classes were held here until 1935, when students began attending school in Spearman. The building is still a community gathering place—the site of weddings, funerals, and community activities such as quilting bees and local theater productions. It also continues to serve as an election polling place. Below is an aerial view of the Holt schoolhouse and cemetery. (Above, photograph by Clay Renick.)

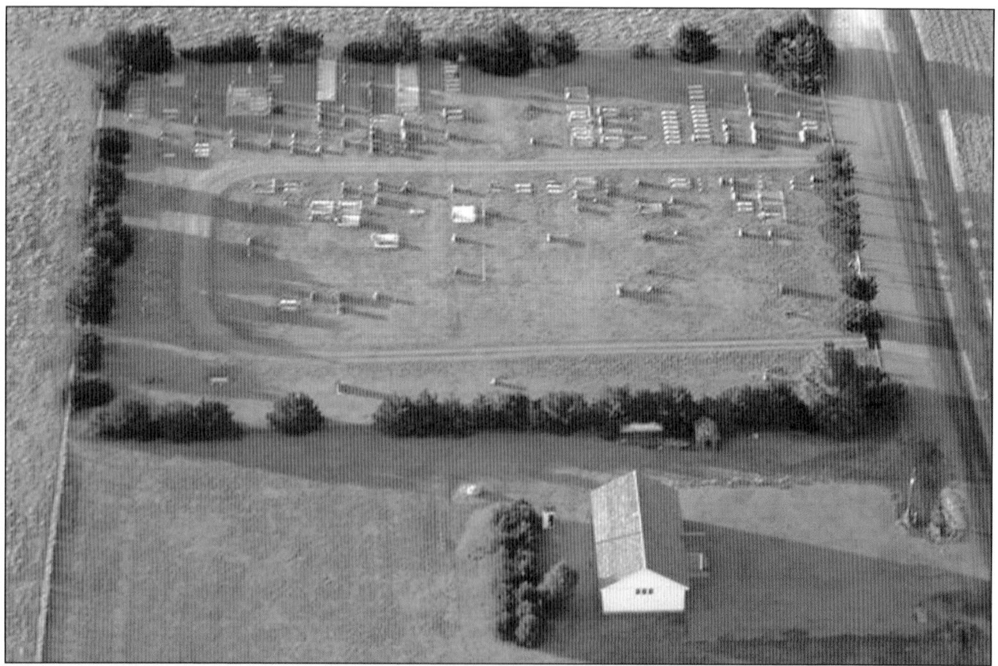

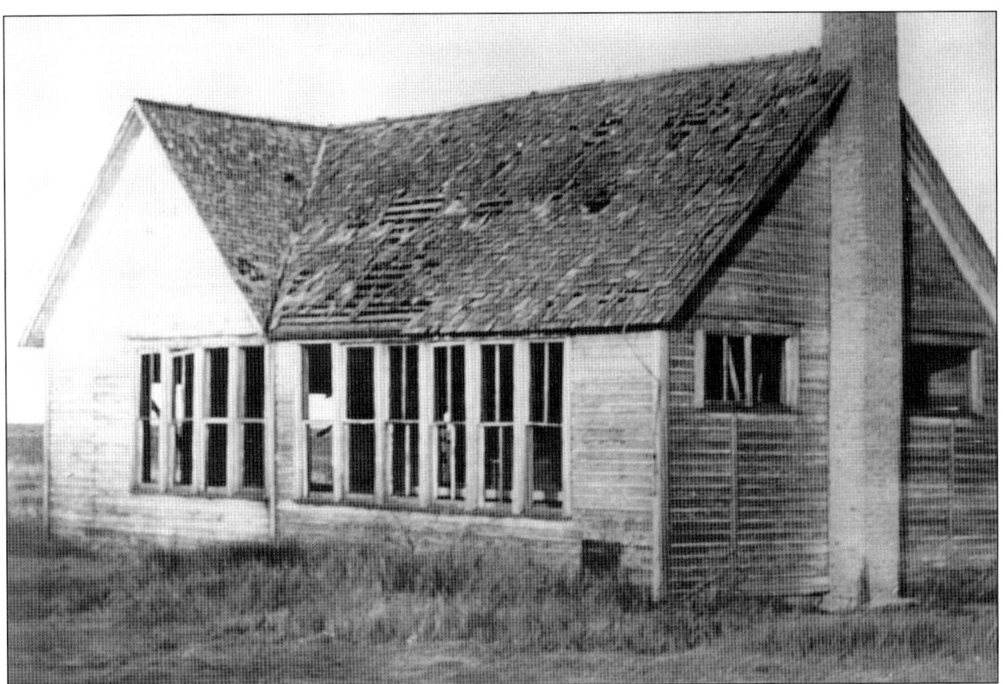

The above photograph shows all that remained of the Lieb School in 1961. Construction on the school started in 1902, and the first term began when the building was finished in 1903. The school was built adjacent to the Lieb cemetery north of Pringle in northwestern Hutchinson County. Seen below in an undated image are teachers and students standing in front of the Spring Creek School in southeastern Hutchinson County. Early Hutchinson County residents greatly valued education and built schools, often with their own money, to ensure that their children were literate.

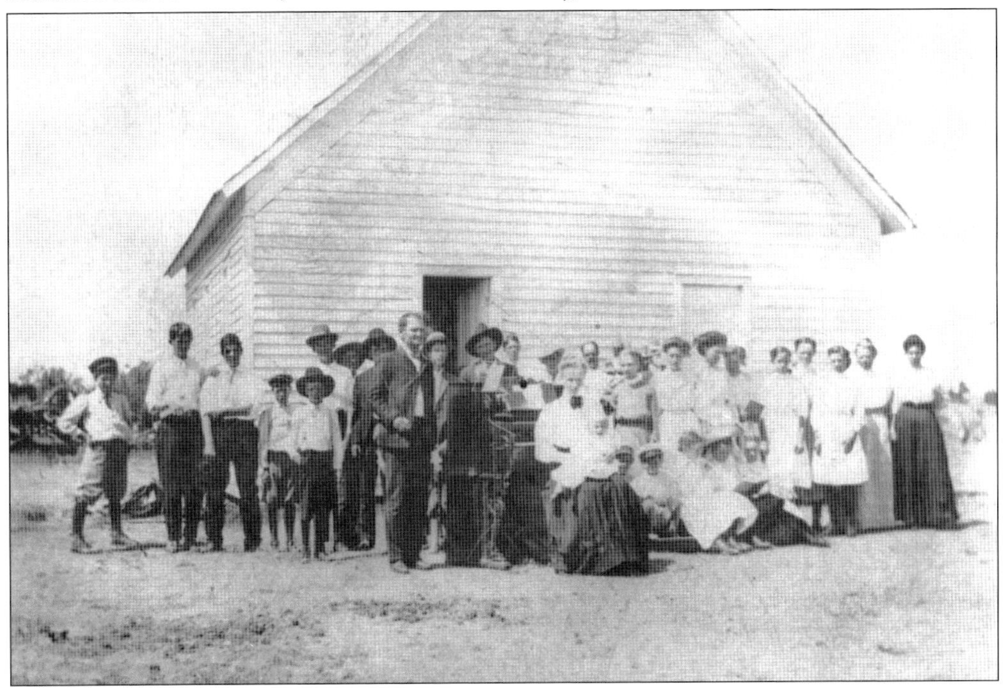

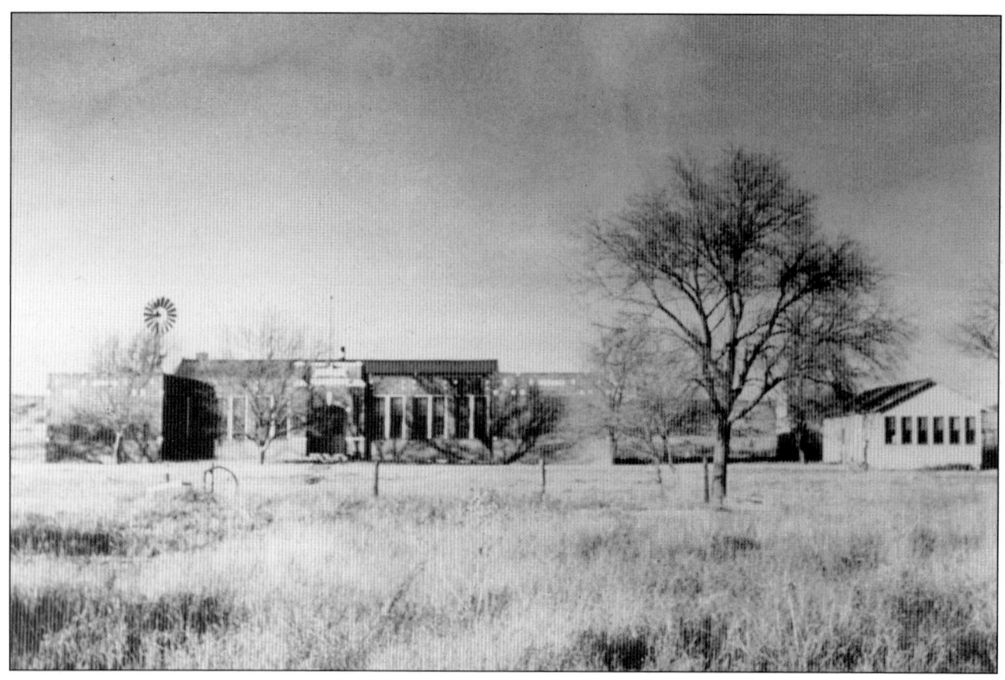

Plemons had a school as early as 1910. The building shown above was built in 1926, and this photograph was taken in 1949. The Plemons school district served a large rural area and educated the children of ranchers and oil workers. In 1987, Plemons, Stinnett, and Phillips consolidated and formed the Plemons-Stinnett-Phillips Consolidated Independent School District, which still exists today. Below is the Weatherly School building in Borger. This building was utilized as the south campus of Borger High School during the 1970s and was demolished in the early 2000s.

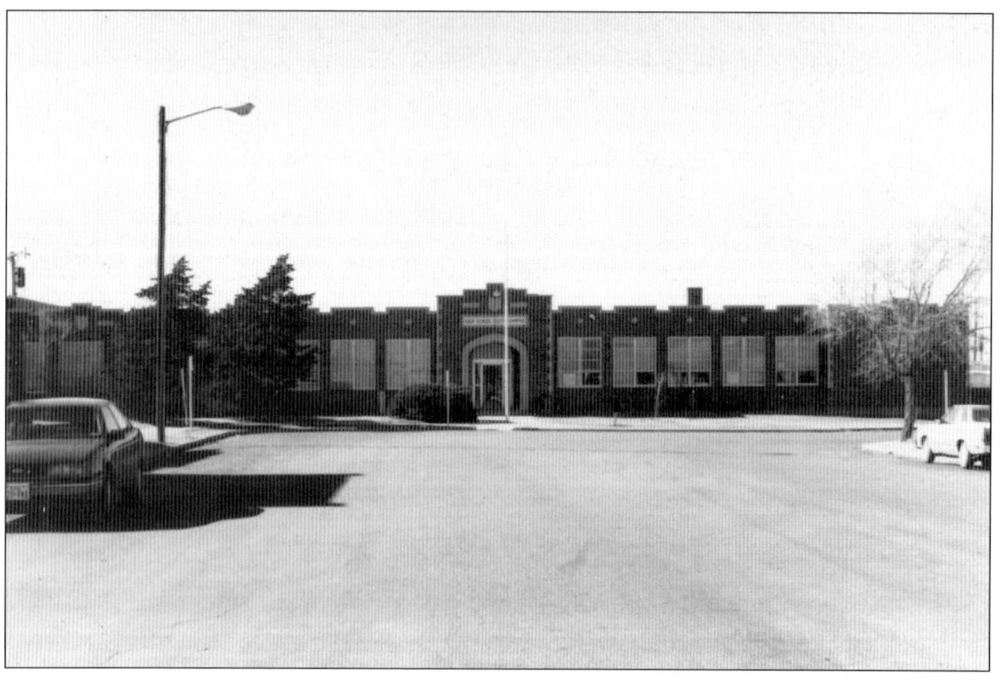

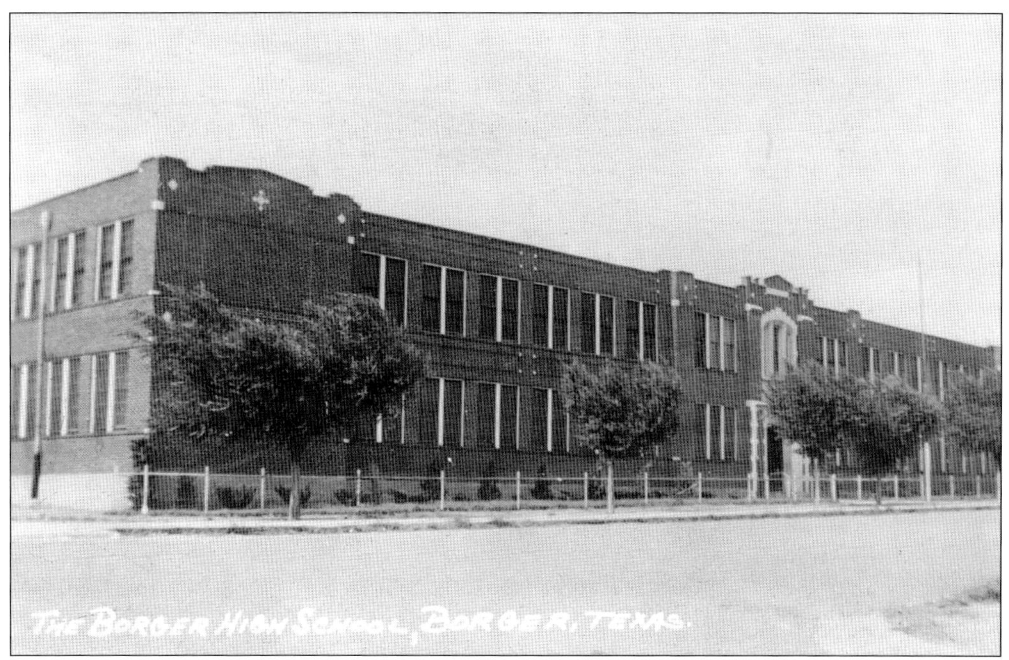

Borger Independent School District was established in 1926. In 1927, Borger High School (pictured above) was erected, as well as East Ward, West Ward, Weatherly, and a gymnasium. The citizens of Hutchinson County realized the vital importance of education. The below image shows the coronation of favorites at Borger High School in 1945.

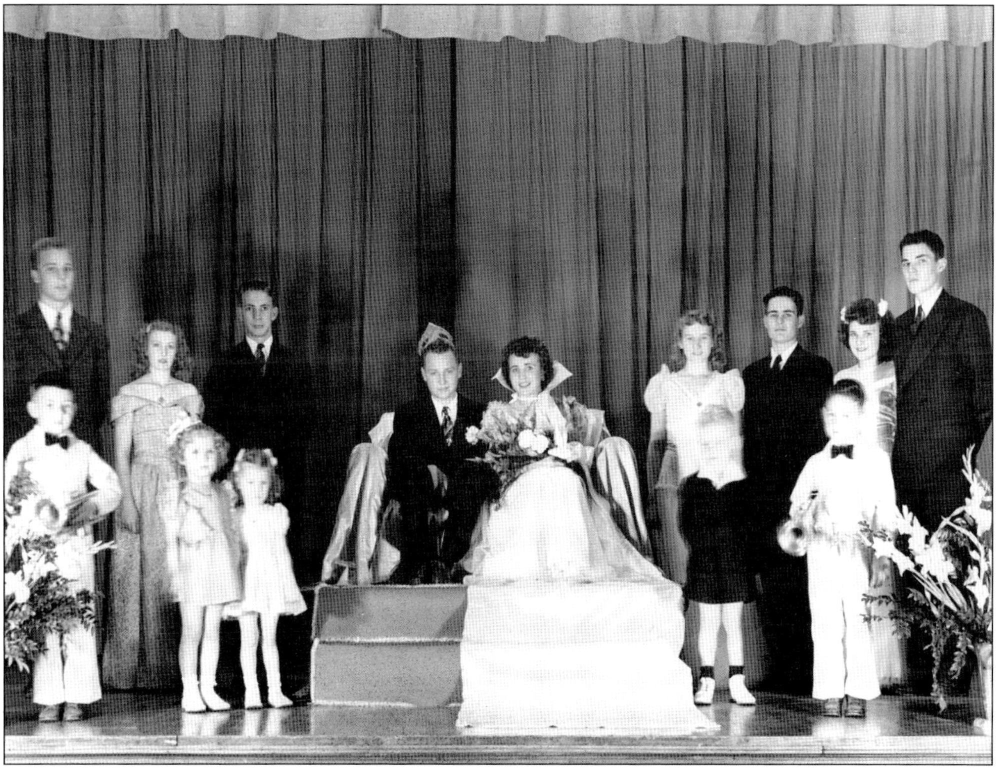

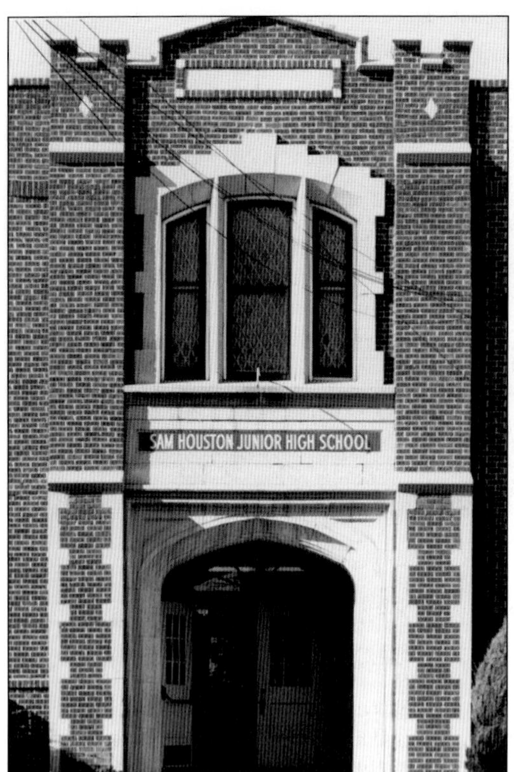

When a new Borger High School was constructed in 1948, the old building became home to Sam Houston Junior High School.

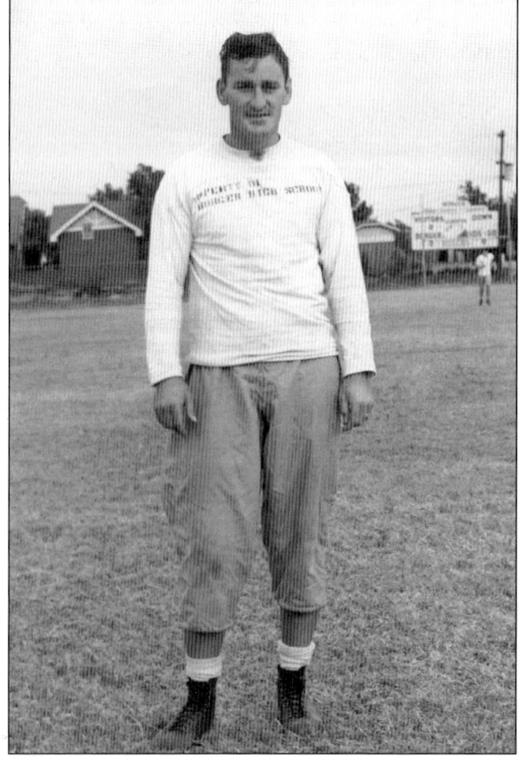

Esther Bryan "Tex" Hanna was a Borger native. He was a graduate of Eastern New Mexico University and served in the US Army. Hanna was a coach and administrator in the Borger Independent School District for 38 years. This photograph was taken at the original Borger football field. Ace Borger's house is visible in the background at left.

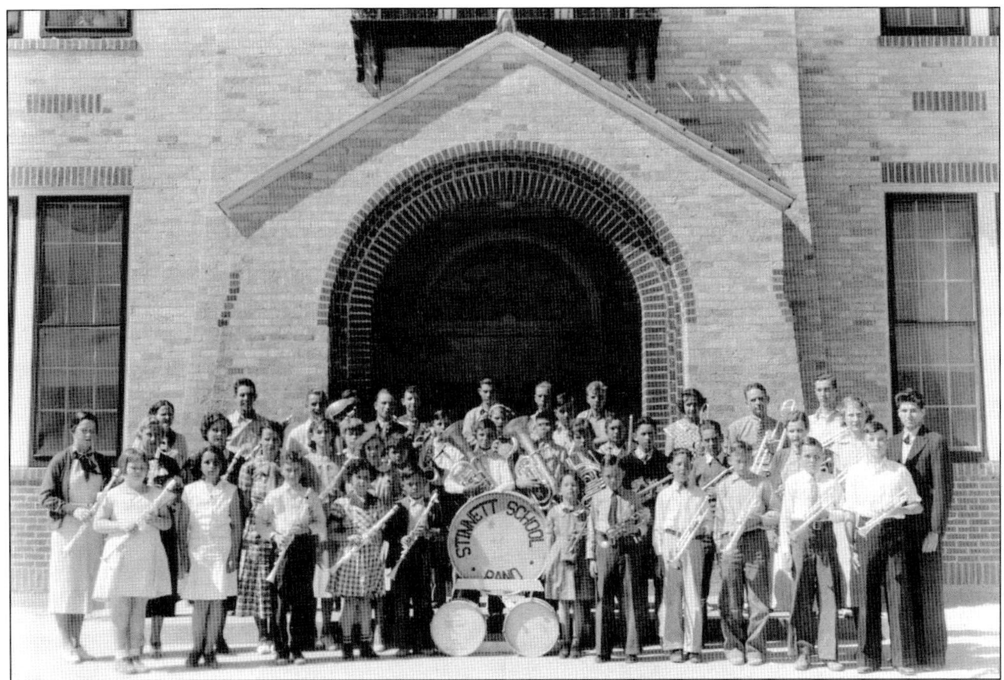

Above, the 1949 Stinnett High School band is pictured at Stinnett High School. Below, Phillips High School students walk in front of the school. After a devastating refinery explosion in 1980, the town of Phillips, built on land owned by Phillips Petroleum Company, was disbanded by the company. All residents had to move. Former Phillips students attended the Plemons-Stinnett-Phillips Consolidated Independent School District in nearby Stinnett. The Phillips High School building was sold to the company in 1989 and served as offices until it was demolished in late 2021.

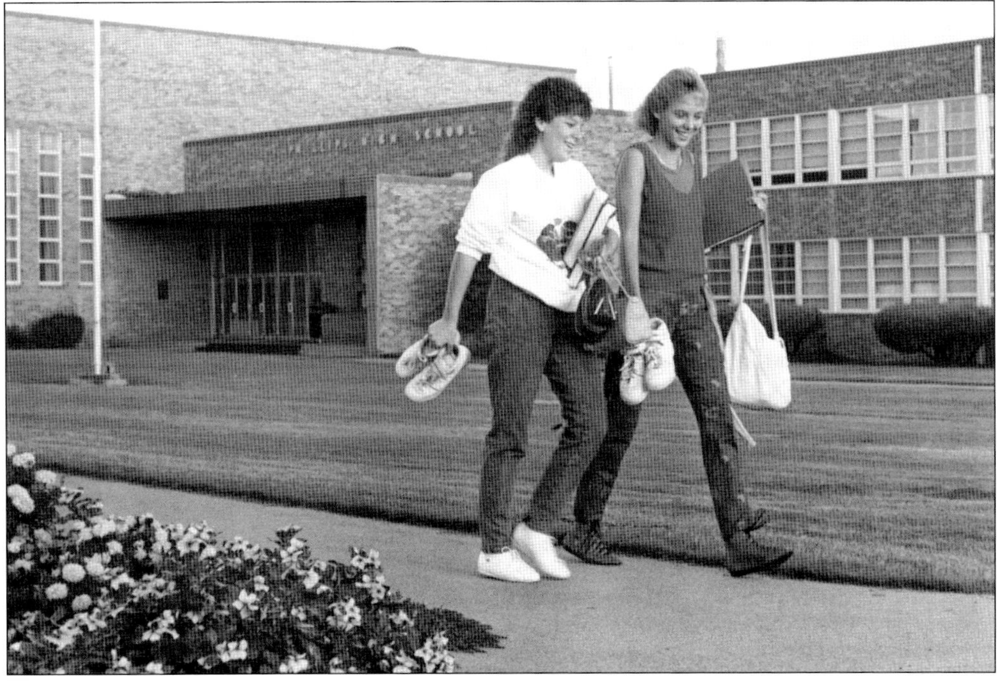

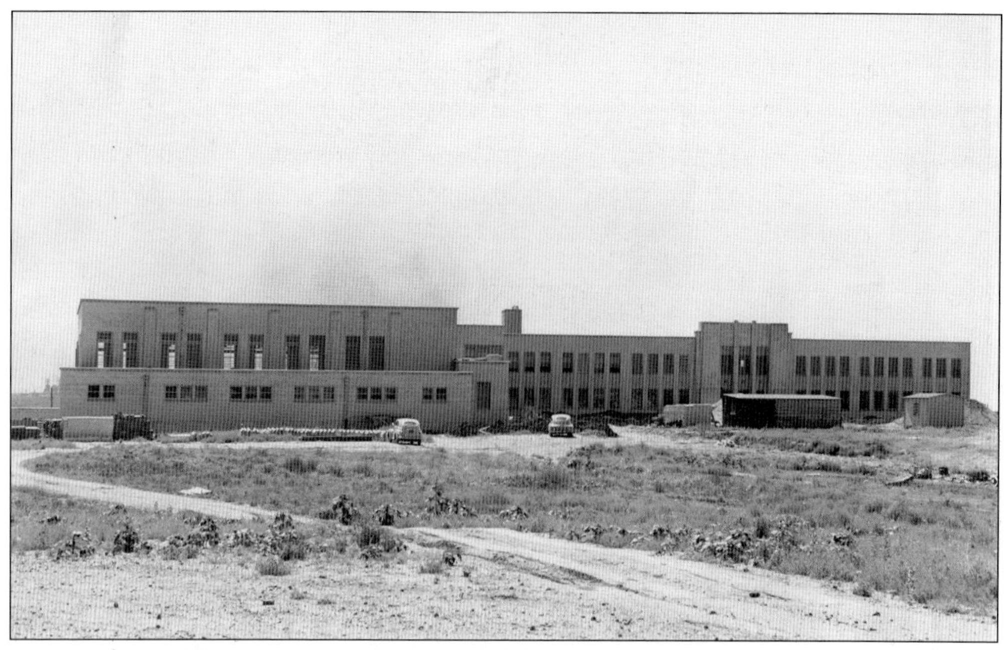

Frank Phillips College was built in 1948 and shared its campus with Borger High School until 1956, when the two districts separated and a new college campus was built. The building shown here is still the home of Borger High School. Note the cloud of carbon black rising behind the building from the plant west of the school. Below is Borger High School as it appears today. The building was renovated inside and out from 2019 through 2021. The 73-year-old structure has been greatly improved. (Below, photograph by Clay Renick.)

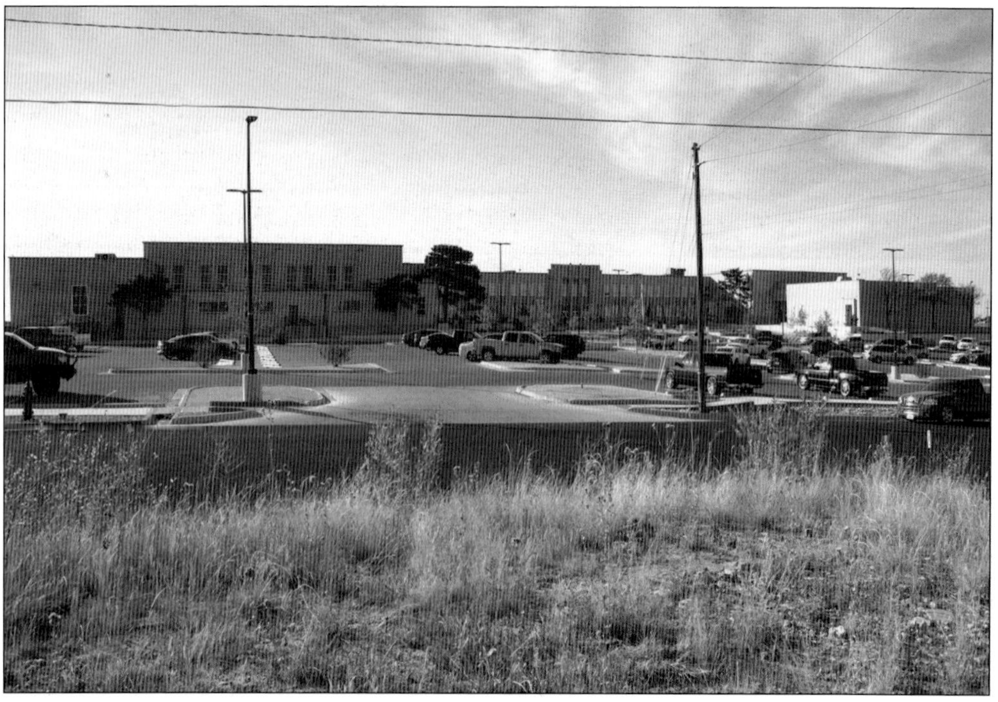

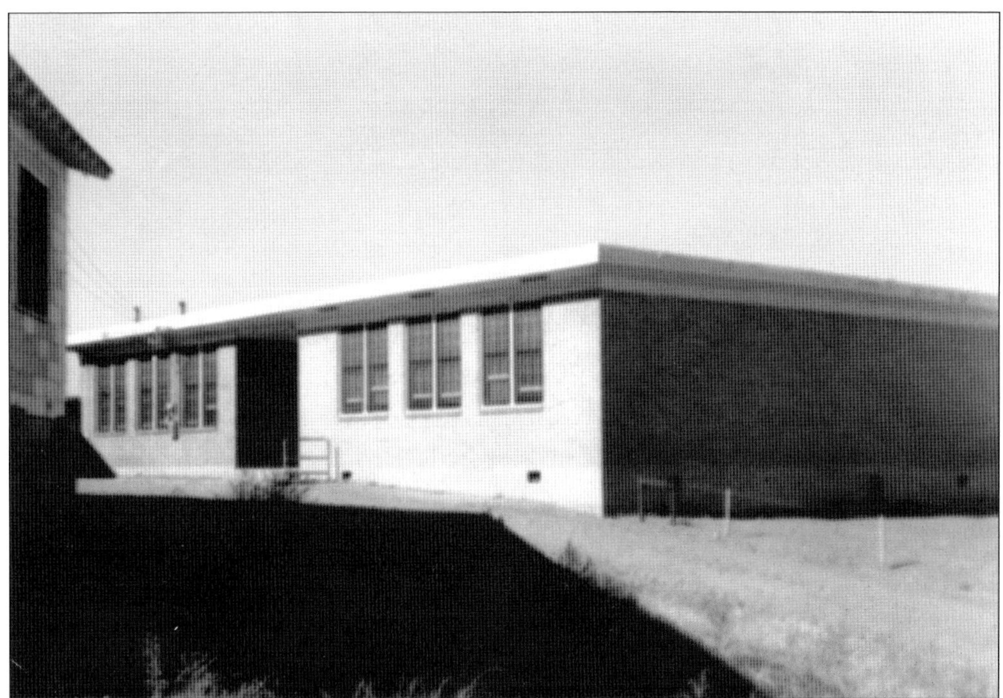

In July 1965, Booker T. Washington School, which served Black students, was closed, and the school's students were transferred to James Bowie Elementary. The Borger Independent School District was among the first in Texas to be fully integrated in the fall of 1965. The Booker T. Washington School building was later demolished; this is one of the few remaining images of it.

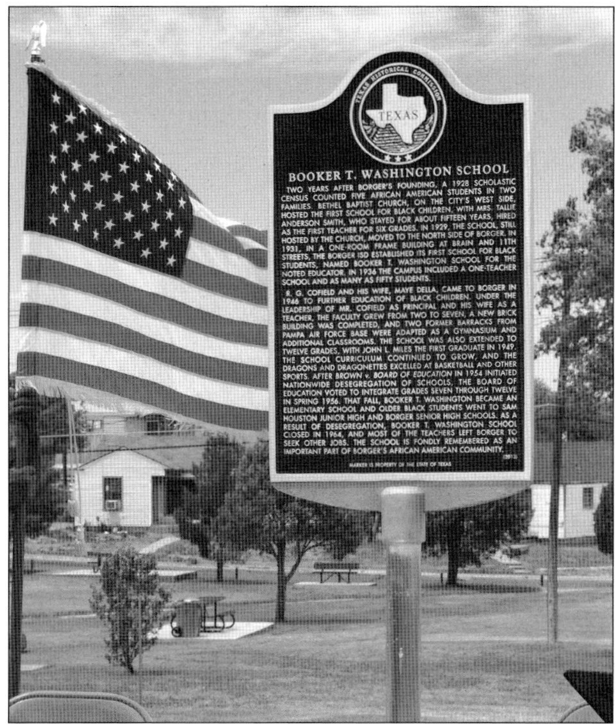

A Texas historical marker was dedicated on June 14, 2013, near the site once occupied by Booker T. Washington School. The marker is also adjacent to the Cofield Community Center, named for R.G. Cofield; he and his wife, Maye Della, came to Borger in 1946 to improve Black education in Hutchinson County. R.G. came from Childress, Texas, with 14 years of experience in education. He both taught and served as principal of the school. The Cofields were instrumental in the improvement of educational opportunities for Black students in Borger.

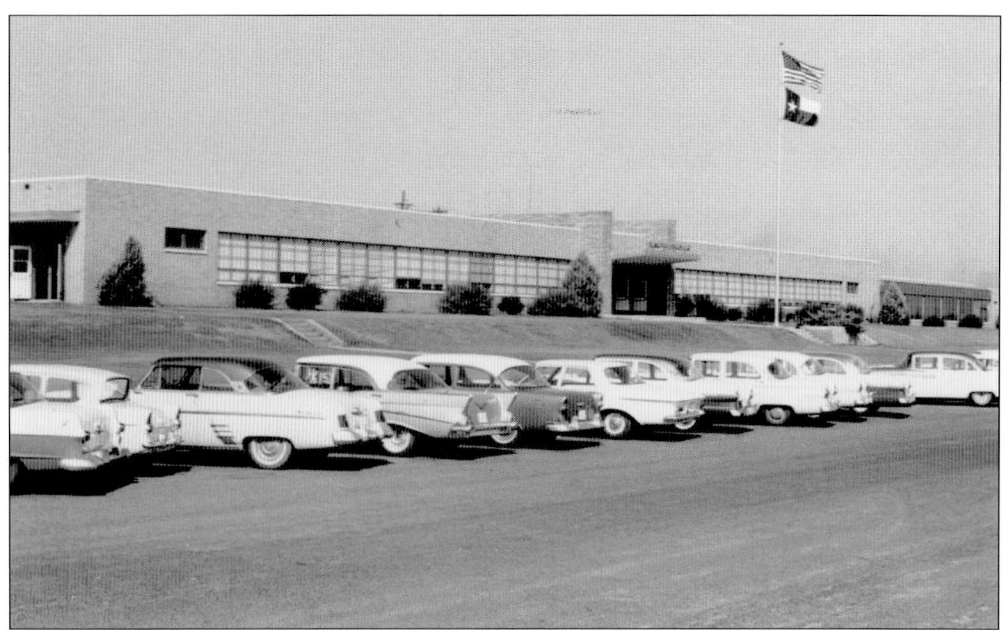

Named for Frank Phillips, the founder of Phillips Petroleum Company, Frank Phillips College was established as Borger Junior College in 1948. In 2021, the community college served 1,484 students, 37 percent of whom attend full-time. The college's student-teacher ratio of 24 to 1 is lower than the state community college student-teacher average of 37 to 1. Minority enrollment is 45 percent of the student body, which is majority Hispanic. The administration building and library of Frank Phillips College are seen below.

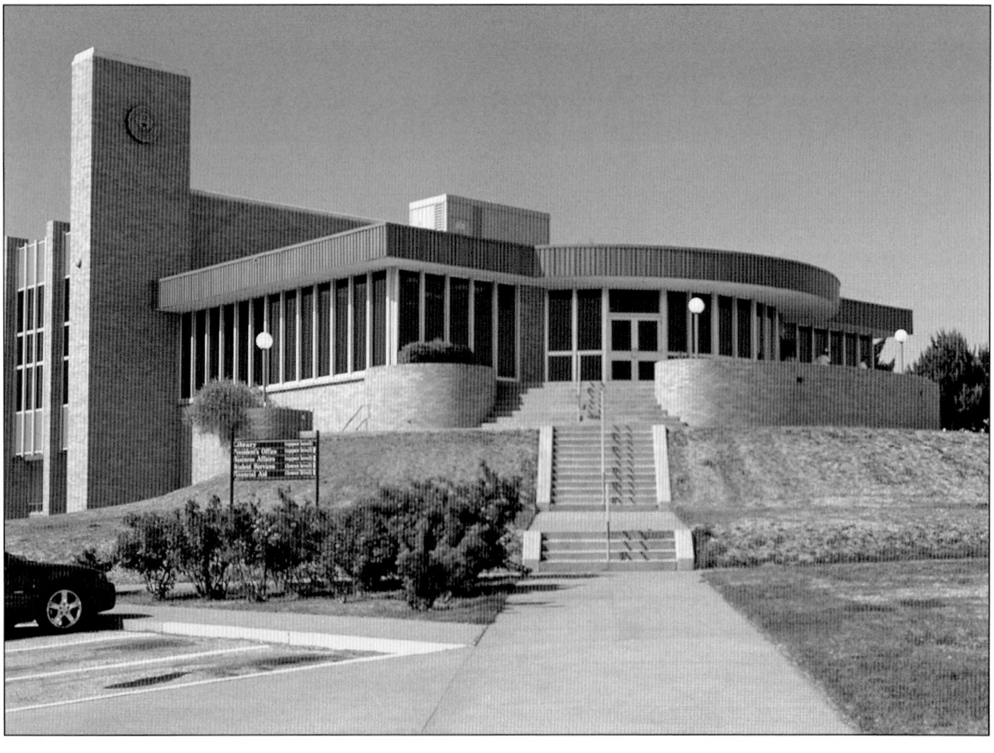

Nine

The Weather, Wildlife, and Terrain

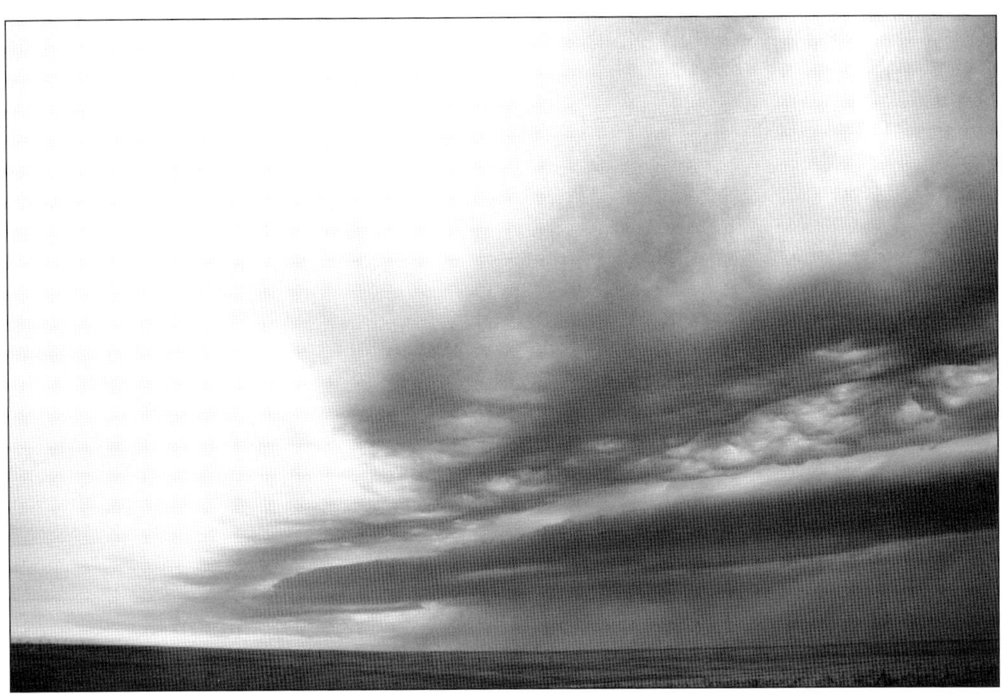

Nature can be violent in Hutchinson County. The weather of the Panhandle Plains includes high winds, thunderstorms, and hail. Tornadoes are common in the spring and summer, and high winds can be expected year-round. Temperatures can range from 20 degrees below zero in winter to as high as 115 degrees in summer. As Texas Panhandle residents are fond of saying, "If you don't like the weather, wait a few minutes, and it will change." (Photograph by Deborah Summers.)

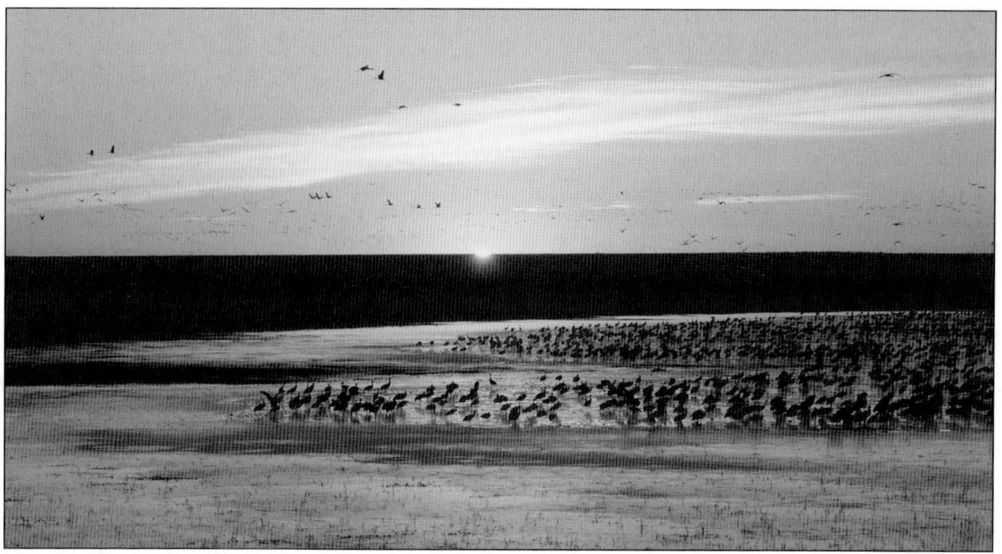

Hutchinson County lies within the North American migratory bird central flyway. Millions of birds migrate north and south along this route each year, stopping for food, water, and rest in the hundreds of water-filled playas on the plains. These cranes are frozen into the ice of the playas at night; at sunrise, the ice can be heard cracking as it falls away from their feet when they take flight. When the sun comes up, the skies are filled with birds in all directions as they rise, reorganize, and resume their journeys. This annual spectacle is a sight to behold. (Photograph by Clay Renick.)

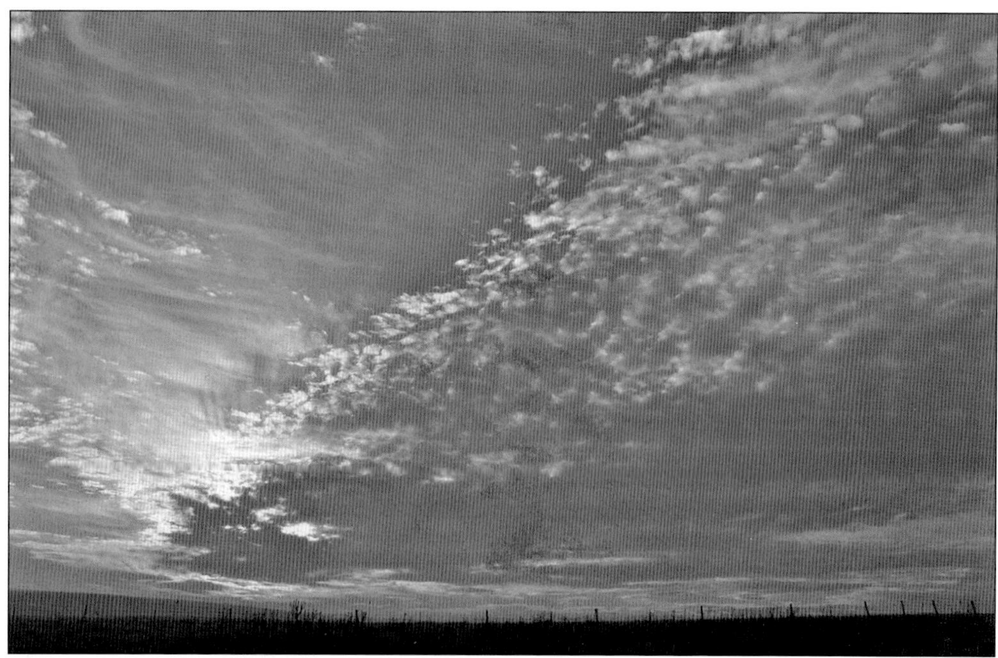

Locals and visitors are treated to spectacular sunrises and sunsets throughout the year. The long views afforded by the treeless plains yield extraordinary displays of light and color each day. (Photograph by Clay Renick.)

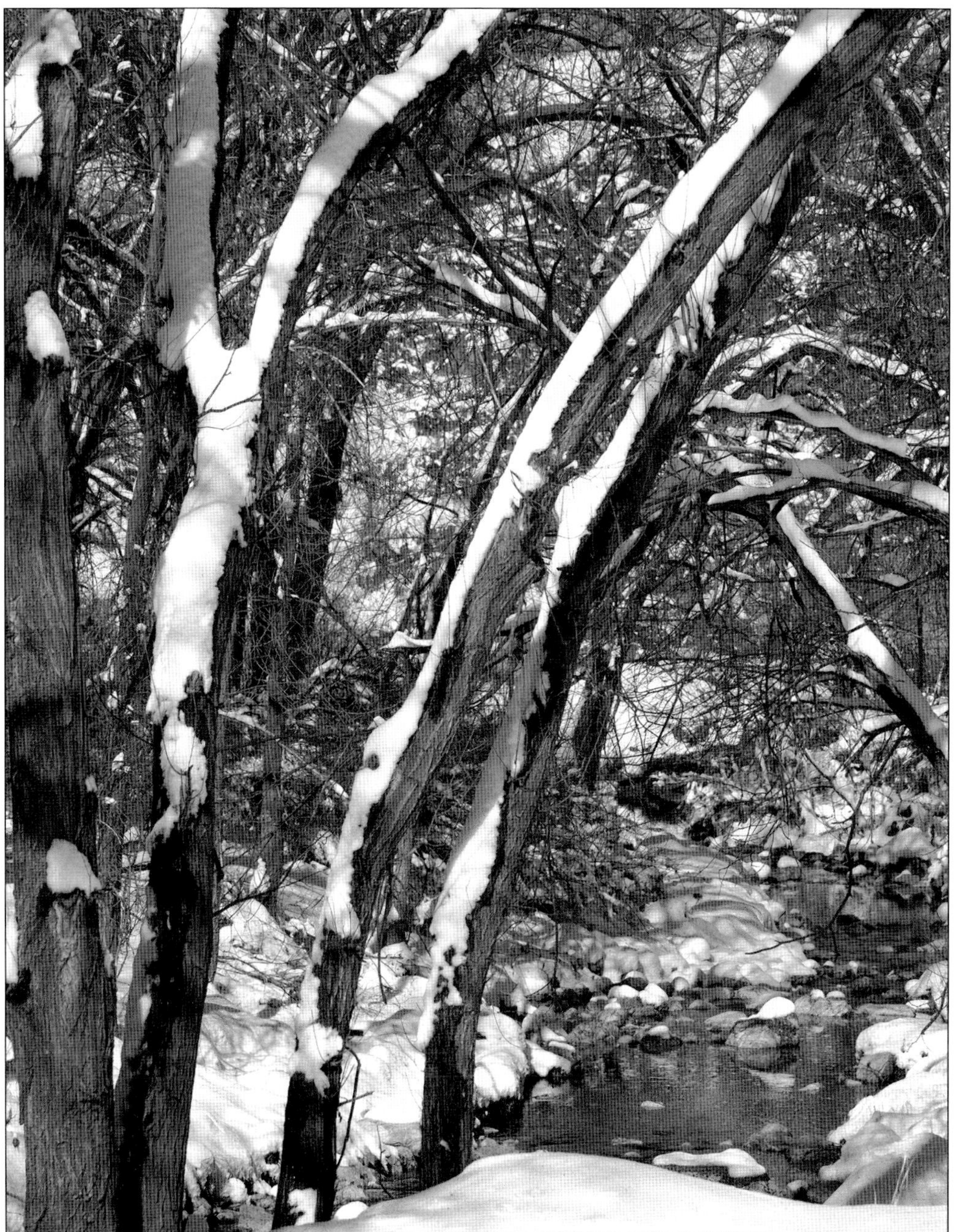

Snow is common during winter in the Texas Panhandle, as are rapid drops in temperature. Snowfall can be soft and beautiful, but can turn violent and deadly. Early ranchers, who were new to the plains in the late 1800s, experienced this phenomenon when temperature drops of up to 60 degrees could occur in a matter of hours. "Blue Norther" blizzards have killed entire herds of cattle when the temperature drops below zero, and winds as high as 75 miles per hour have been recorded. Snowfall can be as much as 12 to 20 inches overnight, and wind chills can reach 30 to 40 degrees below zero during these storms. (Photograph by Clay Renick.)

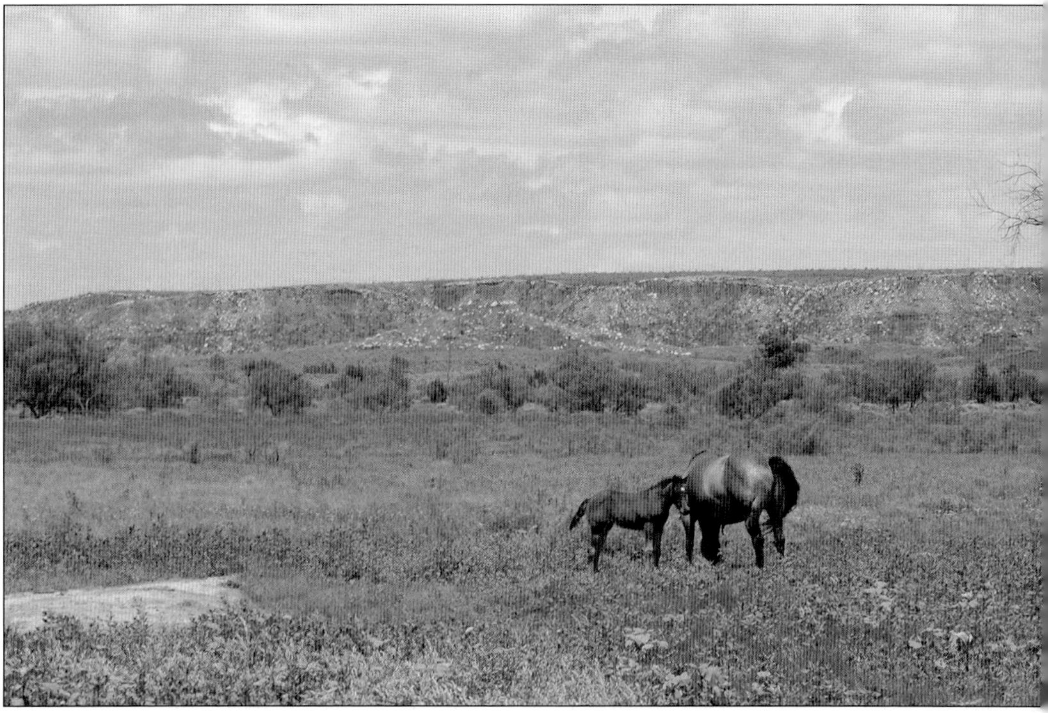

The Canadian River valley is home to pastures for domesticated animals and offers quality habitats for most native species, such as white-tailed deer. Before the Sanford Dam and Lake Meredith were created in the 1960s, the river often flooded violently, which reduced the amount of land

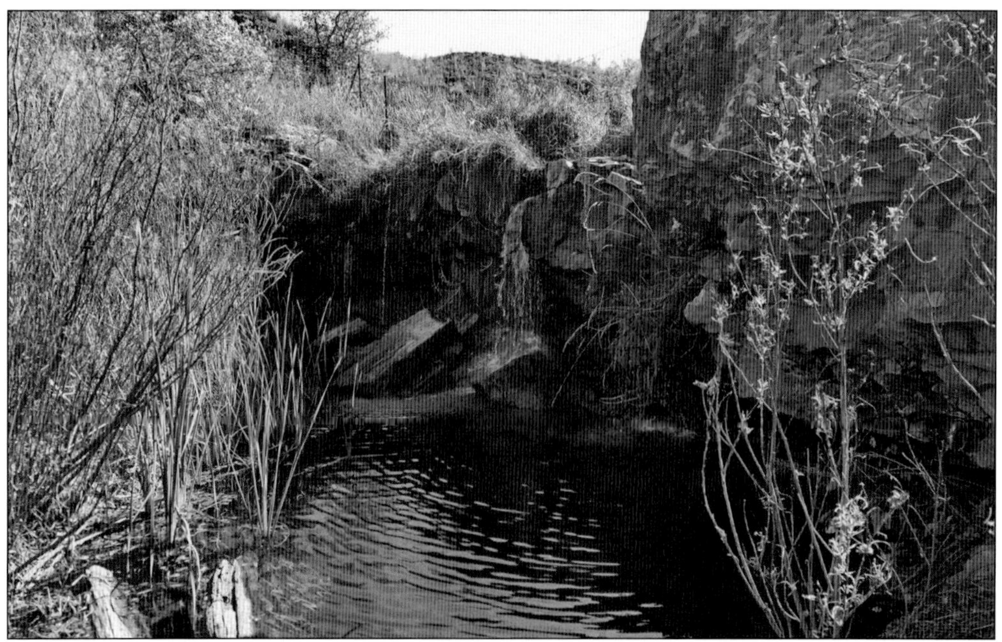

Springs and pools like this are found in the canyons of the Canadian River drainage area. Native Americans and early pioneers knew that in most places where cottonwood trees grow, water can be found near their bases.

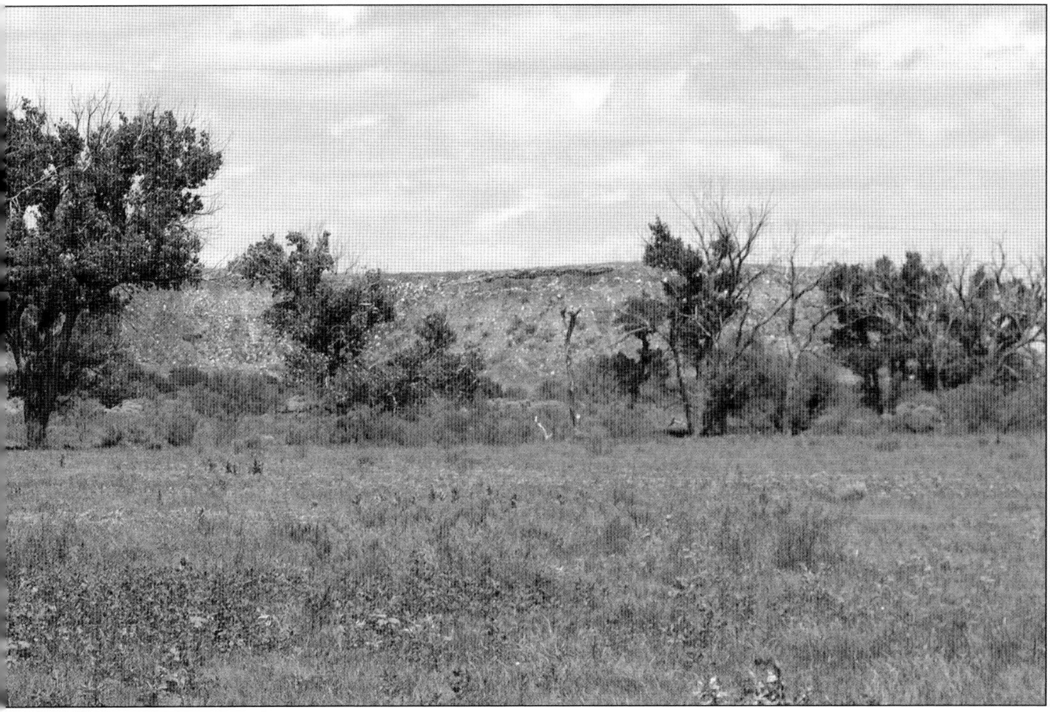

available for domestic agriculture. After the dam was built and flooding could be controlled, greater areas of land became available, and scenes such as this became more common. (Photograph by Clay Renick.)

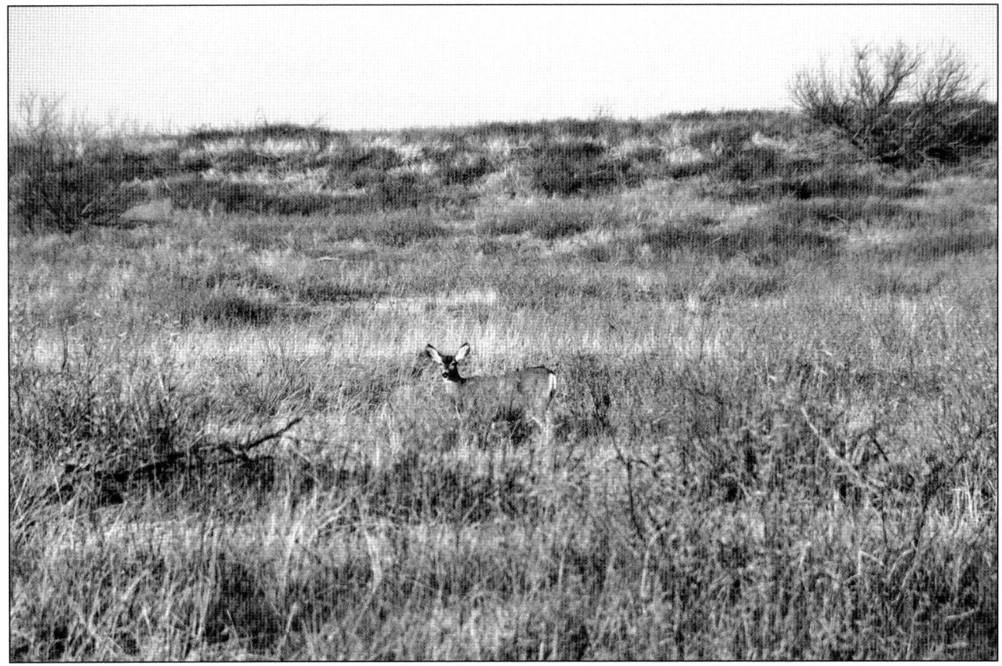

White-tailed deer can be found throughout the county. The oases in the Canadian River valley are safe havens for wildlife, and many are well-known by outdoorsmen.

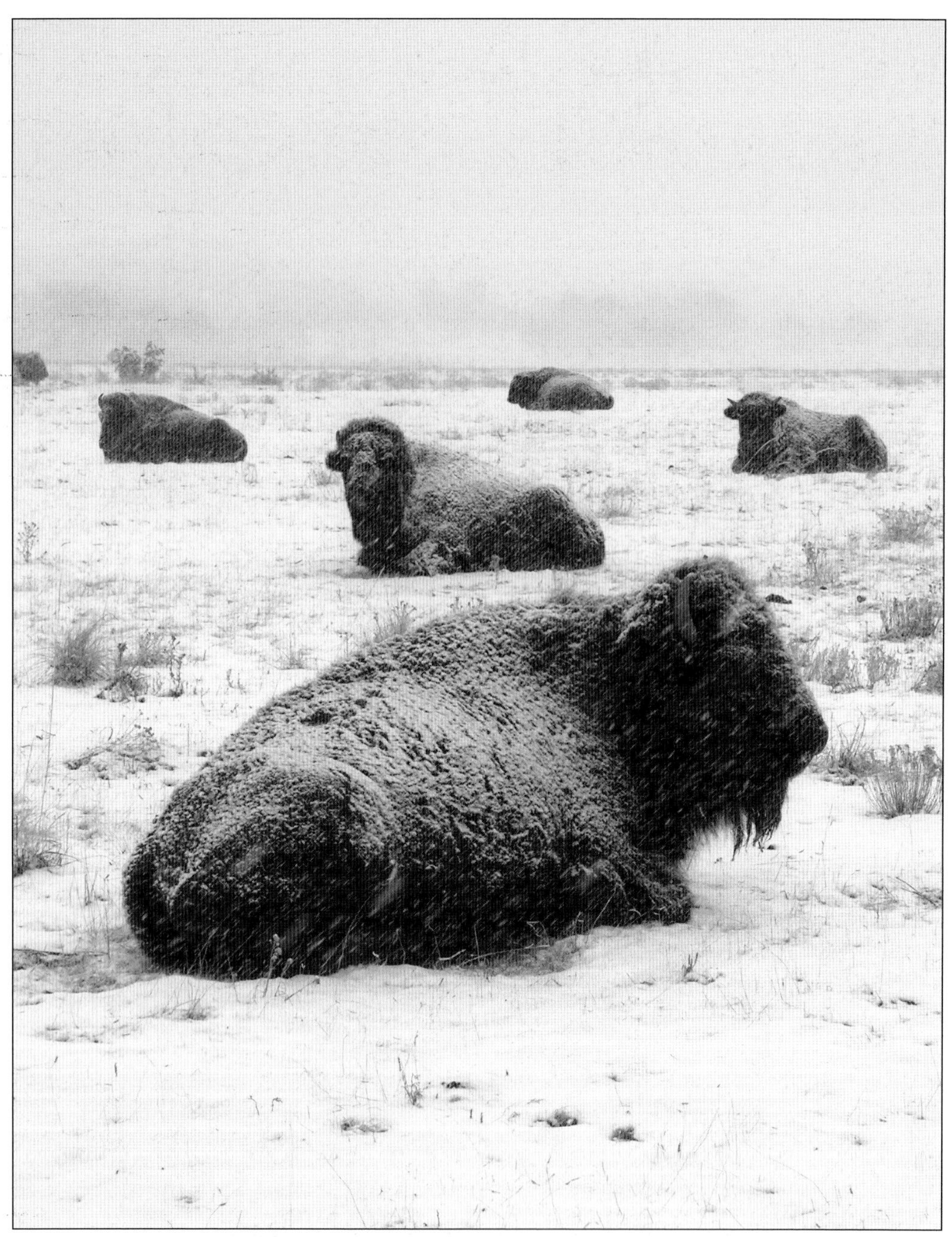

From prehistoric times until the late 1800s, untold millions of bison roamed North America from coast to coast. Due to the rush of new arrivals in the West and market demands for leather and hides in England, the bison were hunted until only a few hundred remained. The US Department of the Interior, several states, and a few companies and individuals saved them from extinction. Bison migrated through the Texas Panhandle for centuries, and their bones are still found in the area. A small herd still roams the range on a private ranch in northwestern Hutchinson County. (Photograph by Clay Renick.)

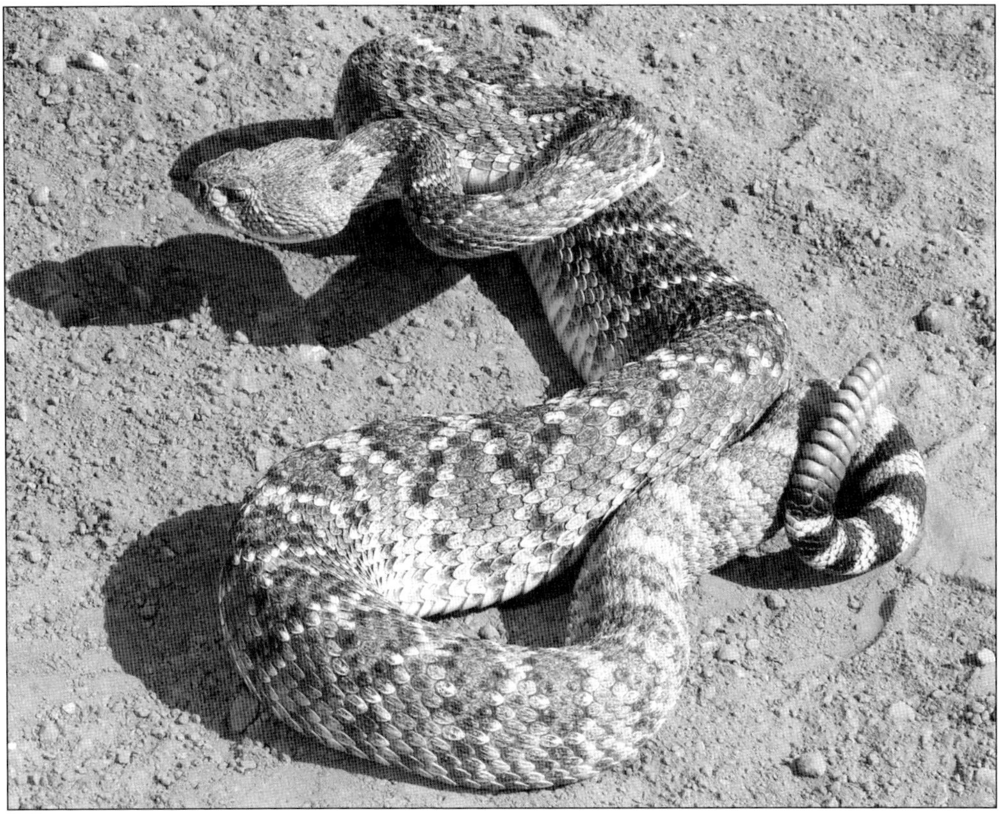

These well-known species of the Texas Panhandle, the diamondback rattlesnake (above) and the horned lizard (below), are still common in Hutchinson County. (Both photographs by Wanda Guinn)

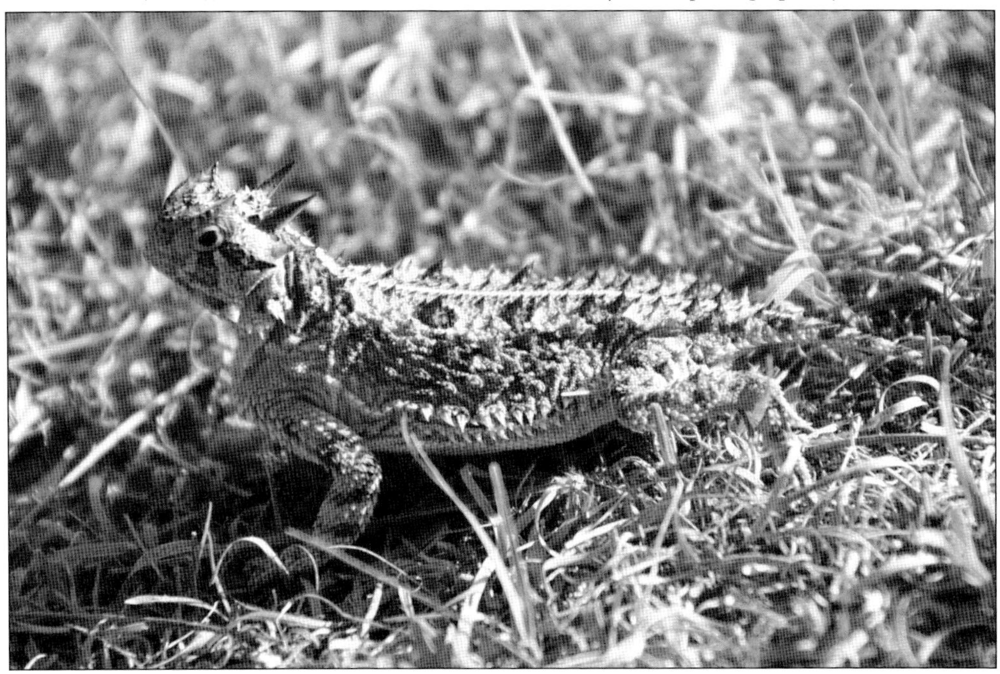

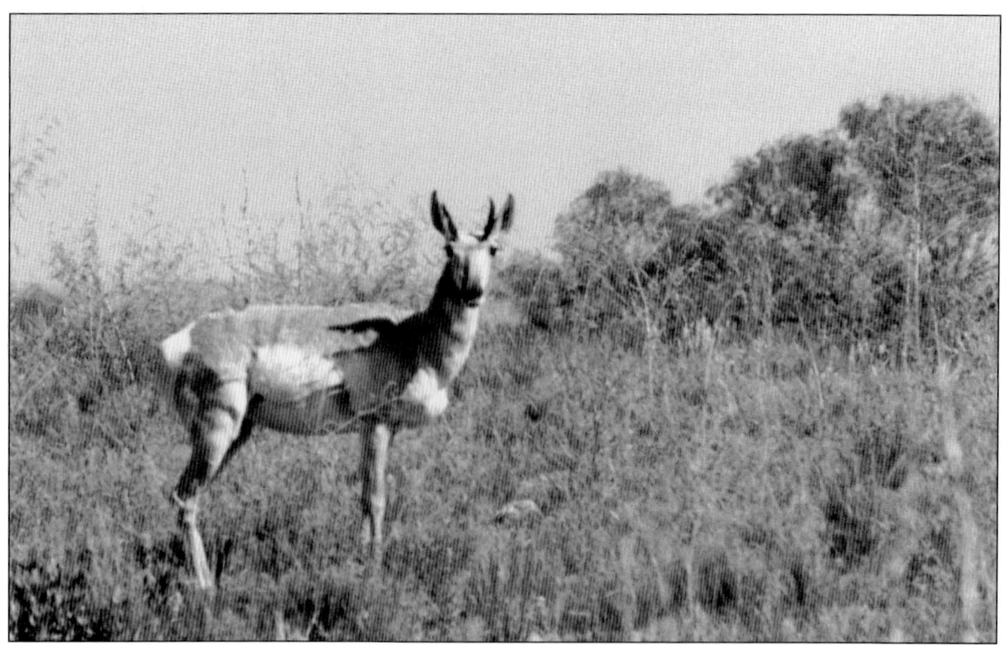

Herds of antelope, white-tailed deer, and mule deer are common in Hutchinson County. Hunting is a way of life for many who live here. Bobcats are solitary animals and are not often seen, as they do most of their hunting at night. Their range varies with food availability and may cover as much as 50 miles or as little as five. (Below, photograph by Deborah Summers)

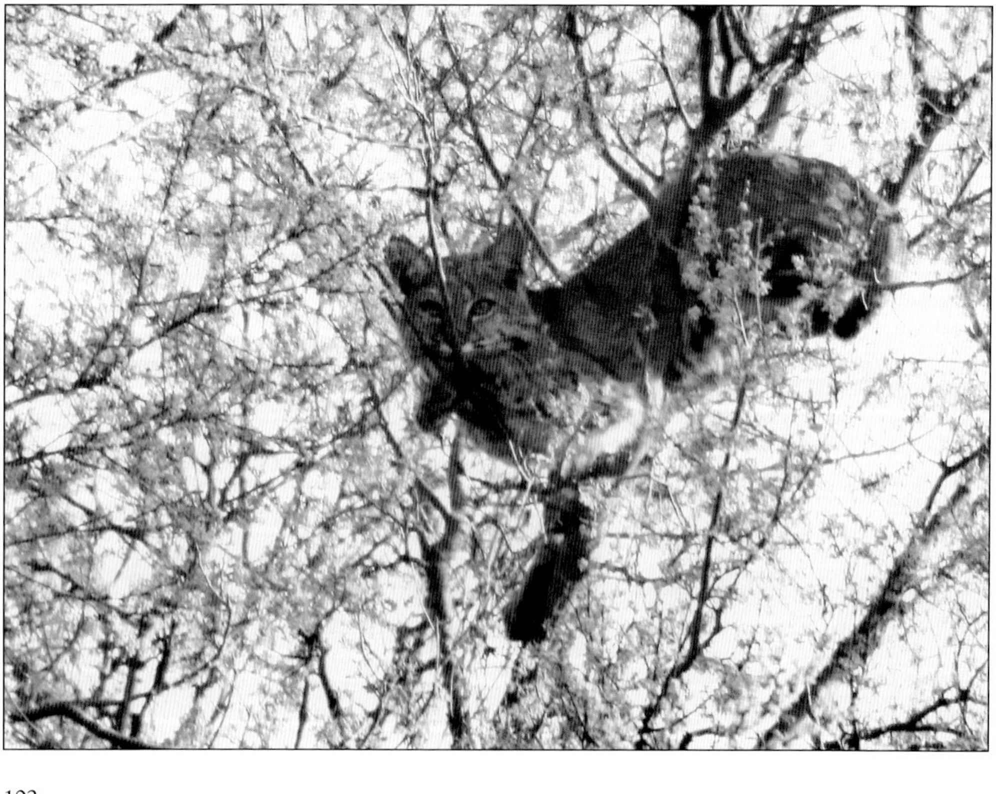

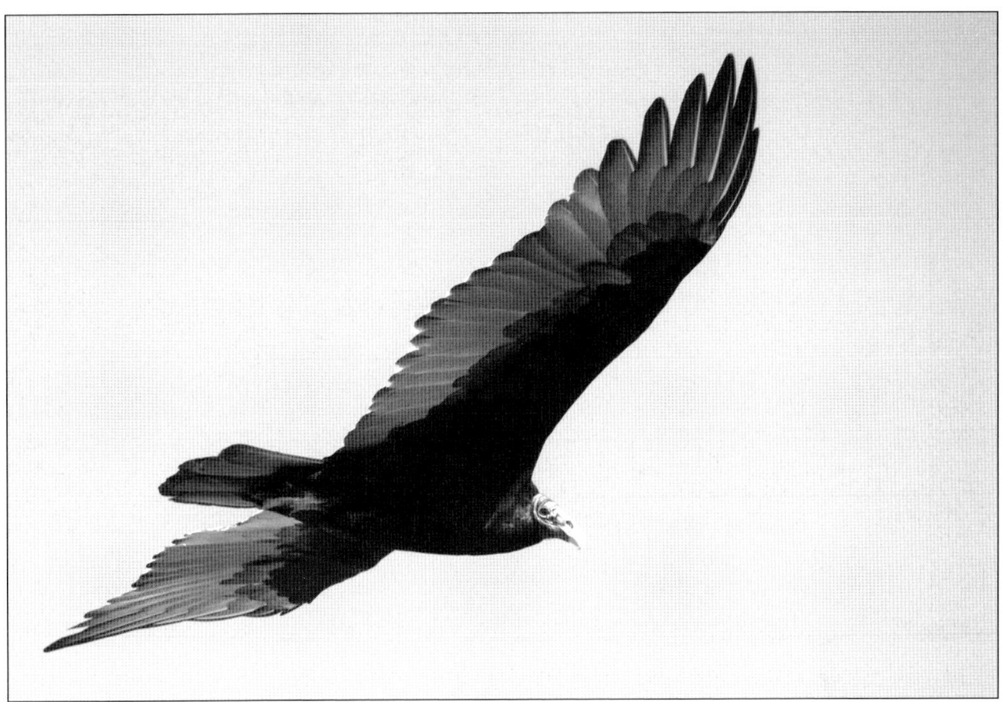

One of the largest birds of North America, turkey vultures are native to the Texas Panhandle and play an important role in the local ecosystem by disposing of carrion that might otherwise become a breeding ground for disease. (Photograph by Clay Renick.)

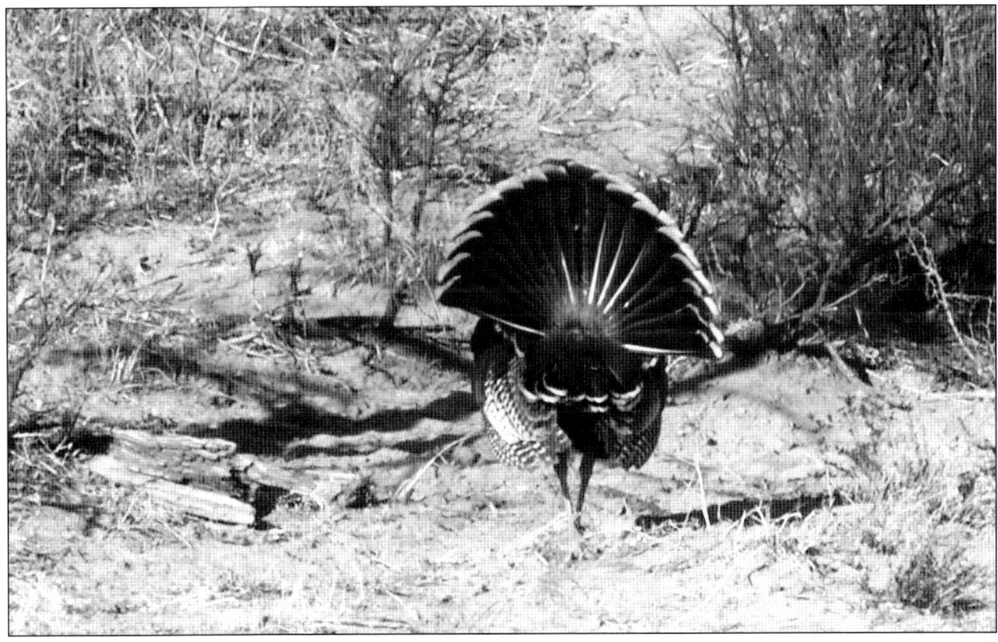

This wild turkey is displaying mating behavior. The Canadian River valley is a perfect natural habitat, but wild turkeys will go anywhere adequate water and food is available. They roost in large trees at night—particularly cottonwoods, which are abundant in the valley. (Photograph by Clay Renick.)

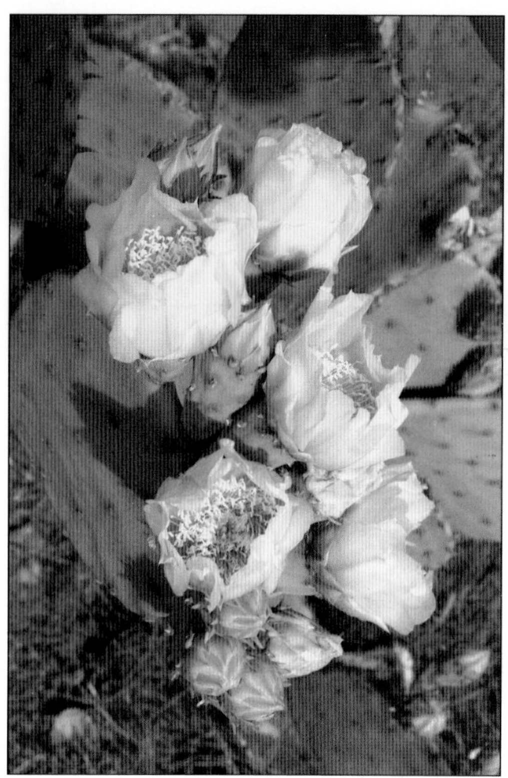

The prickly pear cactus has sharp spikes on its pads, but once they are dethorned, the pads can be cooked and eaten. The plants have yellow, purple, or red flowers. The prickly pear is the state plant of Texas. (Photograph by Clay Renick.)

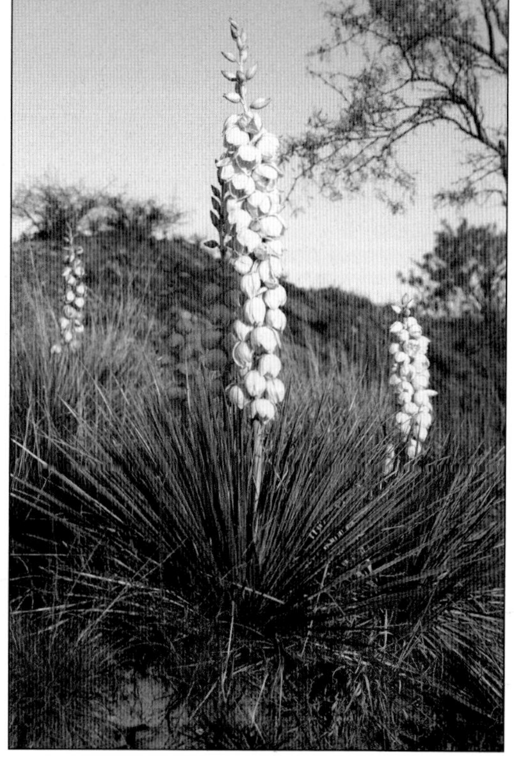

This is one of the most common plants in North Texas—yucca, which has 49 species and 24 subspecies and is notable for rosettes of tough, green, sword-shaped leaves and large white flowers. These plants are native to the hot and dry parts of North and South America and the Caribbean. (Photograph by Tanya Brewster.)

Ten

Hutchinson County Past and Present

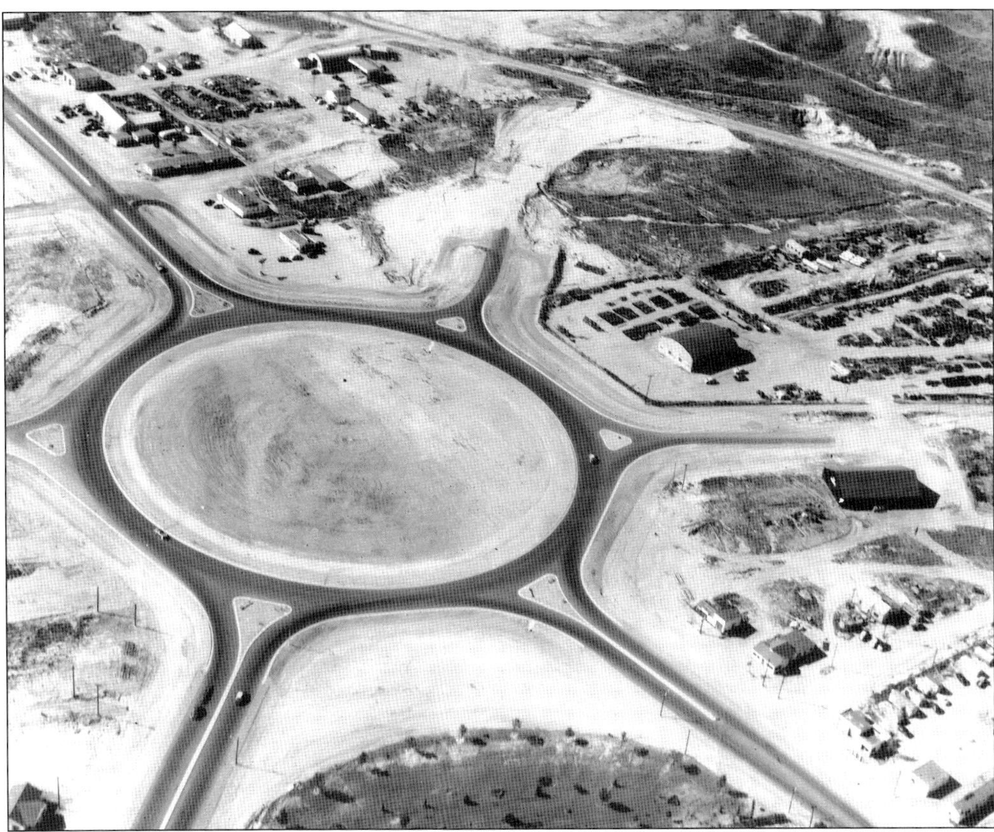

Before construction began on the Interstate Highway System in 1952, this roundabout (better known as the traffic circle) was built on the north side of Borger. It allows many highways and roads to merge and be redirected without stopping traffic. Although it was an unusual design in Texas at the time, it greatly improved safety and efficiency and is still in use today.

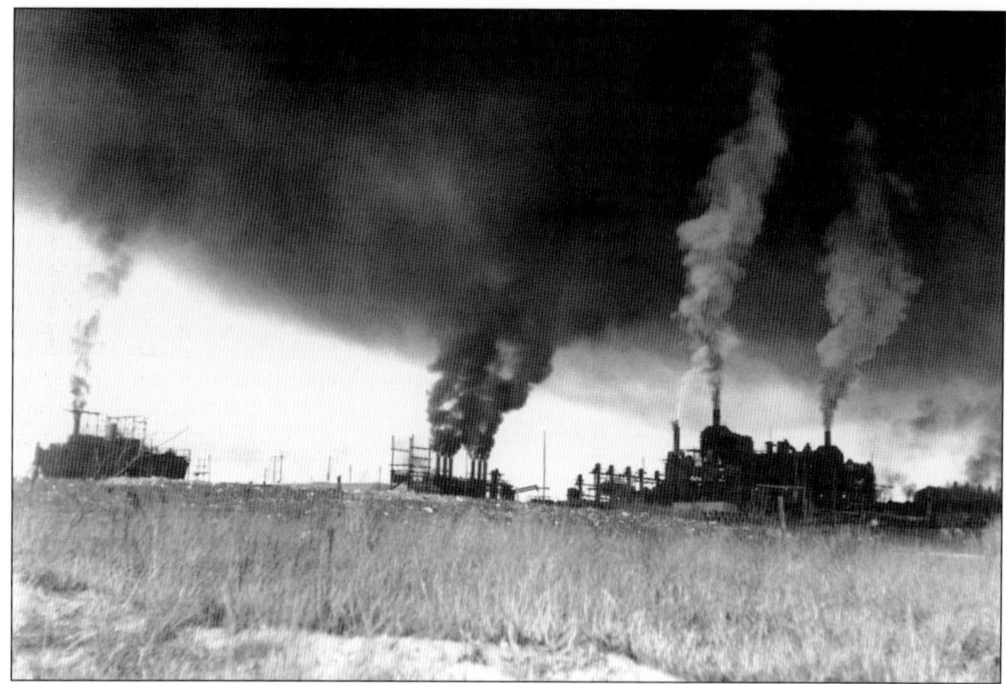

As many as 20 carbon black plants were built after the discovery of oil and gas in the Hutchinson County area. Carbon black is a vital component in making tires, hoses, conveyor belts, plastics, printing inks, and automotive coatings stronger, deeper in color, and longer-lasting. In its pure form, carbon black is a fine black powder composed of elemental carbon produced by partial burning of natural gas at high temperatures under controlled conditions. The carbon black plant currently operating west of Borger occupies the same location as many others before it. Great effort has been expended to make the plant less harmful than it has been in the past. In the present-day image below, only steam is seen escaping from the plant's stacks. (Below, photograph by Clay Renick.)

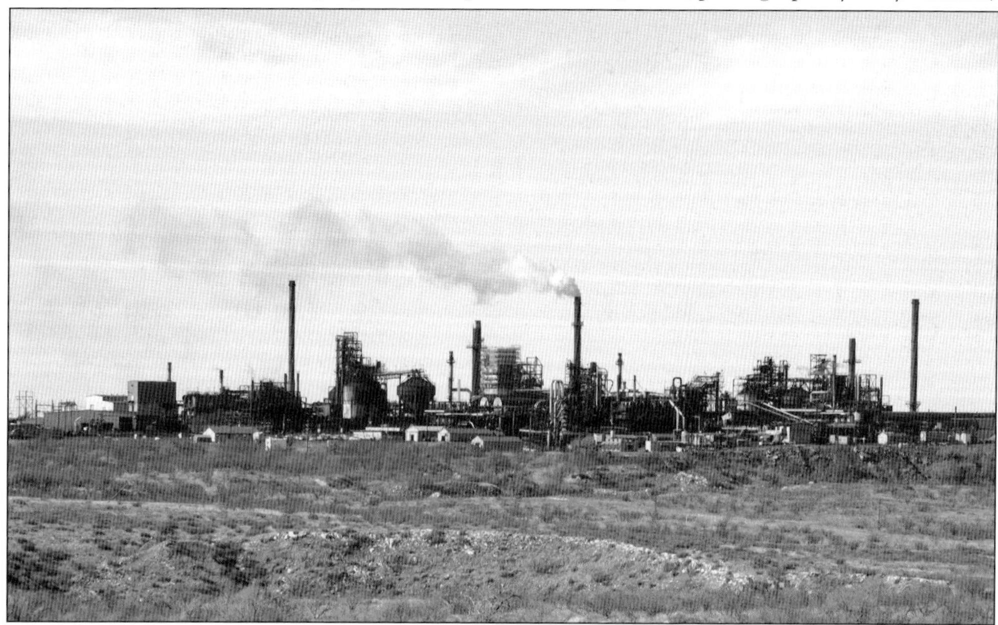

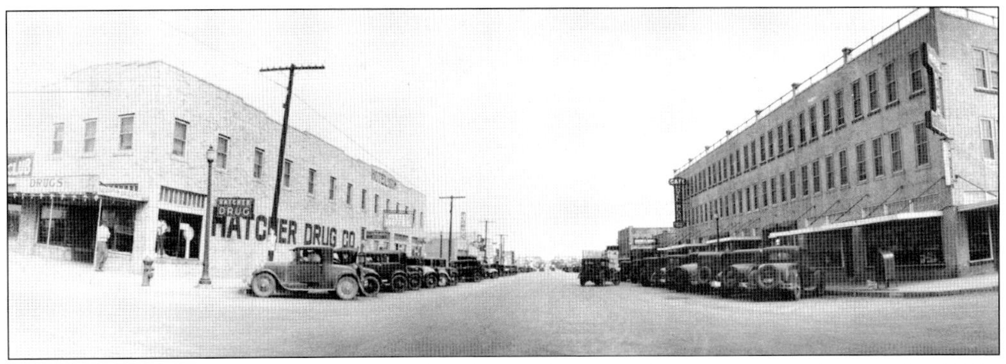

Hatcher Drug and Hotel Black at Grand and Main Streets in Borger are seen here in the 1920s. Hotel Black was an elegant place to stay and featured an unusual feature for its time—a private bathroom in every room. Just two blocks from the railroad station, it was the best place to stay while in Borger.

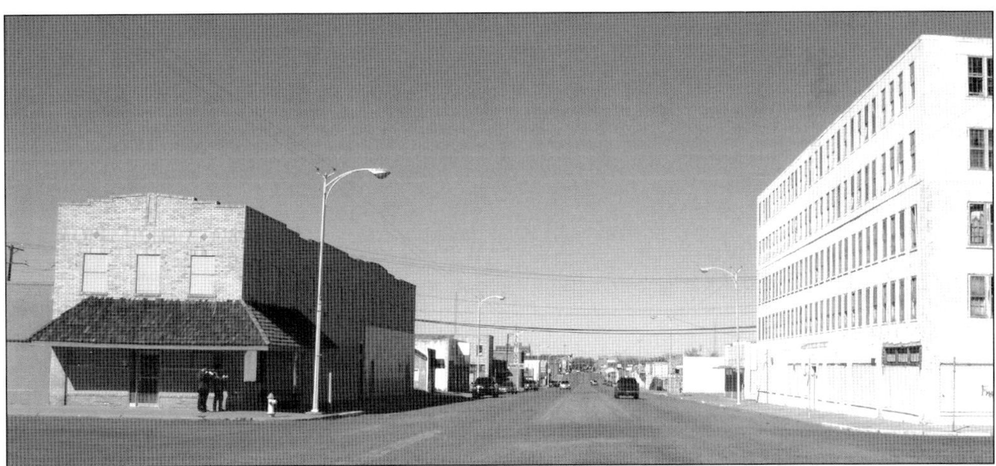

The old Barney's Pharmacy building (left) and the long-abandoned Phillips Petroleum Company building at Grand and Main Streets are pictured here in 2016. Phillips purchased Hotel Black in the 1950s and added two floors to house the administration offices for the refinery three miles away. Phillips moved to another facility in the 1980s, and the building sat vacant for many years until it was demolished to make way for a new industrial building. (Photograph by Clay Renick.)

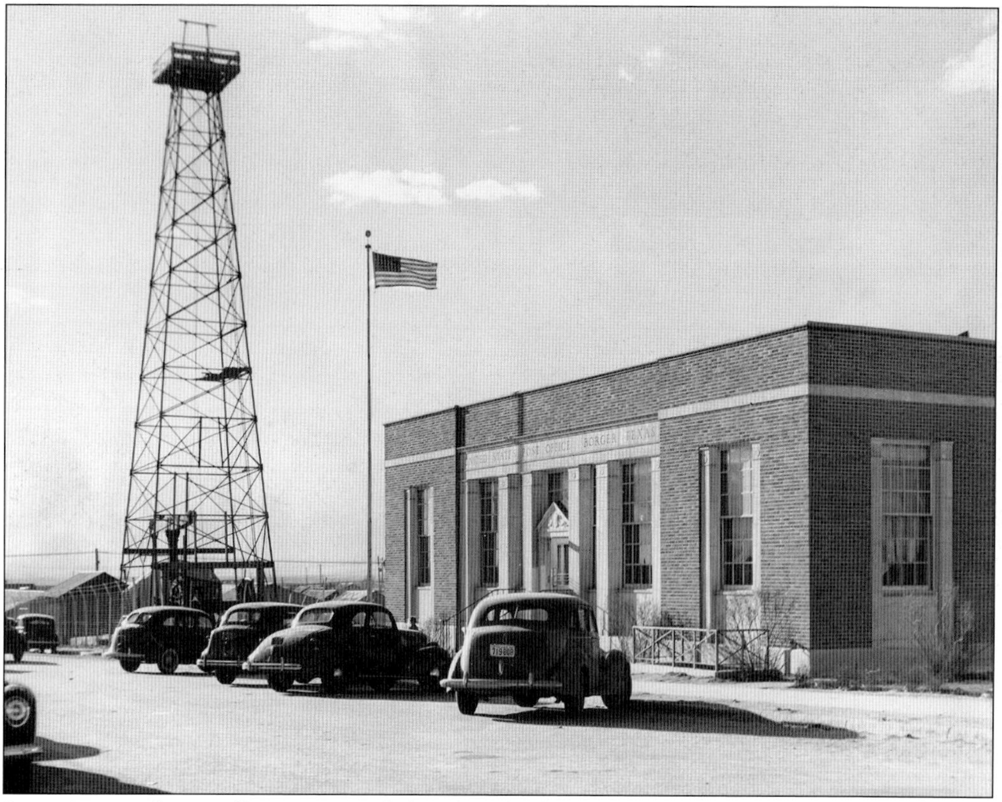

Borger's second post office is pictured above in the late 1930s with an oil well across the street, which was right in the middle of town. The well continued producing oil until it was plugged and removed in the 1960s to make room for a new bank. The below photograph was taken from approximately the same point in 2021. The building is now a greenhouse and gift shop, though it retains much of the charm from its earlier days. (Below, photograph by Clay Renick.)

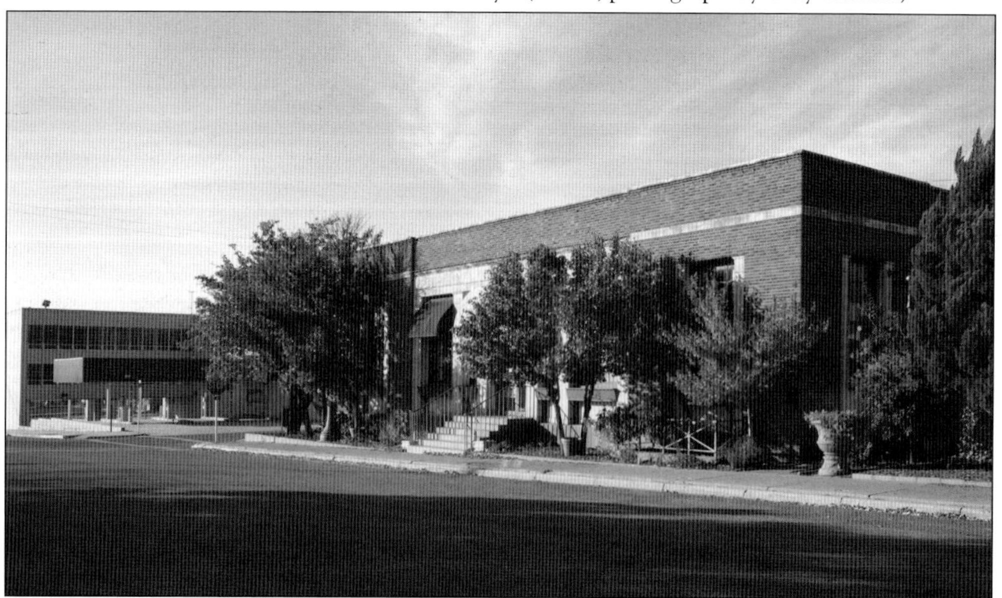

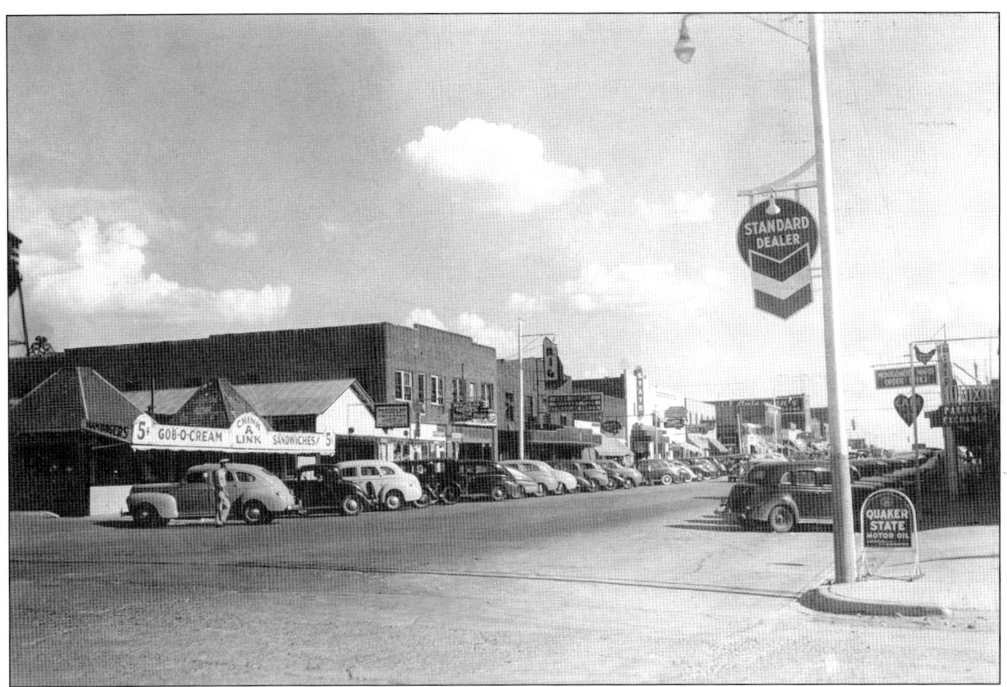

Borger's Main Street is pictured above in the 1930s. The two-story brick structure in the center was built by Gus and John Yiantsou, brothers from Greece, in 1927. The Yiantsous built it to house a hardware store on the first floor and a hotel on the second floor. Below is a view from the same vantage point in 2021. The building was donated to the Hutchinson County Historical Museum in 1976 by Dr. Chris Yiantsou, great-nephew of the original owners. It has been the home of the Hutchinson County Historical Museum since 1977. (Below, photograph by Clay Renick.)

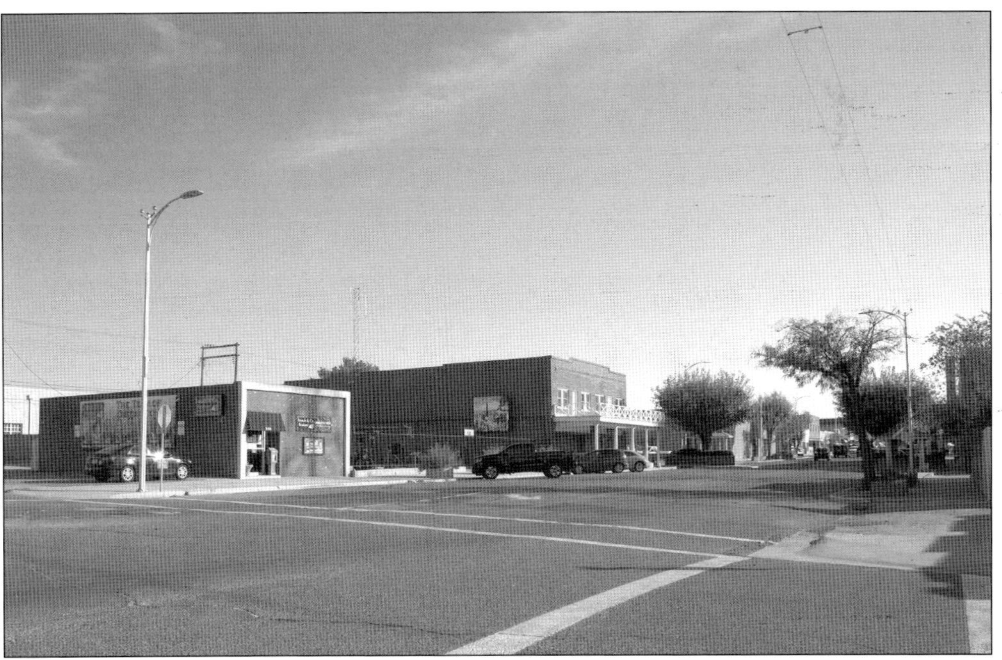

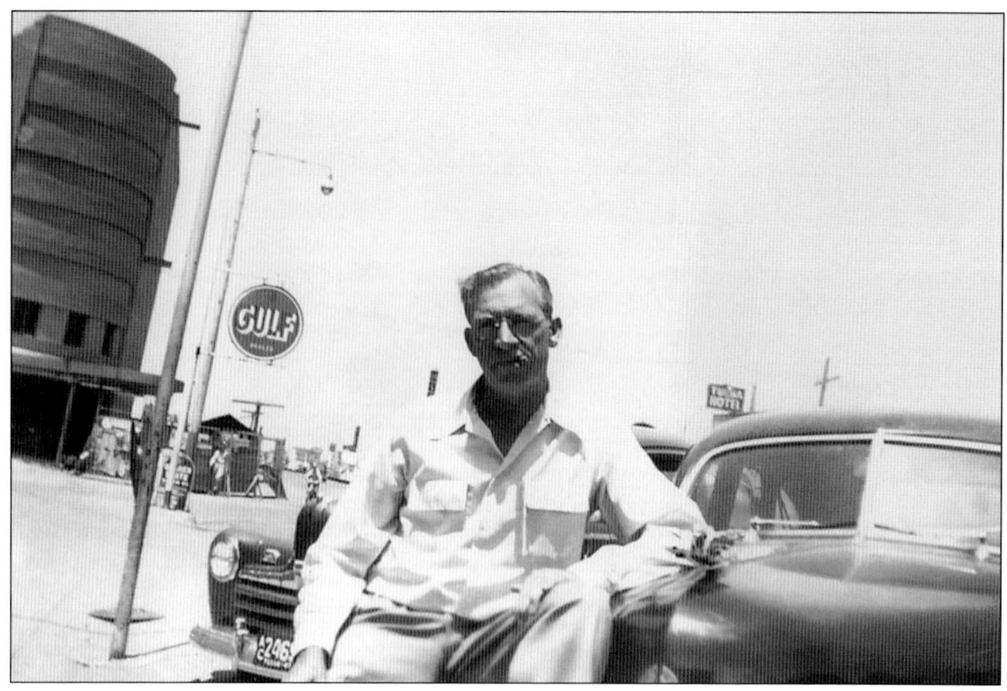

Carl Caywood, the builder of the Morley Theater (visible in the background at left above), is pictured while the theater was still under construction in 1947. Below is the Morley Theater today. A typical 1940s movie theater, the Morley featured a large screen and seating for many. For the time and place, it offered an elegant cinematic environment. It has been updated to its former glory and is still a great place to catch a movie. (Below, photograph by Clay Renick.)

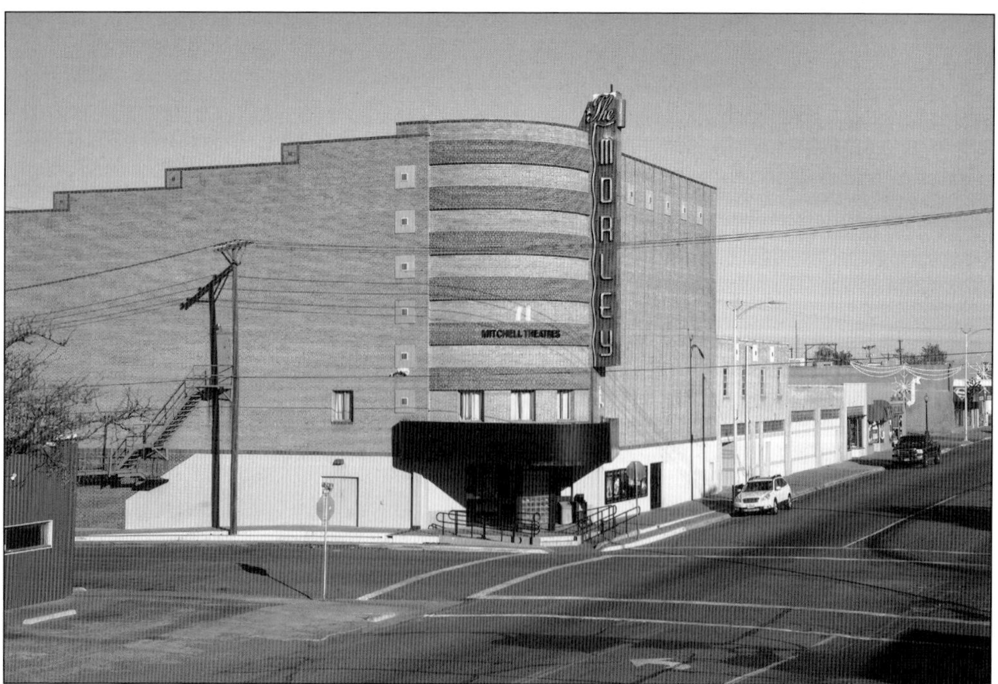

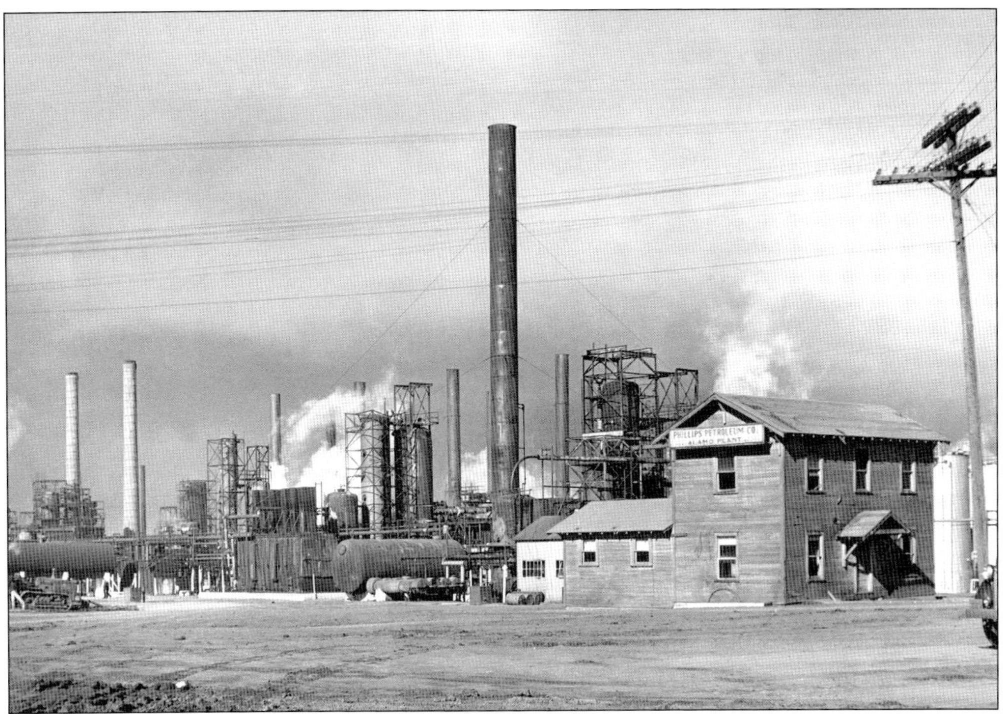

The Alamo petroleum refinery was originally built by another company and then acquired by Phillips Petroleum Company in 1927. The plant shown above was operated by 12 employees. Below is the refinery as it now appears—it has grown into one of the largest inland refineries in North America. Phillips is the largest employer in Hutchinson County and provides a strong foundation for the local economy. (Below, photograph by Clay Renick.)

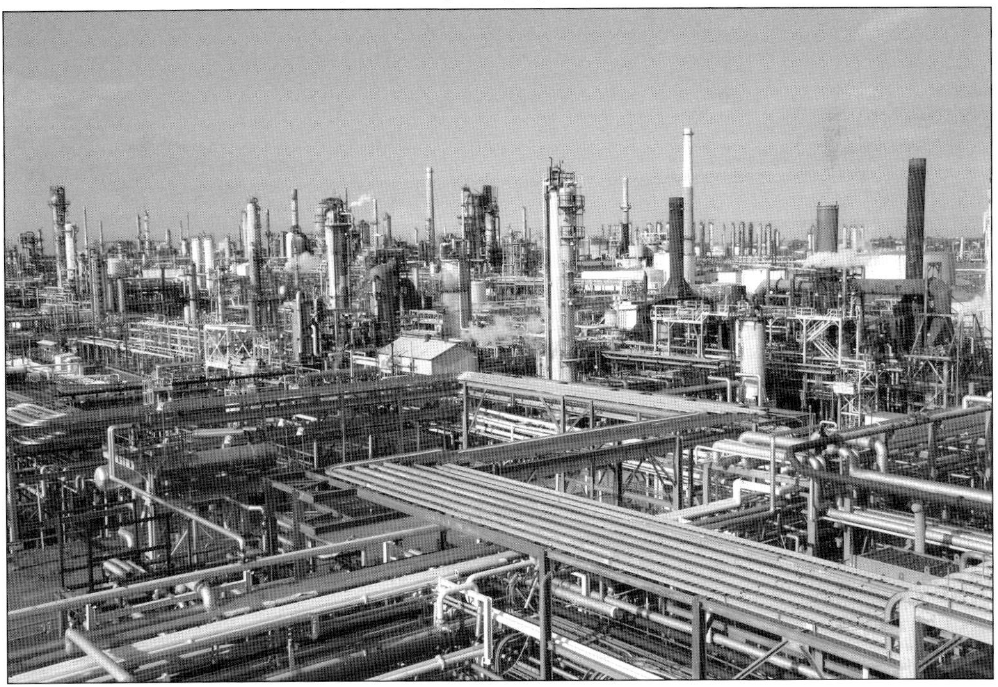

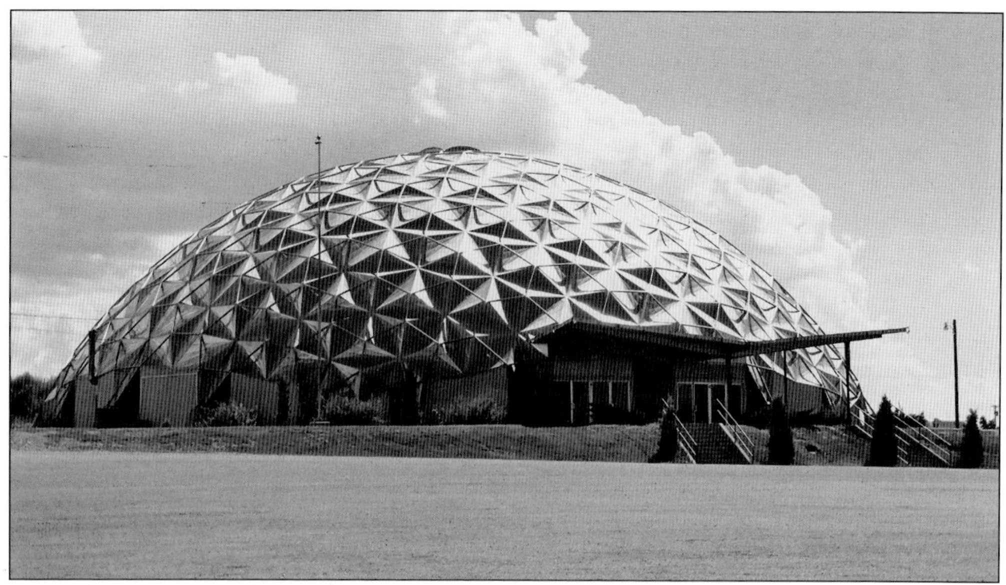

American industrialist Henry J. Kaiser and industrial designer Richard Buckminster Fuller collaborated in 1942 to explore the commercial potential of geodesic structures as a project of Kaiser Aluminum. In the late 1950s, Borger and Hutchinson County experienced an economic boom after the war. The Hutchinson County Commissioners Court decided to build one of Kaiser's domes to serve as a venue for community events. A bond election was held on July 2, 1957, and the project passed with 598 votes for and 378 against. Construction of the Borger dome was completed later that year, one of the first geodesic structures built in the continental United States. Kaiser built three civilian domes in 1957, including one in Virginia Beach, one in Borger, and one in Hawaii. It is unclear which was built first.

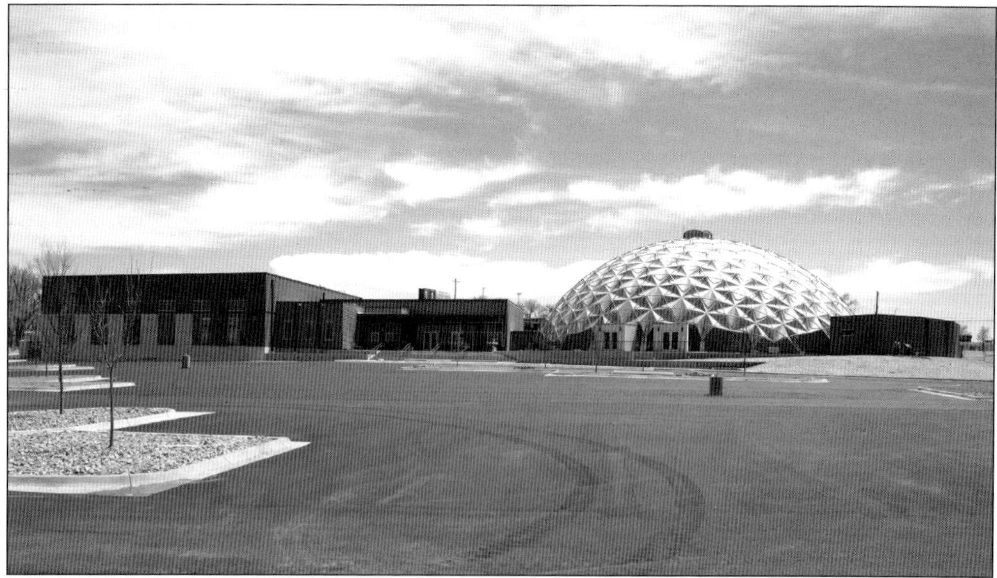

The City of Borger has brought new life to the dome. After acquiring it and nine surrounding acres from Hutchinson County in 2020, the structure was renovated and enlarged in 2021–2022 to make it a modern, multi-functional meeting space and event venue. The renovation is almost complete in this image. (Photograph by Clay Renick.)

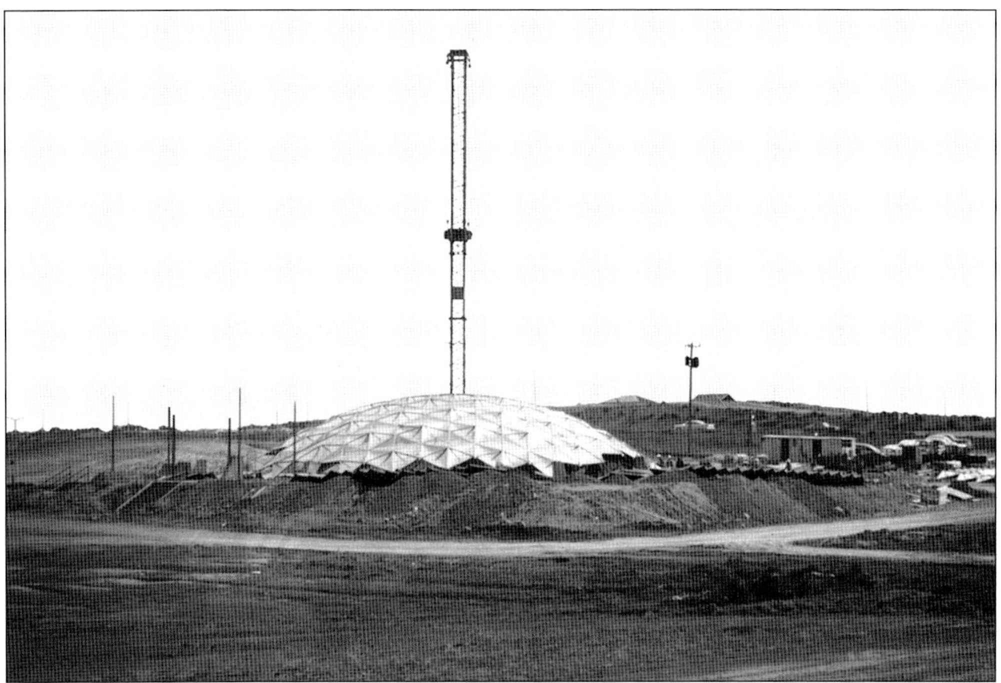

These photographs were taken by Brac Biggers in 1957. His son Curt donated them to the Hutchinson County Historical Museum in 2019; they are the only known images of the dome under construction. The slab was poured, a central mast was erected, and as panels were added to the outer edge, the dome grew and was lifted by cables. Construction was completed in a matter of days. The Borger dome is one of the oldest aluminum domes built by Henry Kaiser still standing in the United States.

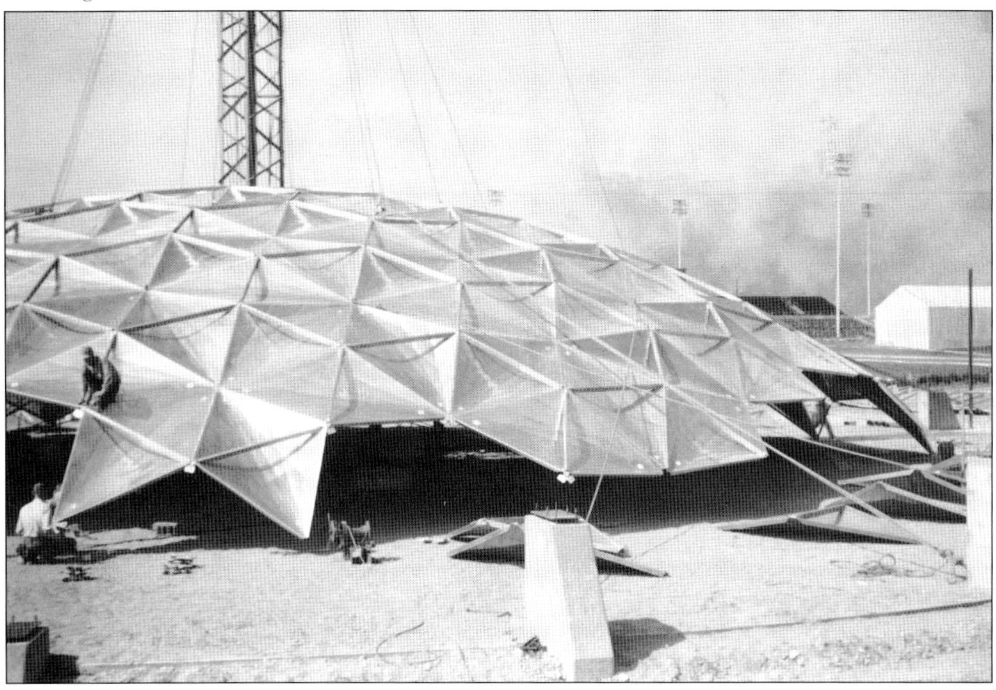

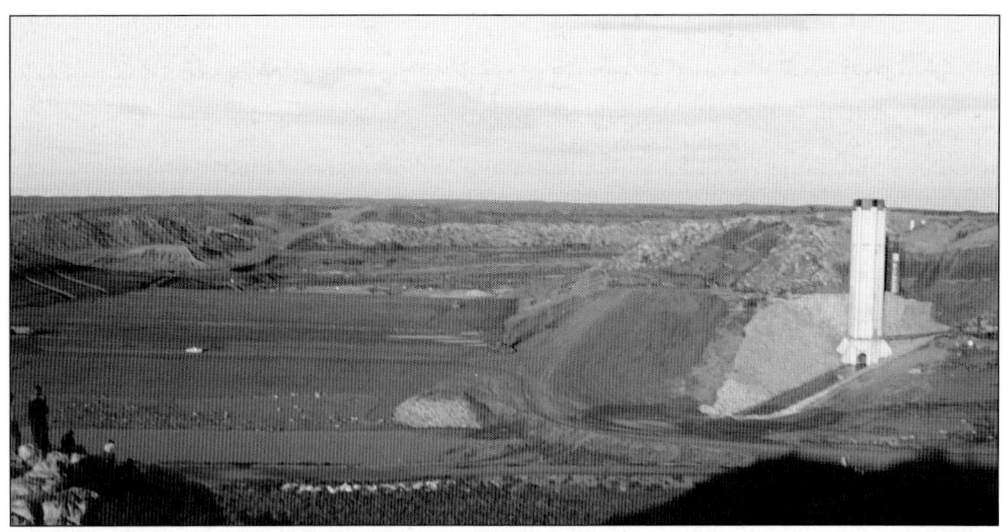

The Canadian River Project was authorized by the US Bureau of Reclamation on December 29, 1950, for the purpose of providing water, controlling floods and silt, and providing fish and wildlife benefits. At a ceremony on July 1, 1962, Former Borger city manager A.A. Meredith and US secretary of the interior Stewart Udall officially opened construction of the new Sanford Dam on the Canadian River. Construction was completed and water impoundment began in 1965. Construction of the aqueduct system to deliver water to the 11 member cities was finished in 1967, and water deliveries began in 1968.

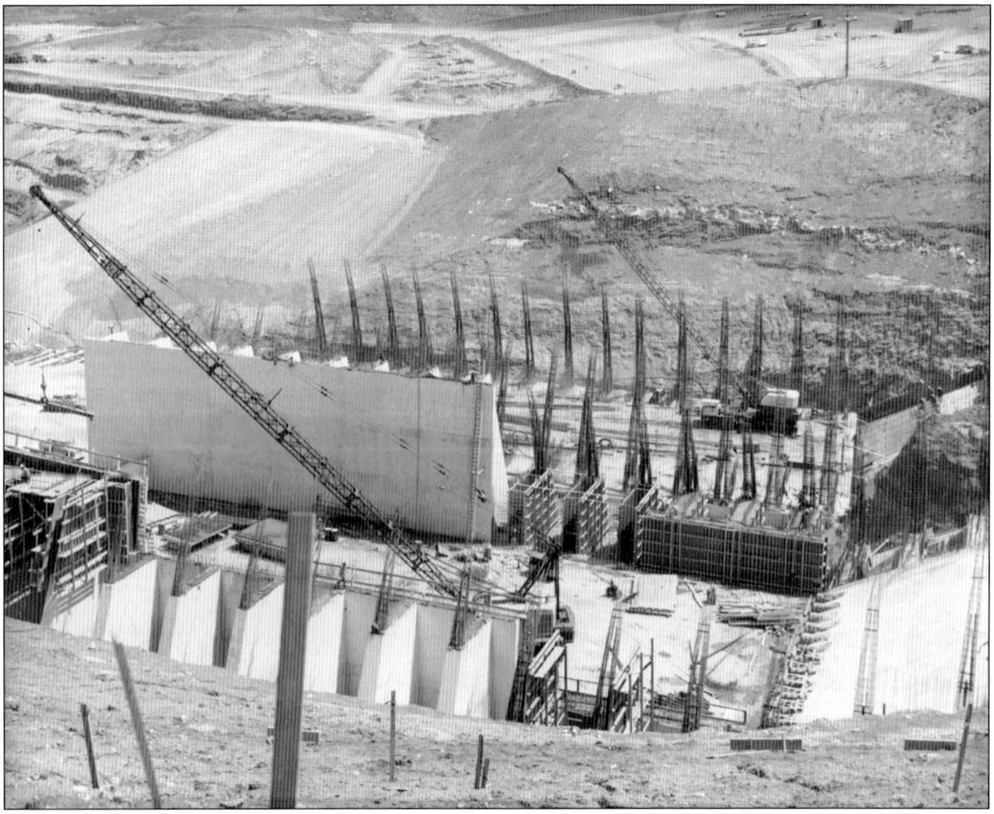

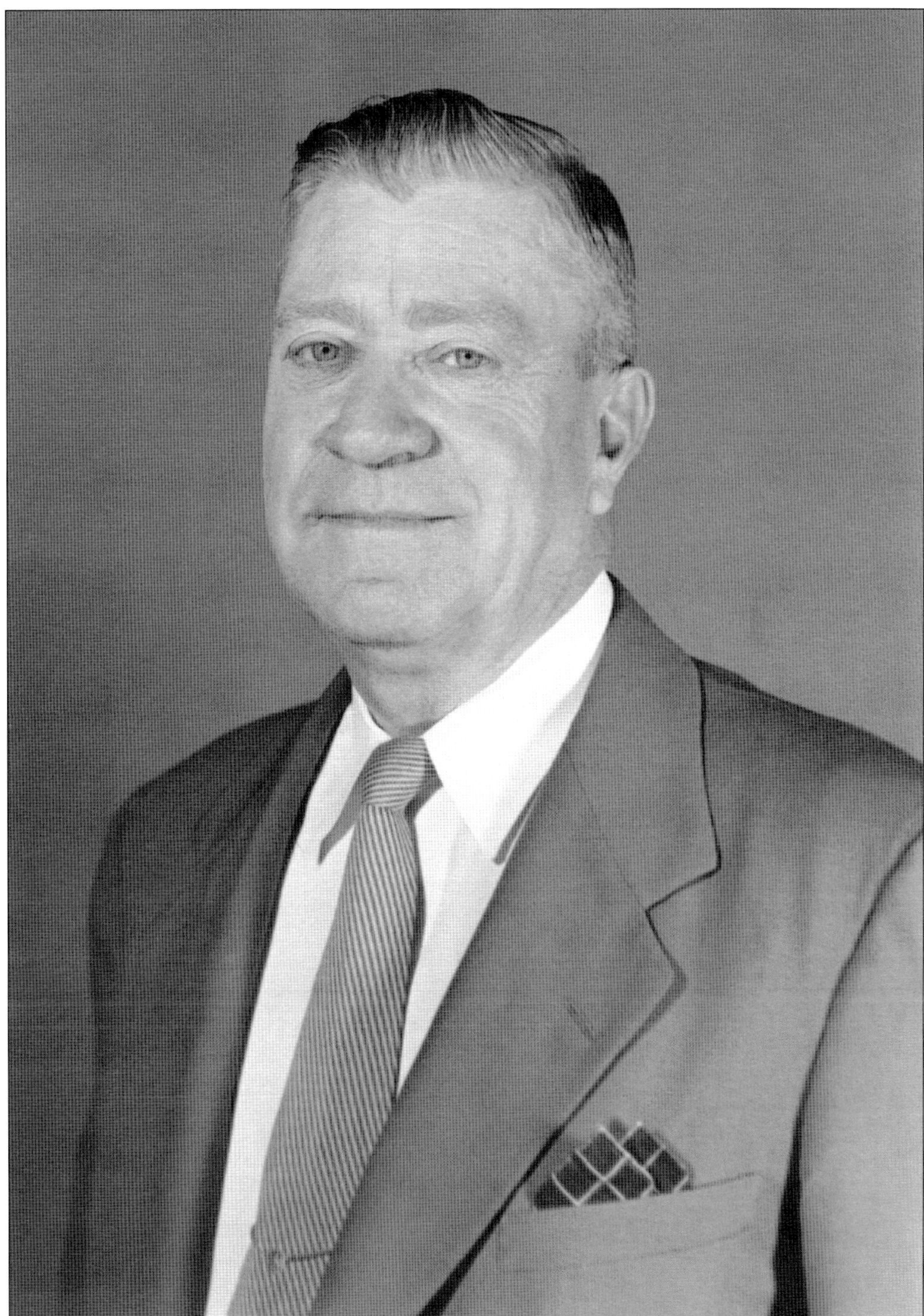

A.A. Meredith devised the Canadian River Project, which is owned and operated by the Canadian River Municipal Water Authority. He died in 1963, and never saw the project completed. In March 1964, Meredith posthumously received the nation's highest conservation award from the US Department of the Interior.

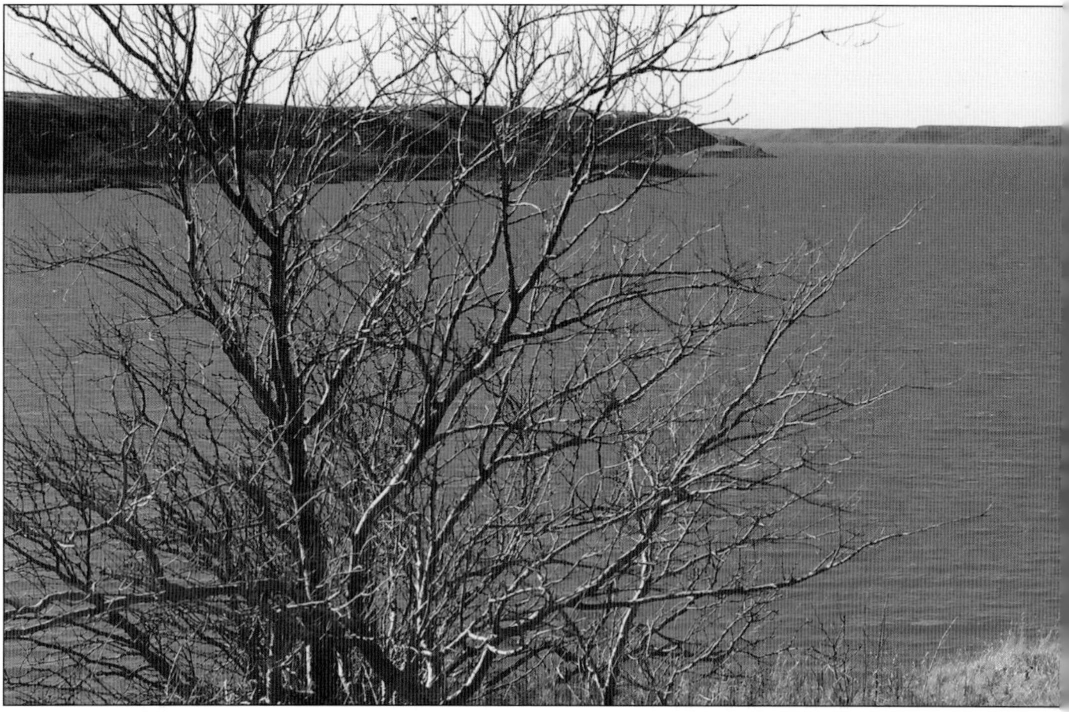

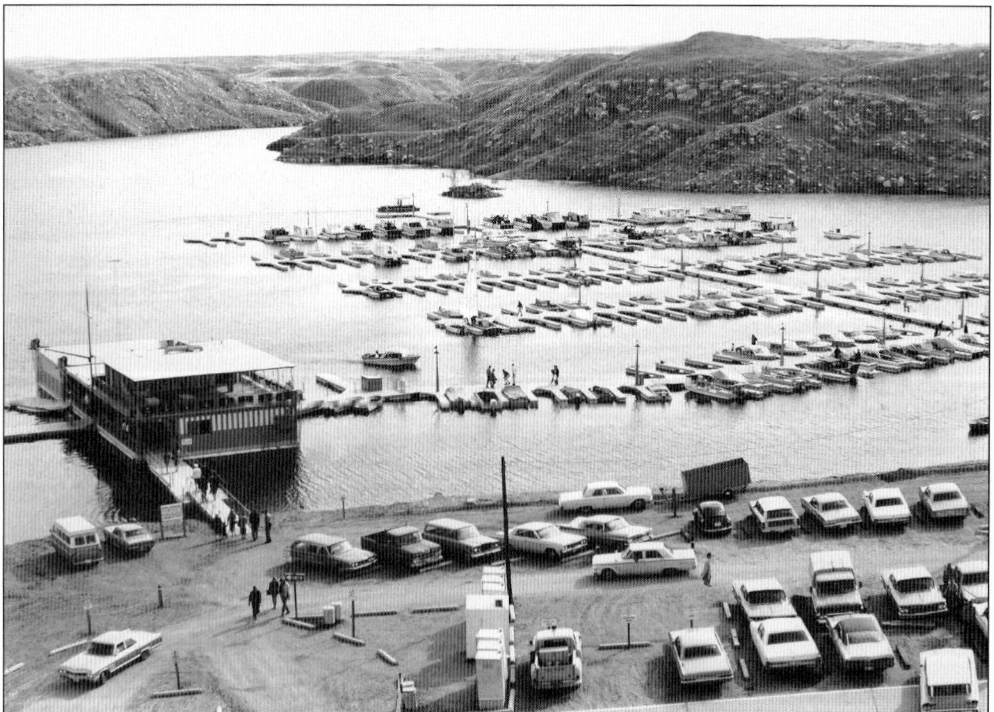

Above is a view of Lake Meredith looking west from near Sanford Dam on the north side in 2019. The lake provides recreational opportunities such as fishing, hiking, waterskiing, hunting, and many other activities to the residents of Hutchinson County and the Texas Panhandle. A recent drought took the level of the lake to record lows, but the return of regular rains in 2018 and 2019 brought the depth almost back to normal, much to the delight of water enthusiasts, hunters, and anglers. (Above, photograph by Clay Renick.)

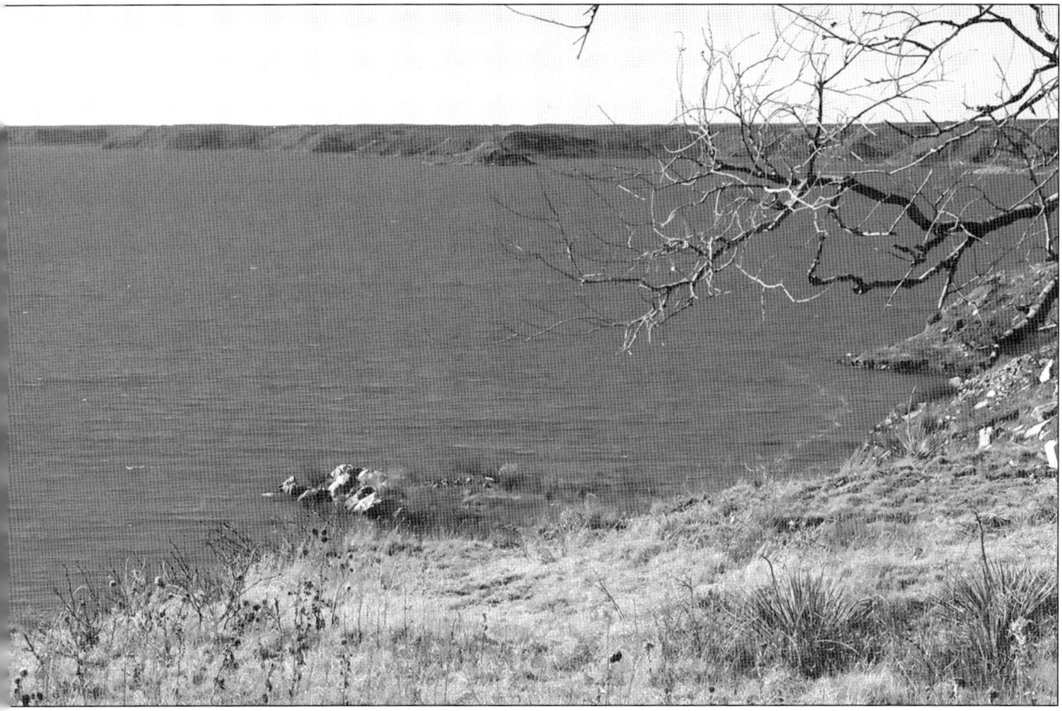

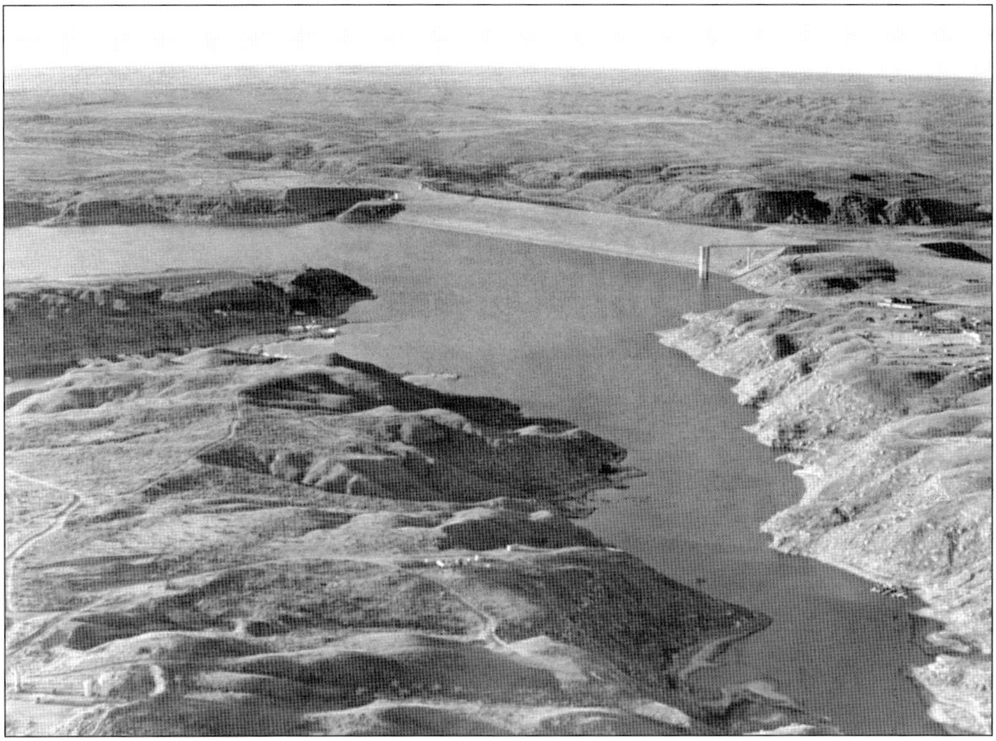

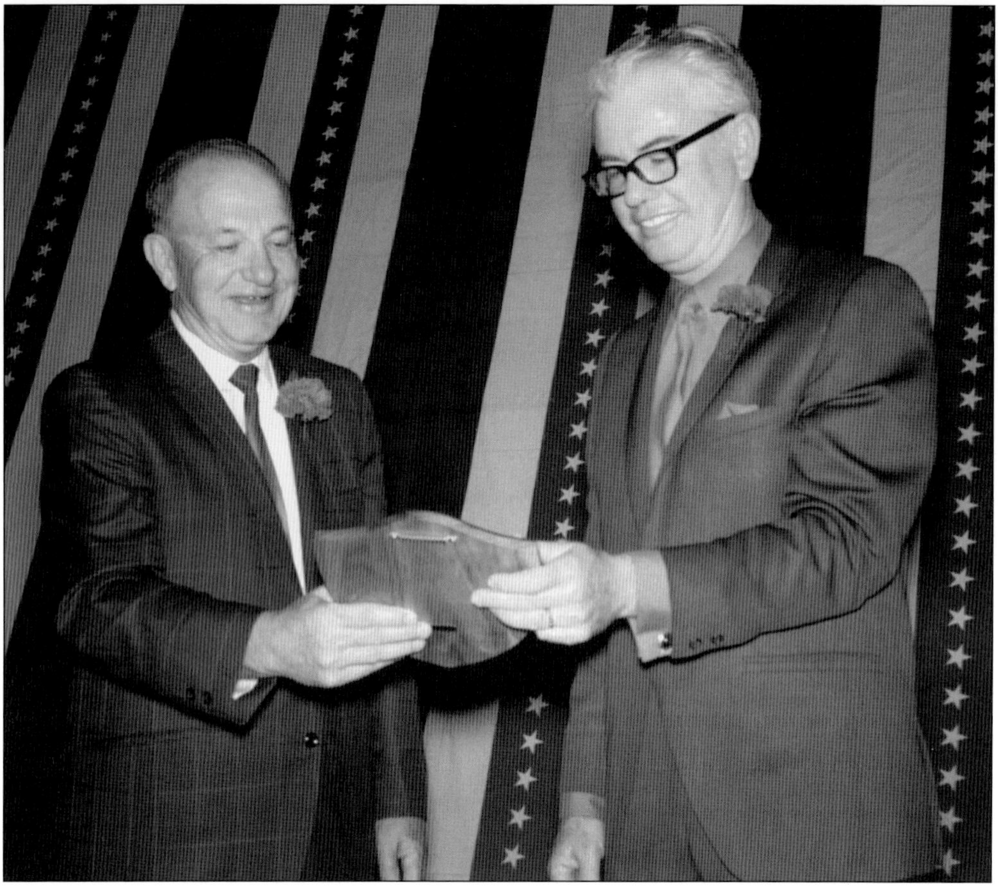

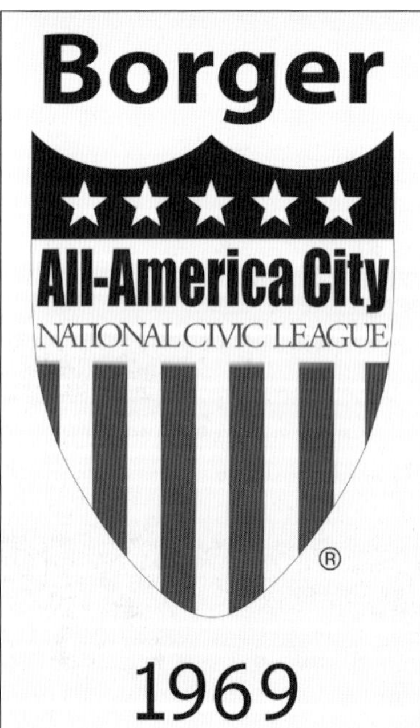

In 1969, the National Civic League and *Look* magazine named Borger an All-America City. The selection committee stated, "Borger is an oil boomtown that refused to be busted. Its citizens win honors for their plans to revitalize their decaying community." A recurring theme throughout the competition that year was community development of human as well as physical resources. The announcement of the award stated that Borger "came on strong in that aspect of the competition." Pictured above are L.D. Patton, president of the Borger Chamber of Commerce at the time (left), and the project head, Brac Biggers. In his presentation to the selection committee, Biggers said, "In the early 1960s, the city of Borger was in decline. . . . It was a renegade community whose citizens had to decide, in later years, whether to abandon it or start with what appeared to be less than nothing and build an acceptable community."

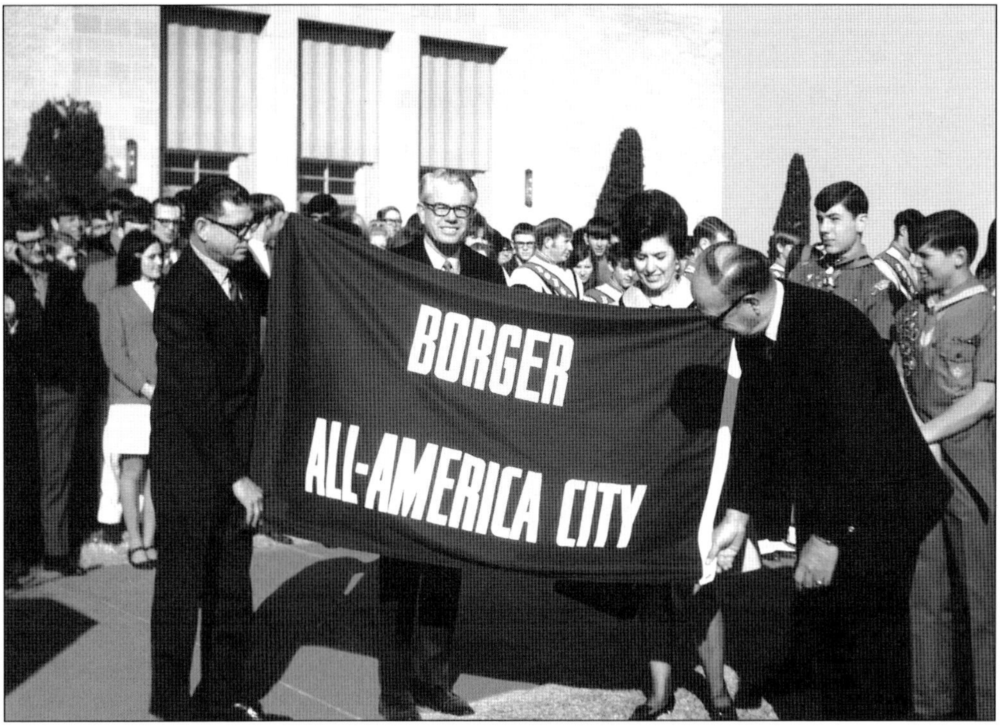

From left to right above, Borger mayor Ed Lewis, Brac Biggers, and L.D. Patton present the All-America City banner at a ceremony at Borger High School in 1969. Below is the billboard that the City of Amarillo placed on the highway leading into downtown Amarillo after Borger received the award.

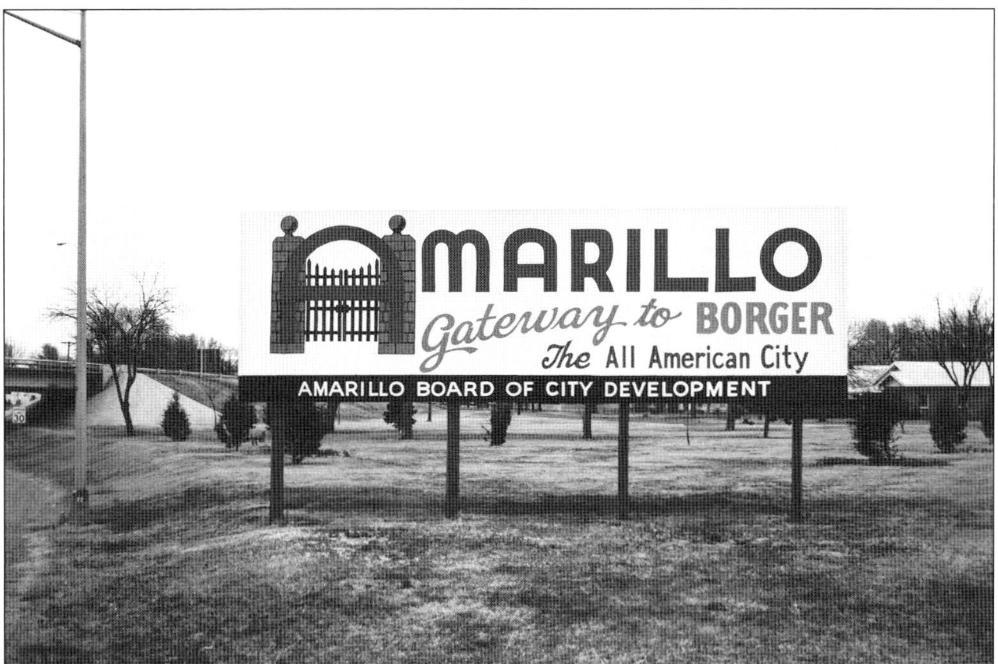

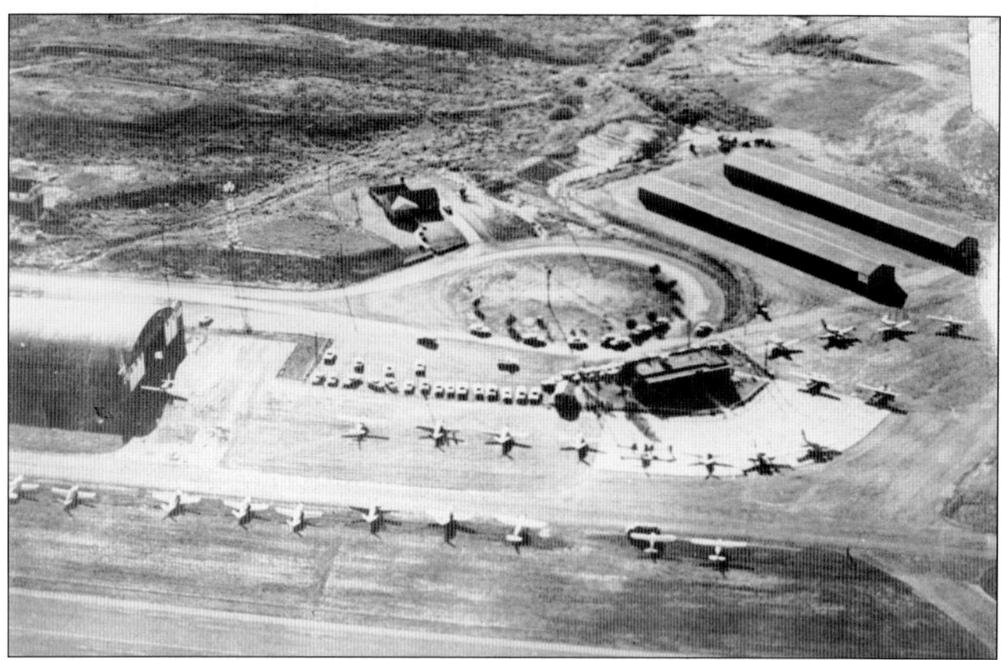

Hutchinson County Airport, north of Borger, is pictured on its opening day in 1951. The class III airport could accommodate all commercial aircraft operating in the area at the time. Over 150 aircraft landed that day, proving that an excellent facility was now available in the county. More than 300 people attended the opening ceremony, including Civil Aeronautics Authority officials and executives from Pioneer Airlines and Central Airlines.

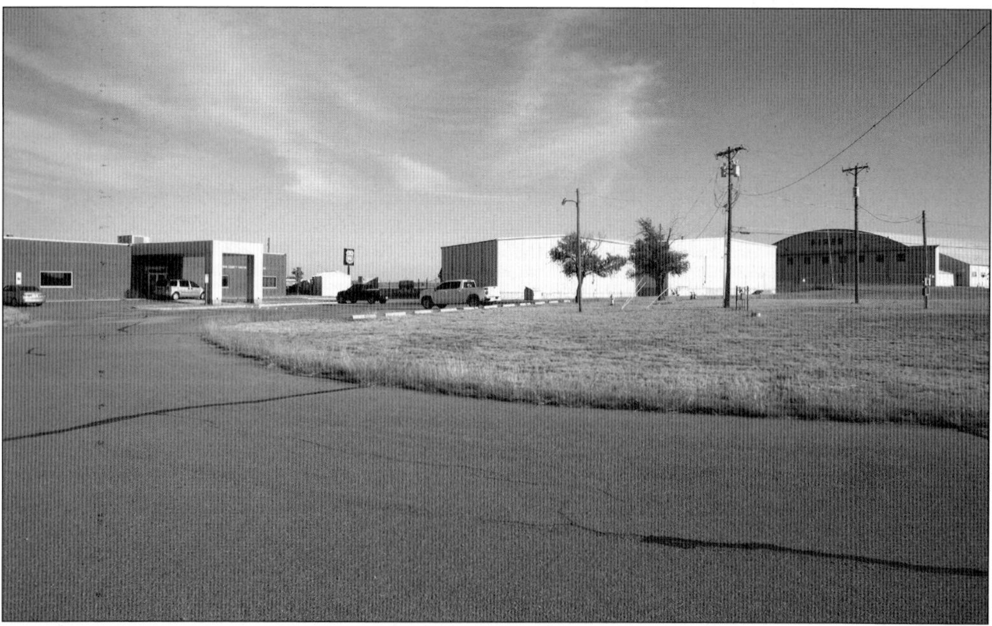

The terminal facility at Hutchinson County Airport was completely rebuilt in 2011. Ramp improvements, resurfacing of runways and taxiways, and 18,000 feet of game-proof fencing were added in recent years. The new facility is a major upgrade, with amenities such as a pilots' lounge, a flight-planning area with Internet access, and a weather briefing area. (Photograph by Clay Renick.)

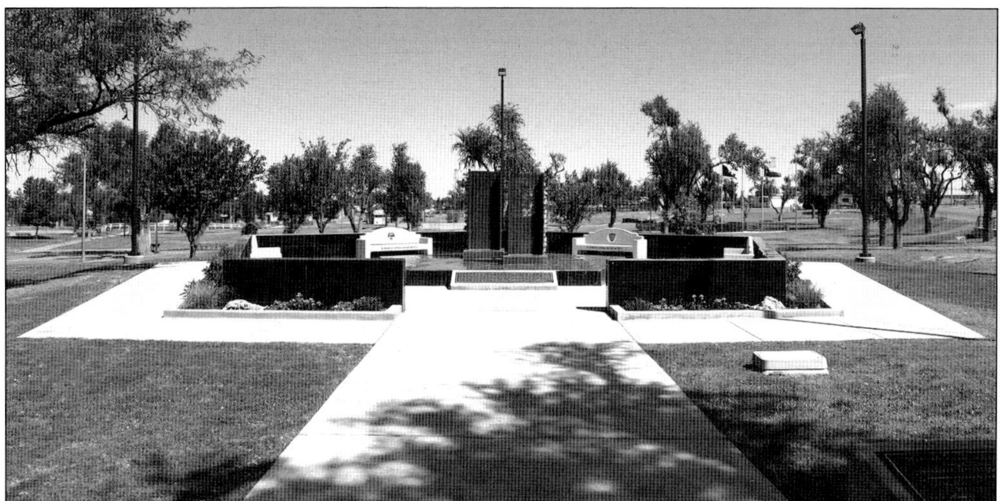

After learning that pieces of steel from the World Trade Center were being given to cities all over the United States, a group of Hutchinson County citizens made their way to New York at their own expense to retrieve two large pieces to build a September 11 memorial in Borger. The city and county combined to produce the monument. Hutchinson County Historical Museum director Clay Renick designed it and worked with a local construction company, which built it for free in Borger's Huber Park. Materials were provided at no cost by several local suppliers. The monument tells the story, on five bronze plaques, of the events of that day. (Photograph by Clay Renick.)

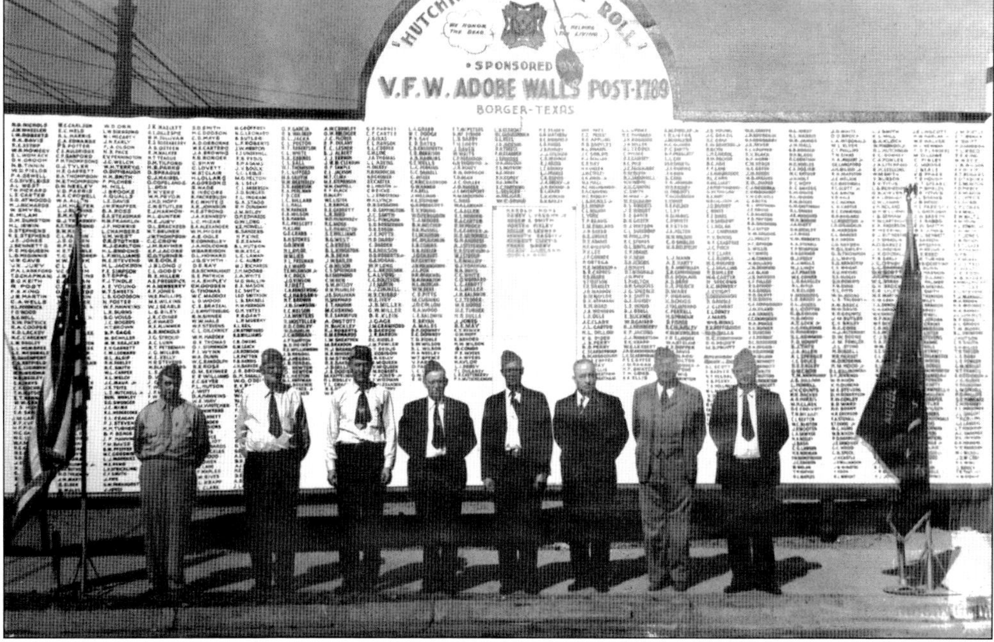

This honor roll was erected at the Adobe Walls post of the Veterans of Foreign Wars in Borger. It lists the names of veterans from Hutchinson County who served during World War II. Although there are over 1,400 names on the sign—974 men and 435 women—it does not include all county veterans who served. When World War II began, there were fewer than 20,000 people living in Hutchinson County, which means about 7 percent of county residents served. Texas had more people who volunteered to go to war than any other state.

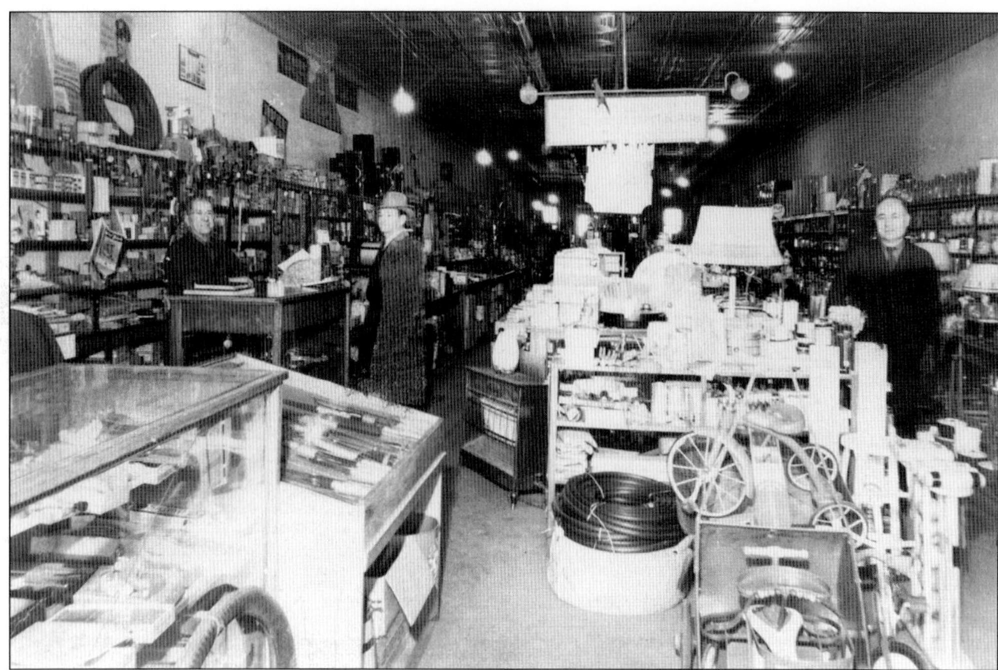

Constructed in 1927, what is now the home of the Hutchinson County Historical Museum is one of Borger's earliest large buildings. Originally a hardware store on the first floor and a hotel on the second, the building was donated to the Hutchinson County Historical Commission in 1976 by Dr. Chris Yiantsou, who was then the owner of the building and a descendant of the original owner, Gus Yiantsou. The facade shown below reflects the many changes and improvements that have been made to the building through the years, but it still appears much like it did in Borger's early days. (Below, photograph by Clay Renick.)

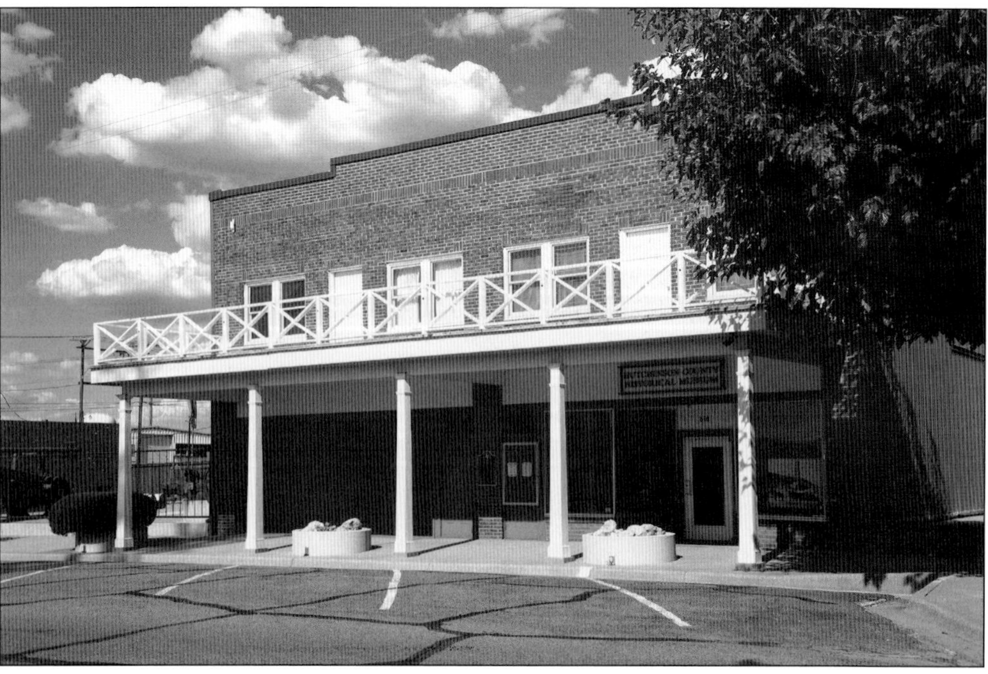

The Texas Historical Commission awarded a Texas historical marker to the Hutchinson County Historical Museum due to the historical significance of the museum's building. The marker was installed on the front wall to tell the story of the building and how it became the home of the museum. (Photograph by Clay Renick.)

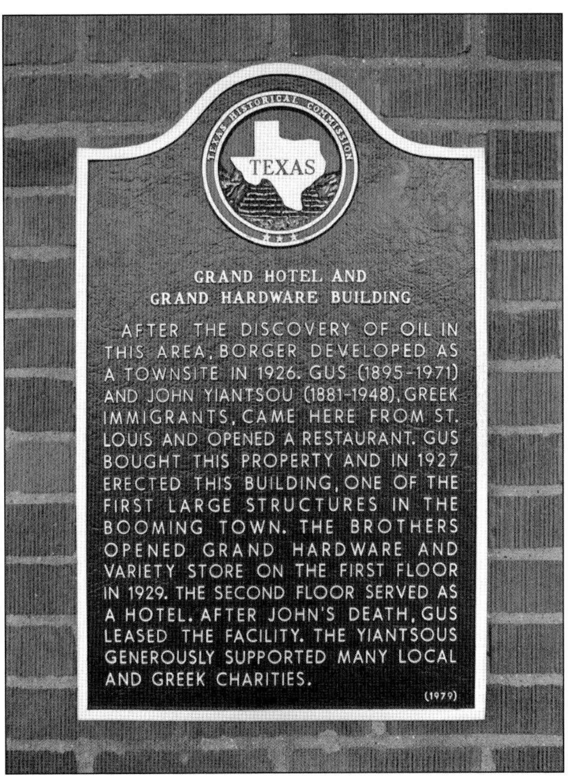

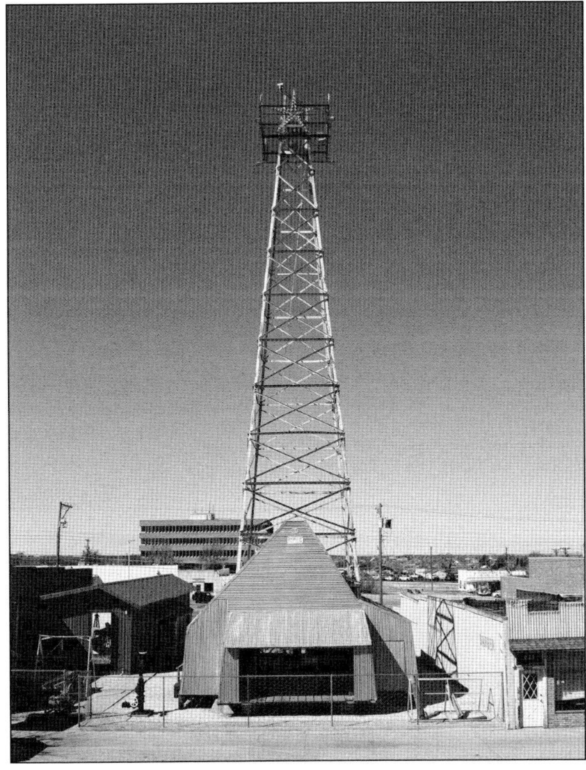

One of the last cable tool drilling rigs used by Gulf Oil Company to drill eight wells on the Dial lease north of the Canadian River was erected directly across the street from the Hutchinson County Historical Museum in 1983. The rig gives museum visitors an idea of the dirty, dangerous life of a roughneck. (Photograph by Clay Renick.)

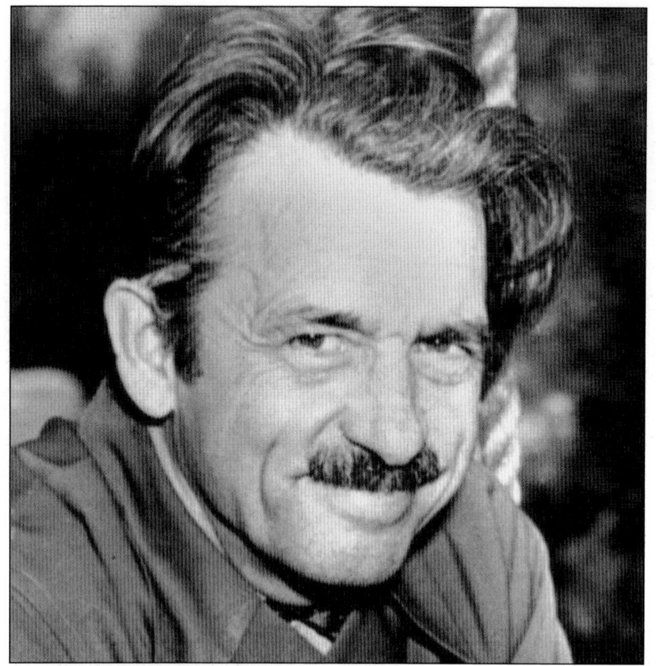

Regionalist painter Thomas Hart Benton (1889–1975) declared himself to be "an enemy of modernism." While on a sketching tour of America in 1928, he visited Borger, where he stayed with friends who owned the Dilley Hotel. Benton made sketches from the window of his hotel room, and upon returning to his studio in New York, he painted *Boomtown* (below). The original painting resides in the permanent collection of the Memorial Art Gallery of the University of Rochester in Rochester, New York.

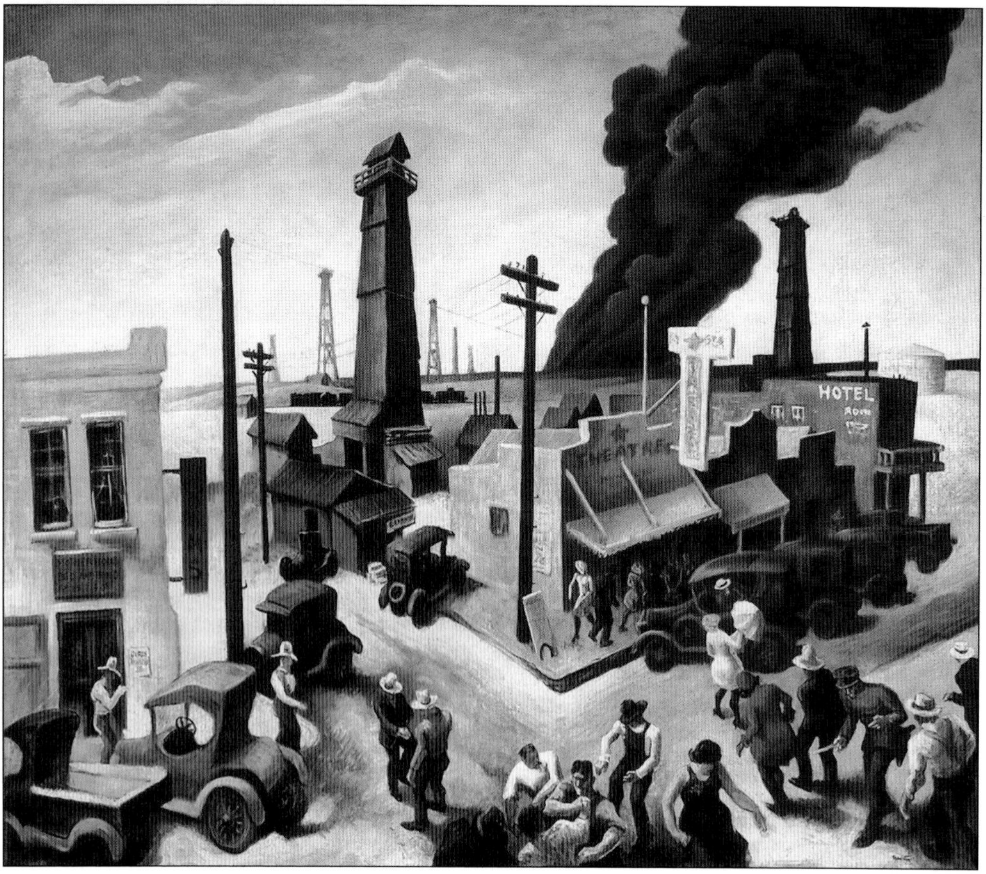

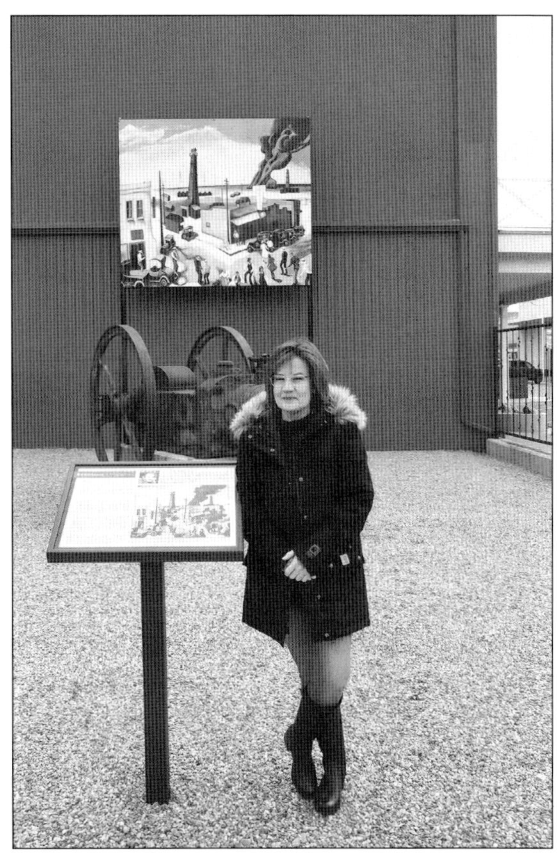

Local artist Michelle Dubiskas volunteered to reproduce Thomas Hart Benton's *Boomtown* and donate it to the Hutchinson County Historical Museum. Dubiskas painted the piece in February 2020. The Friends of the Hutchinson County Historical Museum paid for the materials used to build the painting's steel base, the structure to mount it on, and the paint needed for the project. The steel surface was fabricated at no cost by the Hutchinson County Road and Bridge crew. Many contributed to this effort to preserve the unique history of Hutchinson County. (Photograph by Clay Renick.)

Petroleum Hall, adjacent to the oil rig across Main Street from the Hutchinson County Historical Museum, is home to vehicles, machinery, and tools from the early Hutchinson County oil fields, as well as more recent examples of technology used to produce oil. The 1924 Mack AC truck in the foreground was restored by Don Thompson and several other museum volunteers. (Photograph by Clay Renick.)

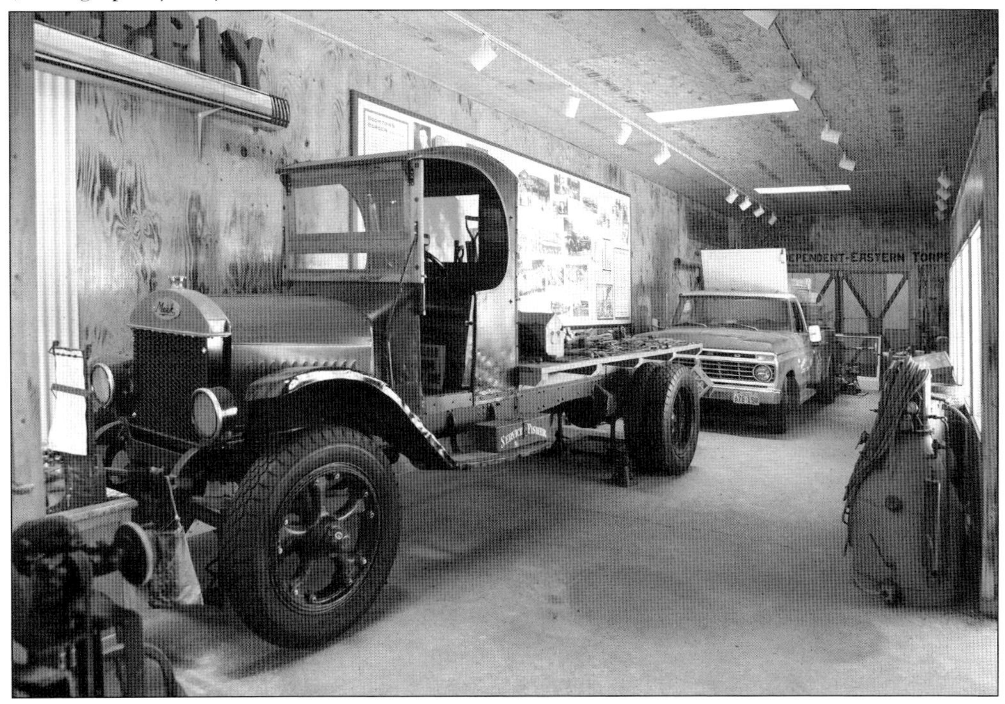

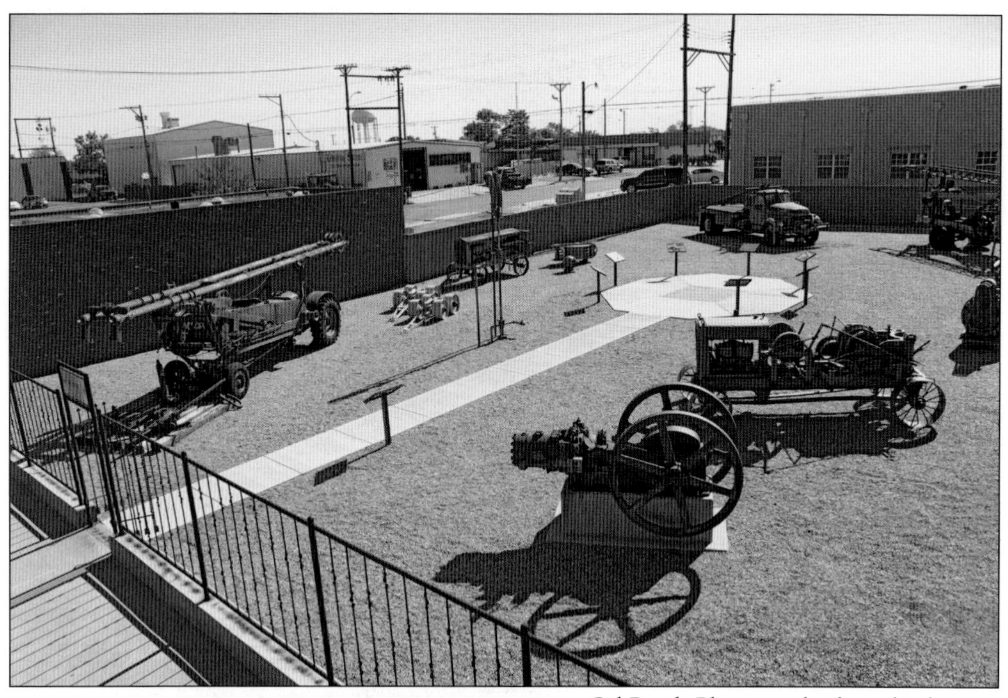

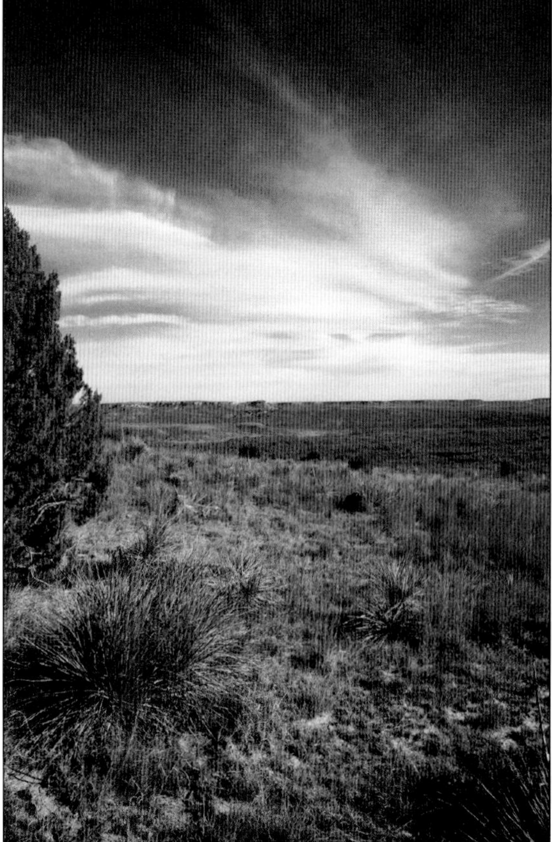

Oil Patch Place was built to display antique oil equipment that had been stored on local yards for many years. These artifacts tell the story of the time when Hutchinson County began the transformation from its agricultural past to a blended economy with petroleum as its powerful partner for a successful future. (Photograph by Clay Renick.)

Hutchinson County is the definition of wide open space. This land is home to amazing history, beautiful distant vistas, wild weather, diverse wildlife, and very friendly people. In 2022, when this book was published, Hutchinson County was only 121 years old—just getting started! (Photograph by Clay Renick.)

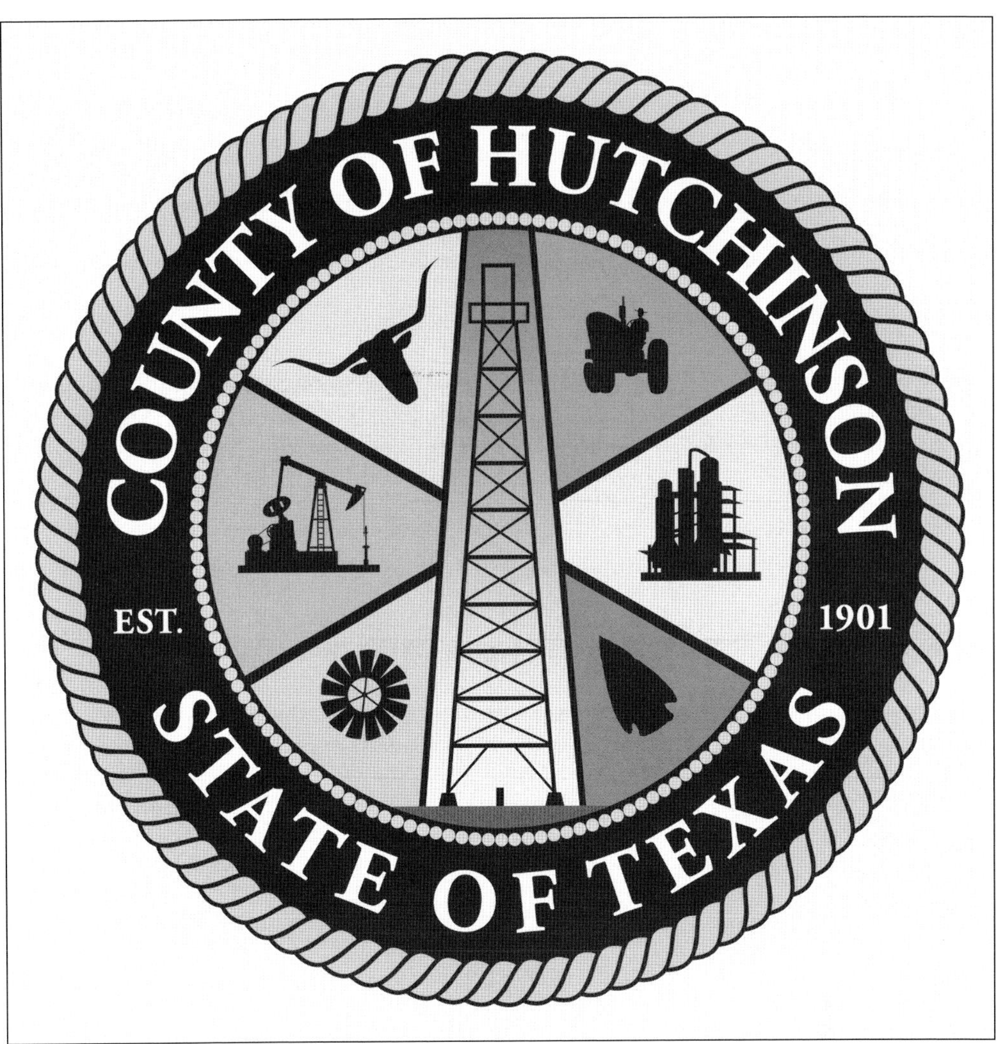

Icons representing agriculture, oil production, cattle, farming, petroleum refining, and Native American culture on the Hutchinson County seal stand for the history of the county and the things that made it what it is today. These icons signify both the heritage and the future of Hutchinson County, which observed its 120th anniversary in 2021 as one of the 253 counties of Texas. The seal was designed in 2019 by Clay Renick.